CW00530985

Conscious Theatre Practice

Consciousness, Literature and the Arts

General Editor

Daniel Meyer-Dinkgrafe

VOLUME 58

The titles published in this series are listed at *brill.com/cla*

Conscious Theatre Practice

Yoga, Meditation and Performance

By

Lou Prendergast

BRILL

RODOPI

LEIDEN | BOSTON

Cover illustration: Production shot taken during rehearsals at the Arches Theatre, Glasgow, July 2015. Photography by Tim Courtney.

Library of Congress Cataloging-in-Publication Data

Names: Prendergast, Lou, author.
Title: Conscious theatre practice : yoga, meditation and performance / by Lou Prendergast.
Description: Leiden ; Boston : Brill Rodopi, [2022] | Series: Consciousness, literature and the arts, 1573-2193 ; vol. 58 | Includes bibliographical references and index. | Summary: "In Conscious Theatre Practice: Yoga, Meditation, and Performance, Lou Prendergast charts a theatre research project in which the notion of Self-realisation and related contemplative practices, including Bikram Yoga and Vipassana meditation, are applied to performance. Coining the term 'Conscious Theatre Practice', Prendergast presents the scripts of three publicly presented theatrical performances, examined under the 'three C's' research model: Conscious Craft (writing, directing, performance; Conscious Casting; Conscious Collaborations. The findings of this autobiographical project fed into a working manifesto for socially engaged theatre company, Black Star Projects. Along the way, the research engages with methodological frameworks that include practice-as-research, autoethnography, phenomenology and psychophysical processes, as well immersive yoga and meditation practice; while race, class and gender inequalities underpin the themes of the productions"– Provided by publisher.
Identifiers: LCCN 2021028148 (print) | LCCN 2021028149 (ebook) | ISBN 9789004467910 (hardback) | ISBN 9789004467927 (ebook)
Subjects: LCSH: Theater–Psychological aspects. | Consciousness. | Meditation. | Yoga.
Classification: LCC PN2051 P74 2021 (print) | LCC PN2051 (ebook) | DDC 792.01/9–dc23
LC record available at https://lccn.loc.gov/2021028148
LC ebook record available at https://lccn.loc.gov/2021028149

Typeface for the Latin, Greek, and Cyrillic scripts: "Brill". See and download: brill.com/brill-typeface.

ISSN 1573-2193
ISBN 978-90-04-46791-0 (hardback)
ISBN 978-90-04-46792-7 (e-book)

For my dear,
dramatic granddaughter,
Sofia-Louise Prendergast

Contents

Acknowledgements   XI
Preface   XII
List of Figures and Tables   XIII

PART 1
Research

1   **Know Thyself**
    Conscious Theatre Practice as Self-Realisation Process   5
    1   Know Thyself   10
    2   Social Self   13
    3   Feminist Self   16
    4   Sick Self   18
    5   Outline of Chapters   21

2   **Bodymind**
    Yoga, Meditation and Theatre Practice   25
    1   Bodymind   26
    2   Philosophical Contexts of Yoga and Meditation   30
    3   Conscious Theatre Practitioners   38
    4   Konstantin Stanislavski   39
    5   Nicolás Núñez   42
    6   Peter Brook   43
    7   Jerzy Grotowski   44

3   **Research Approaches**
    From Embodied Knowledge to Self-Reflexivity   47
    1   Practice as Research   48
    2   Autoethnography   49
    3   Immersive Contemplative Practice (ICP)   51
    4   ICP as Fieldwork   52
    5   Journal Entry Critique   53

4   Immersive Contemplative Practice
    Vipassana Meditation Courses and Bikram Yoga Teacher Training   57
    1   Vipassana   57
    2   Bikram Yoga Teacher Training   70

5   Three C's Research Model
    Conscious Craft, Conscious Casting, Conscious Collaborations   85
    1   The Three C's Research Model   86
         1.1   *Conscious Craft*   86
         1.2   *Conscious Casting*   86
         1.3   *Conscious Collaborations*   87
    2   Higher States of Theatre Consciousness   87

         PART 2
Practice

6   Blood Lines (2014)
    United in Diversity: 'But Who Could Resist You Dad?'   95
    1   Conscious Casting: *Blood Lines*   95
    2   Narrative   100
    3   Staging   101
    4   Ensemble   103
    5   'Fierce and Self-Searching Reflection'   105

7   Tommy's Song (2015)
    Imagining Masculinities: 'Kickin' an Stampin!'   111
    1   Conscious Craft: *Tommy's Song*   111
    2   Writing   112
    3   Casting   113
    4   Directing   114
    5   Performance   118
    6   'Childhood Poverty and Family Dysfunction'   120

8   AWKWARD: A Life in Twenty-Six Postures (2016)
    Love Changes Everything: 'Compassion, Not Passion'   137
    1   Conscious Collaborations: *Awkward*   137
    2   Ensemble   138
    3   Staging   140
    4   Performance   141
    5   'A Space for Reflection; A Space for Sharing'   146

9 **Findings, Lessons and Learnings** 153

    1   Research Recapitulations 154

    2   Outcomes for Theatre Practice 155

    3   Black Star Projects Manifesto 156

    4   CTP Antagonisms and Limitations 157

    5   Implications 160

    6   Applications 162

    7   Back to My Future 166

Afterword 170

Blood Lines 172

Tommy's Song 201

AWKWARD: A Life in Twenty-Six Postures 218

Bibliography 245

Index of Names 251

Acknowledgements

First and foremost, thanks to Daniel Meyer-Dinkgräfe, without whom this book would not exist. Huge to thanks to Dr. David Overend, who patiently attempted to keep the research on track in the early years; and to Dr. Graham Jeffery, who guided the whole project to fruition. I am massively grateful to you all.

Thanks to UWS for the funded PhD, and to Fiona Sturgeon-Shea who has been an important ally. I am indebted to all at Playwright Studio Scotland. As project collaborator, this essential playwriting organisation provided much needed moral and financial support, which turned out to be life changing.

Thank you to the Black Star Projects team who worked on the plays, including the performers on: *Blood Lines* – Sophia Prendergast, Neil Stewart, Graham Campbell and Michael Abubaker; *Tommy's Song* – Tom McGovern; *Awkward* – Laura Fahey and Anna Leckey. You were absolutely the right people.

Special thanks to Alan McKendrick, Gary McNair, Iain Heggie; you were amazing, as was/is designer Colin O'Hara. Thanks Fiona McKinnon. Thank you Ashanti Harris. Thanks to the National Theatre of Scotland. Thank you to the theatre making peers that formed the focus group discussion.

And I say thank you for the music: to the Wee G3 – the house band that the *Blood Lines* musicians formed on the day they met, contributing energy, talent, reggae beats and songs to sing and dance to; a highlight of the production.

A nod of love to Elvis Presley – choosing the songs and working with his lyrics on *Tommy's Song* was one of the most enjoyable parts of making the work. Thanks to Lee Handman for the short clips of the Bowie songs on *Awkward*; a conversation that began in the Himalayas and ended in the Scottish Borders.

Thanks to all collaborators at Ankur, the Arches, Oran Mor and the Swallow Theatre. Thanks Sarah Smith at Glasgow School of Art, for the feminism and autobiographical writing scholarship. Thanks to Katarzyna Kosmala and to Deborah Middleton at the Centre for Psychophysical Performance Research.

Thanks to Stewart Laing and Pamela Carter for being inspirational in theatre.

I am grateful for the yoga, the meditation and the movement, and all the courses and teachers and workshop leaders I met along the way; from Stephen Clark who taught me Bikram Yoga in his flat, to Alex Cat who supervised me through TCTSY training. Keep spreading the love. Namaste.

Preface

This book began as academic research, but is not only for academics. It is for anyone that has left a theatre show, or a performance, feeling elevated; more alive. It is for art practitioners and yoga practitioners and Vipassana meditators. It is for anyone interested in their own potential for evolution as a human being.

The research investigates ways in which creative processes in the making of theatre work(s) can be augmented by contemplative practices, including yoga and meditation. It focuses on three theatrical productions that were publicly presented across three consecutive years: *Blood Lines* (2014), *Tommy's Song* (2015) and *Awkward – A life in Twenty-Six Postures* (2016).

Specifically, the book researches Bikram Yoga and Vipassana meditation as 'bodymind' training systems for performance. It charts the development of a Conscious Theatre Practice (CTP); a theatre in which the ideologies, as well as the physical aspects of these Eastern disciplines contributed to the shaping of a working manifesto for socially engaged theatre company, Black Star Projects.

The theatrical productions forming the practical elements of this research were analysed and deconstructed using the 'three C's' research model. This comparative framework was the paradigm for exploring three aspects of theatre making: Conscious Craft: writing, directing, performance; Conscious Casting and Conscious Collaborations.

Creating a conscious theatre practice has been part of an ongoing self-realisation process. Themes of self-discovery and enhanced somatic harmony have been inherent in this project, informing the field of contemporary performance studies via the philosophies and practices of ancient disciplines.

Research for this book included several ten-day silent Vipassana meditation retreats and a nine-week Bikram Yoga teacher-training programme, contributing to autoethnographic research methods and subsequently, to partly autobiographical play texts and their theatrical performance outputs.

The ancient 'know thyself' adage has been instrumental as a guiding light in both theatre-making and yoga/meditation practices. This research argues that these disciplines can work in unison to transform the lives of individuals, and that personal shifts in consciousness have the potential to improve society.

Figures and Tables

Figures

1   Lou Prendergast performing in *Blood Lines* (photography by Tim Courtney, 2014).   3
2   Tom McGovern performing in *Tommy's Song* (photography by Leslie Black, 2015).   24
3   Lou Prendergast, Laura Fahey and Anna Lecky performing in *AWKWARD* – *A Life in Twenty-Six Postures* (photography by The Swallow Theatre, 2016).   46
4   Lou Prendergast with Bikram Choudhury, 5th December 2015 (photography by Bikram Yoga Teacher Training official photographer).   84
5   Lou and Sophie Prendergast performing in *Blood Lines* (photography by Tim Courtney, 2014).   109
6   Neil Stewart performing in *Blood Lines* (photography Tim Courtney, 2014).   109
7   Michael Abubakar performing in *Blood Lines* (photography Tim Courtney, 2014).   110
8   Lou and Sophie Prendergast performing in *Blood Lines* (photography Tim Courtney, 2014).   110
9   Tom McGovern rehearsing *Tommy's Song* (photography Leslie Black, 2015).   135
10   Tom McGovern rehearsing *Tommy's Song* (photography Leslie Black, 2015).   135
11   Tom McGovern rehearsing *Tommy's Song* (photography Leslie Black, 2015).   136
12   Tom McGovern rehearsing *Tommy's Song* (photography Leslie Black, 2015).   136
13   Bikram Choudhury and *Awkward* performer Anna Leckey at Bikram Yoga TT   145
14   Lou Prendergast, Laura Fahey and Anna Lecky performing in *AWKWARD* – *A Life in Twenty-Six Postures* (photography The Swallow Theatre, 2016).   151
15   Lou Prendergast, Laura Fahey and Anna Lecky performing in *AWKWARD* – *A Life in Twenty-Six Postures* (photography The Swallow Theatre, 2016).   151
16   Lou Prendergast, Laura Fahey and Anna Lecky performing in *AWKWARD* – *A Life in Twenty-Six Postures* (photography The Swallow Theatre, 2016).   152
17   Lou Prendergast, Laura Fahey and Anna Lecky performing in *AWKWARD* – *A Life in Twenty-Six Postures* (Photography The Swallow Theatre, 2016).   152

Tables

1   Tommy's Song Company member's daily yoga and meditation entries   122
2   Tommy's Song post performance audience questionnaires   124

PART 1

Research

∵

FIGURE 1   Lou Prendergast performing in *Blood Lines*
SOURCE: PHOTOGRAPHY TIM COURTNEY, 2014

But who could resist you dad?
As London's early Ska music scene burst into life
Your brethren bringing forth the 'black music' from your island
You meet my mother in the Roaring Twenties nightclub, on
Carnaby Street
So handsome in your straw hat, and cane, and she
With fringes round the hem of her dress, caught your eye.
"He made some comment and I was hooked ..."
I hear you were creative, could draw; and sing
A sign writer my birth certificate tells me.
But another kind of creativity surfaced in your life-below-the-law

No public transport work for this immigrant bwoy!
Flash Harry had bigger fish to fry ...
And he ends up here. In Glasgow
Not a bus driver – nor a hospital auxiliary
But providing commodities that this city demanded
Hashish. And women ...

PRENDERGAST, 2014

CHAPTER 1

Know Thyself

Conscious Theatre Practice as Self-Realisation Process

Theatre (is) a spiritual practice that for both the performer and her audience can bring about experiences that help heal the world
BRASK & MEYER-DINKGRÄFE, 2010

⋮

I am a theatre artist with an interest in academic research. I worked on a PhD in partnership with the University of the West of Scotland and Playwrights' Studio Scotland, to combine theatre and performance practice with academic research. The starting point for the research is the practice. Through the practice, I explore ideas around self-realisation and the ways in which these ideologies might contribute to theatre-making, through the contemplative practices of yoga and meditation.

The practical elements of the research materialise through three semi-autobiographical theatre productions. The processes involved in the creation of the work(s) were motivated by the ideological teachings and embodied knowledge from Bikram Yoga in particular, and Vipassana meditation. Bringing these disciplines to bear upon my emerging theatre practice facilitated an enquiry around the creation of a 'conscious theatre practice' (CTP). This is a term I coined to define the overarching project methodology; marking out a territory for arts making both within academic modes of production; and out with the academy, where creative outputs became public presentations in the wider field of theatre.

Autoethnography is used as a correlative method, facilitating an analysis of journal entries, scripts and performances as autobiographical texts. This research method fits with the use of self-reflection and writing to explore personal experience. Beyond the self, autoethnography broadens out to question the potential for cultural, political and social change. The project takes an embodied approach; connections between mind and body interrogate the conjoined term 'bodymind' as the core of the research.

© KONINKLIJKE BRILL NV, LEIDEN, 2022 | DOI:10.1163/9789004467927_002

This book provides insights around the formation of conscious theatre practice (CTP). It emerges through ways of 'doing' in theatre, that are shaped by ways of seeing, and of being, ascribed to yoga and meditation. The research feeds directly into the development of new theatre company, Black Star Projects, of which I am Artistic Director. Apropos of this role, I designed the 'three C's' research model as a framework for investigations into conscious craft: writing, directing, performing; conscious casting: the 'how and why' of recruiting cast and company members; and conscious collaborations: proactively seeking ethical working relationships with collaborators. Specifically, CTP continues to influence a working manifesto, guiding the organisation's artistic processes and outputs. In the following 'sound bite,' I use creative writing as an appropriately abstract means of capturing the transformative energy of the organisation:

> black star, black sheep, black dog, underdog, underling, underlying, lies, truths, empathy, love, light, luminously bright, humble human beings.
> PRENDERGAST, 2015

Black Star works with anomalous performers and sharp-edged stories from society's margins. 'Black' in this context signifies that which is alternative to society's dominant group (Wirth, 1945). It includes, but also extends beyond racial diversity, to 'otherness' across class, age, sexuality, physicality, mentality, or indeed any 'other' marginalised position that leads to discrimination, including being female. Human suffering is acknowledged as embodied wisdom: 'who feels it, knows it'.[1] From this empathetic basis, Black Star embraces yoga and meditation as body and mind performance training methods. Yoga increases physical strength and flexibility, but equally important, both disciplines encourage a stillness of mind; augmenting an inner confidence to take risks with creative processes and content. Working with self-acceptance, we deepen our compassion for others in an ideal situation. This can happen off stage, within intra and interpersonal relationships, and on stage, through 'true' narratives drawn from 'real' life. A further realm for potential transformation is among the audience, who may also experience some shift in consciousness through contact with the work.

---

1   This phrase is a Rastafarian slogan relating to oppression. It was used by my late father and is also the album title of reggae artist Rita Marley (Shanachie, 1981).

In the following chapters, these research questions will be examined: 1. How might 'contemplative practices' that create some shift in consciousness inform the creative processes of a 'conscious theatre practice' in which the work is derived from lived experience? 2. How might the creative outputs of a 'conscious theatre practice' (in which work is drawn from lived experience and influenced by contemplative practices) contribute to processes of socio-cultural transformation? 3. How might a research methodology aligned with theatre practice contribute to an evaluation process that questions the degree to which 'conscious theatre practice' might contribute to a shift in consciousness?

My theatre and yoga practices became my inner work; utilising both disciplines to unravel some of the knots and voids of my own consciousness; my Self. Daniel Meyer-Dinkgräfe's research into the intersection of theatre and consciousness will be drawn upon throughout, providing key theoretical insights. His approach, to better understand theatre via 'the model of consciousness proposed through the Vedic Science developed by Maharishi Mahesh Yogi' is particularly pertinent (Meyer-Dinkgräfe 2005: 4). Further to Indian philosophical concerns with the development of human consciousness, the Natyashastra is the scripture dealing with drama. Meyer-Dinkgräfe's exploration of theatre aesthetics through this text demonstrates an established body of knowledge around the ancient connections between these disciplines. Furthermore, the assertion that a 'shift in consciousness ... though spiritual, is not ethereal but rooted in doing, in actions, in breathing' speaks directly to my embodied commitment to theatre and yogic practice; and the shifts in consciousness that have manifested via immersive practice (Brask and Meyer-Dinkgräfe 2010: vii).

The ongoing process of self-realisation was kick-started when I walked away from journalism. Having been writing for agendas other than my own, I took up art study to express myself. (New) life did indeed begin at forty. Arts practice set me on a path of self-enquiry that continued throughout a string of concurrent academic qualifications and arts projects, culminating in this book. The research was mainly for me; to benefit my practice. By sharing my findings, I hope that something in this book may benefit yours. To this end, I unravel the research project in its own contexts, both conceptual and methodological, beginning with Practice as Research (PaR) as the overall methodology. As Robin Nelson observes, 'advanced students engaging in PaR bring with them to the praxis a baggage of educational, experience and specialist training ... many have significant personal experience. Accordingly, they know how to engage in their practice ... their 'know-how' will be inscribed in the body' (Nelson 2013: 42). As I go on to discuss, my central role as practitioner is crucial to the bodily 'know-how' imperative in the yoga and meditation techniques that inform my theatre making.

Vipassana meditation was originally developed by Gautama Buddha, on whose teaching Buddhism was founded. Today, it is practiced through the lineage of U Ba Khin under the auspices of the late S. N. Goenka, who deems that 'direct experience of reality is essential ... at the experiential level one must understand one's own nature, mental and physical' (Goenka, 1987: 2). Bikram Choudhury, founder of Bikram Yoga through the Bishnu Gosh lineage, echoes this sentiment thus, 'real knowledge is practical knowledge, not book-reading knowledge' (Choudhury, 2007). These ideas are embedded in PaR as a theatre-making methodology, through:

> the recognition that arts making, across disciplines, can represent a form of research that generates and communicates knowledge. This is a field that has, at its defining core, the ideas of embodied knowledge and the dissemination of knowledge through the body and through experience itself.
>
> NELSON, 2009: 21

The epistemological concerns of this research involve lived experiences represented as scripts, which then become live performances. During the writing process, the knowledge gained from living my life is captured, and transforms through the embodied knowledge drawn from the writing process. The new knowledge is again reinterpreted through the creative processes involved in the making of performance, and further enhanced by the embodied knowledge of the contemplative practices used to know myself better. Autoethnography also facilitates the capacity to know oneself better, through an approach of reflexivity (Richardson, 2000). Thus, the dissemination of all this knowledge is through the practice of arts making, described as research for the purposes of this book.

As a methodology that also validates the tacit insights of experience, PaR emerges as an appropriate research modality. This method is further exemplified by Haseman and Mafe's argument that 'practice needs to be understood in its wider sense of all the activity an artist/creative practitioner undertakes: Practitioners think, read and write as well as look, listen and make' (2009: 32). The three creative outputs of this research are multi-layered, drawing upon several creative forms. *Blood Lines* (2014); *Tommy's Song* (2015); and *AWKWARD – A Life in Twenty-six Postures* (2016), facilitated experimentation across a range of creative disciplines. These included conventional playwriting, lyrical writing, song lyrics, performing, directing, selecting and sampling recorded music, working with live musicians, choreographers, designers and yoga teachers. The creative practices contribute depth, and layers of feeling, to the theoretical paradigms presented here through academic discourse.

In addition to arts making activities, my position as researcher within the project became interchangeable with a host of ancillary roles brought forward from earlier careers, including producer, band manager and PR executive. My lived experience forms my own consciousness and is subsequently brought to bear on my practice through bodily know-how; what Susan Mower terms 'corporeal consciousness' (Mower, 2010). In her discussion of corporeal mime artist Etienne Decroux (1898–91), Mower suggests that 'as theatre may change the consciousness of those partaking in its creation or its consumption, (he) changed the consciousness of modern theatre itself' (Mower, 2010: 195). Mower cites Decroux thus:

> I can remember having been a painter, a plumber, a mason, a tile-layer, a butcher, a construction worker, a docker, a coach-repairer, a dishwasher and a hospital attendant. I even put rubber tubing on refrigerator doors to make them airtight. I gathered the hay and reaped the harvest.
> After all, there were so many things to see.
> There are some poor wretches who have not seen any of that.
> I wonder how they go about producing a play.
> These things, seen and experienced first-hand, gradually moved into the back of my mind, down the back of my arms, and finally down to my fingertips where they modified the fingerprints.
> MOWER, 2010: 195

This extract demonstrates how Decroux's background impacted upon his consciousness and subsequently informed his practice, metaphorically 'modifying' his fingerprints from the inside out; from the lived experience held in his body (embodied knowledge) to the outward expression of his creativity (practice). This consideration can also be applied to this project, not only through diverse past experiences, but also embodied knowledge gained via contemplative practices, which continue to modify my consciousness. Theatre is 'an art form understood as part of a whole, as taking place in total consciousness as well as expressing consciousness(es)' (Brask & Meyer-Dinkgräfe, 2010: vii). Shifts in my consciousness were implicit in my work; with performance practice sparking the beginnings of self-diagnosis.

Meyer-Dinkgräfe outlines two separate areas of consciousness reflected in drama: 'states of consciousness, such as sleep, dream, all kinds of waking states, and altered states of consciousness; and development of consciousness, also more commonly referred to as development of character' (Meyer-Dinkgräfe,

2005: 35). In addition to the contexts of the drama itself, I propose that CTP invites the exploration of further dimensions of theatre consciousness. CTP is concerned with consciousness in relation to all the processes involved in the crafting of performance. As these are collaborative processes, it opens the potential for company members to develop their consciousness as we make the work; as well as the spectators, who may also experience some 'shift' by coming into contact with it. Jill Dolan believes that 'being passionately and profoundly stirred in performance can be a transformative experience useful in other realms of social life' (Dolan, 2005: 15). I suggest the same can be said of yogic and other contemplative practices, which equip practitioners with techniques that enable them to perform better and/or contribute more positively socially and/or globally.

1   Know Thyself

Meyer-Dinkgräfe describes a scholar 'whose thought has been influenced by non-Western philosophy, in which a more holistic, all-encompassing view of consciousness is not only theorized, but where numerous physical and mental techniques are provided' (Meyer-Dinkgräfe, 2005: 22). This portrayal resonates with my own trajectory, which aspires towards the Indian philosophical contexts of 'higher' states of consciousness (Meyer-Dinkgräfe, 2005: 24). As I go on to discuss, I have undertaken intensive 'fieldwork' within my role, described by Gold as 'complete participant,' in which the researcher 'takes an insider role, is fully part of the setting' (Gold, 1958: 217–223), while also adopting Tammy Spry's disposition of 'Performative-I subject(ive) researcher' (Spry, 2011: 53). These methods involved immersing myself in several ten-day, silent Vipassana meditation courses; and an intensive nine-week Bikram Yoga teaching training course.

Knowledge transferred from this fieldwork corroborates the Vedic Science belief that the embodiment of 'altered consciousness' has a bearing on artistic inspiration and creativity (Meyer-Dinkgräfe, 2005: 23). In addition to the phenomenology of lived experience and the reflexivity embedded in the interstices of autoethnography, the use of more conventional qualitative research methods expands the scope of the investigation. This 'data' is presented as part of the practice analysis. Hence, the research explores an aspiration towards 'higher' consciousness as a means of making distinctive work; in a conscious avoidance of producing 'deadly theatre,' described by Peter Brook as that which 'not only fails to elevate or instruct, it hardly even entertains' (Brook, 1968: 10). This ambition to 'elevate' (myself at the very least) is reflected in the key concepts 'know thyself' and 'self-realisation' inherent in CTP. I will therefore expand upon these interchangeable definitions at this juncture.

The phrases can be broken down into two cyclical, constituent parts: 1. 'know thyself,' which is linked to 'self-realisation': processes involved in 'the development of one's faculties, abilities,' (Concise Oxford Dictionary, 1990) thereby including material, physical, and socially constructed elements of self, as well as any spiritual basis; 2. 'conscious theatre practice,' which feeds out of, and back into the above, through self and others, throughout the multi-facets of performance practice.

Each concept is examined in further detail below, while simultaneously relating the separate parts to yoga and/or meditation practice. The relevance of this lies in the contribution to praxis of these specific disciplines. The term 'conscious' is defined at its most literal as 1. 'awake and aware of one's surroundings and identity,' 2. 'knowing,' and 3. 'realized or recognised by the doer' (Collins Oxford Dictionary: 243). The state of being conscious, 'consciousness,' is described as 'the totality of a person's thoughts and feelings' (COD: 343). At another level, consciousness can relate to subjective or phenomenal experience; as Susan Blackmore proposes, 'the way things seem to me, as opposed to how they are objectively' (Blackmore, 2005: 7). Embarking upon knowing oneself involves sharpening, deepening or raising one's consciousness. The concept of conscious theatre practice as a rich and manifold self-realisation process will be revealed throughout this book.

Self-cultivation is a pertinent concern of the key theorists this project draws upon, including Peter Brook and Richard Shusterman. Brook believes that 'the theatre is a vehicle, a means for self-study, self-exploration: a possibility of salvation' (Brook, 1968: 59). Moreover, for Shusterman, 'know thyself' exemplifies 'an awareness of one's vulnerability, shortcomings, mortality, or inferior stature' (Shusterman, 2012: 69). Yogic practices deepen this self-exploration. Bikram Yoga is derived from Hatha Yoga, the ancient roots of which are grounded in Hinduism, as Vipassana meditation's roots are in Buddhism. The 'know thyself' adage is common to both philosophical traditions. Buddhism expounds the importance of ' "knowing thyself" – from superficial, apparent, gross reality, to subtler realities, to the subtlest reality of mind and matter' (Goenka, 1987: 2); and in Hinduism, the phrase is referenced in the *Bhagavad-Gita*, a 700-verse Hindu scripture. Set on a battlefield, it forms the main part of epic sacred text, *Mahabharata*. Brook's theatre production *Mahabharata* (1985) will be discussed in relation to an analysis of the practice at the heart of this study.

Meyer-Dinkgräfe draws parallels between the *Bhagavad Gita's* Prince Arjuna, and Shakespeare's *Hamlet*, noting similar principles of characterization around the changes in both heroes. While representation of the divine is suggested in the form of the ghost in *Hamlet* (Meyer-Dinkgräfe, 2005: 50, 52), in the *Bhagavad-Gita* it is made explicit through dialogue between a God and a man. Deity Lord Krishna responds to Prince Arjuna's moral dilemmas with the commands 'wake up! be thyself!' and also, 'this is true knowledge, to seek the Self'. Meyer- Dinkgräfe draws upon a further major Vedic text, Patanjali's *Yoga Sutras*, dating from around 350–250 BCE. Patanjali is also responsible for the original eighty-four yoga *Asanas*, or postures, from which Bikram Choudhury adapted his contemporary sequence of twenty-six postures and two breathing exercises. Described by Choudhury as 'the father of yoga,' Patanjali was among a group of 'ancient sages' for whom yoga practice 'improves our powers of concentration, the quality we all need to recognise and achieve our Karma Yoga and Self-Realization' (Choudhury, 2007: 32). For Choudhury, self-realisation is our 'ultimate destination' (Choudhury, 2007: 5).

Vipassana meditation also teaches that 'we must begin by knowing our own nature; otherwise, we can never solve our own problems or the problems of the world' (Hart, 1987: 25). This ancient technique purports to be a cure for the ills of humanity:

> Everyone faces the problem of suffering. It is a universal malady which requires a universal remedy, not a sectarian one [...] a code of living which respects the peace and harmony of others [...] developing control over the mind and insight into one's own nature. Vipassana is a universal path'
>
> VIPASSANA MEDITATION, n.d.

Shifting between the personal and the universal, via theatre, the project attempts to apply ancient Eastern systems of self-enhancement to the processes involved in contemporary theatre making. Self-realisation is associated with embarking upon the correct and 'truthful' path that the individual should be following in line with their true 'nature'. This path is known through the philosophy of yoga as *dharma* (*dhamma* in Buddhist meditation). For Meyer-Dinkgräfe, the concept of *dharma* functions as a means to achieve higher states of consciousness and is described by Maharishi Mahesh Yogi as 'that invincible power of nature which upholds existence. It maintains evolution and forms the very basis of cosmic life. It supports all that is helpful for evolution and discourages all that is opposed to it' (Meyer Dinkgräfe, 2005: 31, 32). Self-realisation does not end with the individual; personal transformation leads in turn to social transformation.

My understanding of supporting 'all that is helpful for evolution' goes beyond Self to society. For me, this is through theatre, where 'the performer and her audience can bring about experiences that help heal the world, a shift in consciousness' (Brask & Meyer-Dinkgräfe, 2010: vii). In performance, I have the potential to raise consciousness through the scripts, performances and/or direction I give to actors, and subsequently to the audience. This is my true path, my *dharma*. One indication of this 'truth' is 'by way of enjoyment of the chosen path, and success, both inward and outward' (Meyer Dinkgräfe, 2005: 32). I am most fulfilled when I am able to express insights from my own life, or self-realisations, in a way that has moved or inspired others. This can happen during rehearsals with collaborators (inward) or through performer-spectator exchanges during performance (outward). It can also occur during yoga classes in which students experience a bodymind shift. This is truly rewarding.

2   Social Self

This project thus reflects the aspiration that CTP can contribute to social and cultural change: change that begins within, and connects to wider contexts. Utilising embodied knowledge as the raw materials of the research provides a barometer of that which, in the present or from the past, needs to be transformed or transcended, physically and/or emotionally. Hence, I locate this project within the framework of autoethnographic work, outlined by Carolyn Ellis as 'research, writing, story, and method that connect(s) the autobiographical to the cultural, social and political' (Ellis, 2004: xix). Ellis further suggests that 'autoethnographic forms feature concrete action, emotion, embodiment, spirituality and self-consciousness' (Ellis, 2004: 38). Emotion, which is inherent in my practice, surfaces as a recurrent theme in the canon of literature around this methodology. As Tami Spry asserts:

> in performative ethnography, the heart, body, spirit et al are openly and critically reflective, as such, epistemologies of pain and hope often emerge. The transdisciplinary desire addressed by alternate methodologies is motivated by our want to understand how we know what we know about pain, perhaps to quell it or console it, but at least, to speak it and introduce it into the human body of knowledge.
>
>   SPRY, 2011: 35

Autoethnographic projects are about 'putting the self into research' (Ellis, 2004: 86) and to this end, the use of the pronouns 'I' and 'my' become necessary to its written articulation. As Norman Denzin explains, 'the pronoun

I is performative; it is waiting to be used by the autobiographical subject ... along with its referent, self' (Denzin, 2014: 10). I am the 'subject' of my research, which utilises conventional and alternative modes by which the creative, emotional, physical and metaphysical 'me' can be interrogated.

A further aspect of one's identity is in relation to social structures. Denzin argues that lived experience is constructed through 'discourse in discursive systems, which often overlap and contradict one another' (Denzin, 2014: 41). Furthermore, the narratives and performances recounted by the 'subject' can only be *that* person's interpretation of the real. Within those interpretations, new realities, new truths are brought to the fore, giving credence to anecdotes and first-person accounts; my own and those of others, which are often recounted verbatim in the performances.

Jane Gallop, who coined the term *Anecdotal Theory* (2002) asserts that 'to dismiss something as "merely anecdotal" is to dismiss it as a relatively rare and marginal case; anecdotal theory would base its theorizing on exorbitant models' (Gallop, 2002: 7). As theatre research, in which the practice attempts to address the marginal, and to take risks through an avoidance of mainstream narratives and conventional processes, Gallop's use of the phrase 'exorbitant' associated with 'the excessive, romantic, perverse, unreasonable, and queer' becomes an appropriate approach for an analysis of marginal subjectivity (Gallop, 2000: 7). Anecdotal theory is a useful critical underpinning of this research. It allows for a shift in mainstream thinking, facilitating ways in which accepted epistemologies can be challenged.

Dee Heddon states that 'autobiographical performance can engage with the pressing matters of the present which relate to equality, to justice, to citizenship, to human rights' (Heddon, 2007: 15). For Spry, it is this 'language we use to articulate/represent' that forms connections between personal life and broader social issues,' giving agency to a diversity of experience (Spry, 2011: 52). Heddon notes that the majority of artists who use autobiography in their work are 'marginalised subjects ... many of these performers are lesbian, gay and/ or black and/or transgender, and their work also addresses explicitly their particular location(s) and the experiences that are inscribed there' (Heddon, 2008: 2). I too am marginalised, through the diverse core identities intrinsic to the work I create.

Situating my Self within wider socio-economic frameworks that inform the autobiography of this project is perhaps salutary at this early stage as a means of signposting the relevance of the theory engaged with throughout. There is intentional slippage between third and first-person modes of writing in the following brief outline of the circumstances that inform my subjectivity. Here and now, in this present moment, the 'subject' of the research is a 55-year-old female, single, mixed race, Scottish identified; working class, a housing association tenant on a low income, with one sibling residing permanently abroad; the mother of a 37-year-old homosexual son in a semi-stable relationship, and a 27-year-old heterosexual daughter with three children, seven-years-old and under, now separated from an unstable relationship. This grandmother, a Bikram Yoga teacher is perhaps perceived as an inspiring figure; an apparent picture of health in the yoga studio 'performing' postures requiring strength and flexibility. She is however, suffering from a hidden autoimmune disorder, Mixed Connective Tissue Disease; with Lupus and its associated Nephritis, manifesting as the deadliest of the 'mix' of conditions falling under that umbrella term.

I was born in London, the second illegitimate child (my sister preceded me by exactly one year and one day) of a 21-year-old Londoner (mother) and a 29-year-old (perhaps – this is unverified) Jamaican migrant of Irish heritage, who arrived in the UK at the age of 17 (possibly) and lived a life of criminality. My parents, many years deceased, separated when I was 7 years old. Contact with my father was sporadic from then on and I saw him for the final time at 15-years-old. My mother raised us alone and in poverty in the village of Tullibody, Clackmannanshire, where we were subjected to racism and a feeling of exclusion from the dominant group; being racially different, without a father, without a working parent and subsequently poorer (although it was an area of deprivation in general). We were the daughters of a mother who was 'different' on a number of levels: culturally, in her style, her English dialect and her comparatively 'bohemian' behaviours by 1970s social standards. My mother practiced yoga and had a keen interest in Eastern philosophies. Her parenting style was particularly 'hands-off' however, bordering on neglectful and even abusive, by contemporary understandings of child welfare. These unconventional and somewhat emotionally unstable beginnings were offset by alternative ways of seeing, and of being in the world, and afforded an inherited tendency to view life through an artistic lens. I graduated from Glasgow School of Art in my forties, precisely as my mother had done, exactly twenty-five years before me.

These contributory socio-psychological factors manifest in the socially engaged practice in which I situate my work. My creative practice is realised via a feminist perspective, a mixed-race sensibility and a social conscience. In theatre, I bring synthesis to my intellectual, political and visual ideas. My writing found form in journalism, transformed through visual art practice and makes its foray into theatre. Here, new creative skills marry with old; the reporter's nose for narrative possibilities and innate acquiescence to deadlines, meets the sculptor's consideration of site and the vision to transform space. Gay McAuley gives meaning to these former experiences, explaining that 'contemporary performance has a complex genealogy, deriving as much from the visual arts as from different theatre practices' (McAuley, 2000: 121). Fine Art training has an ongoing bearing upon my theatre-making trajectory. It is where autobiographical work took tangible form, culminating in a degree-show installation about my late mother and the Eastern philosophies that expanded her world-view perspectives (Prendergast, 2011). Themes around the demise of my parents, and my own mortality, bleed into my theatre-making. New challenges arose around artistic processes that formerly involved still forms, that now involved performing bodies: from the static to the dynamic.

3   Feminist Self

Glasgow School of Art is also the location in space and time where feminism scholarship began in earnest. The scope of my research is around the creation of a conscious theatre practice as self-realisation process, which derives from an informed feminist perspective. As Willet et al attest, 'the topic of the self has long been salient in feminist philosophy, for it is pivotal to questions about personal identity, the body, sociality and agency that feminism must address (Willet et al. 2016). A crucial element in my 'self-realisation' has been the understanding, through lived experience, that I am subject to patriarchal systems and social structures of power and control. My performance practice emerges from this basis. Chimamanda Ngozi Adichie's *We Should All Be Feminists* (2014) highlights what I already knew: that women do more housework than men, that the word 'feminism' has negative connotations, that women do not enjoy the same male freedoms, that it is more difficult for a woman to challenge her boss at work, and that society expects women to be married. Life taught me those lessons, not books.

   In 2011 my GSA dissertation explored 'other' feminisms that were pertinent to me. Writing before the word 'intersectionality' had arrived as a buzzword in my academic consciousness, I structured this semi-autobiographical work around four anecdotal and interrelated themes: 'Go Back to Where You Came From: Colour Prejudice, from Racial Abuse to Eurocentric Aesthetics'; 'Nobody's Going To Marry You Now: Lone Parents, Changing Families, Changing Feminisms'; 'You Smell Like a Fish Factory: Gay Misogyny, a New Expression of an Ancient Problem'; and 'Smacking Bottoms, Twisted Sisters: Women Playing Dirty in the Workplace' (Prendergast, 2011). There are interlocking layers of female denigration. As Nina Lykke explains: 'intersectionality today has become a central theoretical paradigm for conceptualising multiple identities, multi-layered workings of power in social relations (and) institutional arrangements' (Lykke, 2014: 5). My work speaks to a range of interweaving marginalities that inform my autobiographical arts-making. The theatre productions encapsulate almost a decade of feminist struggles. Feminism is in me. My plays are of me.

Feminist positionality is not explicit in this book; it resides in tacit female wisdom and in stories I choose to tell through arts making. The feminism in my work aligns with Chandra T Mohanty's vision of feminism, which is concerned with 'making connections between the many levels of social reality we experience' and the 'interwoven processes of sexism, racism, misogyny, and heterosexism that are an integral part of our social fabric, wherever in the world we happen to be' (Mohanty, 2003: 3). From the narrative around the Jamaican prostitute and the experience of female slaves on Scottish owned Caribbean plantations in *Blood Lines*; the blatant sexism of the male character in *Tommy's Song* and his insecurities around his masculine identity; to the plethora of race, class and gender inequality presented in *AWKWARD: A Life in Twenty-Six Postures*, these are feminist works. I am a feminist artist.

The idea that 'gender, race and class stratification do not operate in isolation from one another but rather interact to produce compound effects' is further augmented in the article 'Feminist Perspectives on the Self' (author unknown, 2015). I identify as an intersectional subject by dint of belonging to more than one subordinated group: female, poor, mixed race, and also unmarried, a lone parent, and intermittently less than able-bodied. Perhaps less than able 'body-minded' is the more salient phrase within the realms of this research. Of further interest to my investigation, it is noted that 'while intersectional theorists bring forward race, class, ability and other socio-economic markers as central to physical-historical locations of agency, power and connectivity, a number of feminists are increasingly paying attention to somatic-organic factors in selfhood' (*ibid*). Following this line of enquiry, I suggest it remiss of any philosophies of Self to ignore the neurobiology of childhood trauma.

In the Adverse Childhood Experiences (ACE) survey, a series of ten 'yes or no' questions are presented, with a point for each affirmative answer. They concern life experiences up until the age of 18 that might have had a developmental, traumatic effect. I scored six. Donna Jackson Nakazawa's study of the latent costs of childhood trauma reveals that 'a remarkable, disproportionate number of individuals who had experienced childhood adversity were later hospitalised for an autoimmune condition – and a disproportionate number of these individuals were women' (Nakazawa, 2015: 98). It was found that 'for every ACE Score a woman had, the higher her risk became, and the more likely she was to end up in the hospital at some point in her adult life in order to be treated for an autoimmune condition' Nakazawa, 2015: 98). Furthermore, if a person is diagnosed with one autoimmune disease, they are three times more likely to develop other autoimmune conditions. As mentioned in the previous section, I have a few.

Health also features in Mohanty's feminism in her vision of 'a world where women and men are free to live creative lives, in security and with bodily health and integrity ... a vision in which economic stability, ecological sustainability, racial equality, and the redistribution of wealth form the material basis of people's well-being' (Mohanty, 2003: 3). I am fortunate to have found ways to live a semi-creative life; through education and/or arts funding, while living simultaneously with the stress of poverty. Arts making is richer than any monetary value that could be attached to it. In the section of Nakazawa's book that addresses strategies to help heal from childhood trauma, the 'twelve steps to help you come back to who you really are' offers insights around 'writing to heal' (Nakazawa, 2015: 158) and 'mending the body by moving the body' including practicing yoga (Nakazawa, 2015: 177). It is not surprising then, that I have been drawn to writing and yoga practice. Nakazawa's theory is that one's biography becomes one's biology; and that children who experienced adversity in childhood grow into adults akin to the 'walking wounded' (2015). Nakazawa terms it 'the new psychosocial theory of everything: our early emotional stories determine the body and brain's operating system and how well they will be able to guard our optimal physical and emotional health all our adult lives' (Nakazawa, 2015: 58). Trauma impacts health. My 'early stories' reside in Lykke's 'in-between spaces between monolithic identity categories'. Writing them is agency; facilitating an engagement with social structures and power dynamics (Lykke, 2014: 3).

4   Sick Self

The prospect of death focuses the mind. In November 2014, I developed Nephrotic Syndrome, 'a collection of symptoms that indicate kidney damage' (Nephrotic Syndrome in Adults, n.d.). This in turn caused a blood clot on my lung; or pulmonary embolism: 'a blockage in the pulmonary artery, the blood vessel that carries blood from the heart to the lungs' (Pulmonary Embolism – Causes – NHS Choices, n.d.). Contrary to my earlier position, resisting medication that would further weaken my immune system, I reluctantly began an intensive course of steroid and immunosuppressant drugs. The renal consultants made it clear that this treatment, if effective, might save my life. From their use of the word 'if,' I surmised the precariousness of my predicament. I was dying. When faced with such a choice, I elected to live. Secondary to an inherent obligation to stay alive as long as possible for one's family, there was theatre to be made, a book to complete: something to live for, something to leave behind. I was fortunate to have a creative outlet; a cathartic means of expression that became a coping strategy. Paramedics' eyebrows rose as their patient edged into the ambulance clutching a laptop. In hospital, I wrote myself though my crisis. My body, even as it was failing, was providing inspiration.

Gay McAuley writes of the way in which the body of the performer has taken precedence in the last 25 years, constituting something of a paradigm shift

> in the way the body is conceptualized in Western philosophy, sociology, and even medicine; no longer ... seen simply as the material container for mind and spirit, it is now increasingly perceived to be at the centre of a complex web of interrelationships with every aspect of the individual's being and with the world surrounding that individual.
>
> MCAULEY, 2000: 120

For McAuley, this presents deep ramifications for theatre praxis, 'for the theatre,' as she explains, 'more than any other art form draws on, plays with, and exploits the reality of the human body' (McAuley, 2000: 120). This transformation of scholarly thinking on the body has been termed the 'corporeal turn' by Maxine Sheets-Johnstone (1990), promoting further understandings of the way in which conceptualisations of the body have shifted. She states that 'through its Cartesian legacy, the body was consistently presented as mere material handmaiden of an all-powerful mind, a necessary but ultimately discountable aspect of cognition, intelligence and even affectivity' (2009: 2). Sheets-Johnstone likens this 'misrepresentation' to a '350-year-old wound that has been covered over – not healed – by the lexical band-aid of embodiment' (Sheets-Johnstone, 2009: 2). For the purposes of research through practice, however, the notion of embodiment serves this study well. Nelson argues that 'some practice-as-research (PaR) projects that advance the idea of 'embodied knowledge' pose a challenge to the privileging of mind over body in the Western intellectual tradition in respect of the locus of knowledge' (Nelson, 2009: 20). This project is among them, as will become evident in the following chapter, which seeks to unpack prevailing body and mind polarity as a central concern of the research.

The idea of the body as repository for the mind is again challenged through Havi Carel's use of phenomenology, which she defines as 'a philosophical approach advocating a description of lived experience and consciousness' (Carel, 2008: 13). It is from this premise that she writes about her illness, intersecting her personal story with insights gleaned from her work as a philosopher.

The actual experience of the disease-bearer, socially, physically and psychologically forms the focal point of her work. Carel asserts that:

> the body is not an automaton operated by the person but the embodied person herself. We are our bodies; consciousness is not separate from the body [...] Disease cannot be taken as a mere dysfunction, because there is nothing in human existence that is purely biological. We are embodied consciousness, so consciousness is inseparable, both conceptually and empirically, from the body. Therefore, the concept of illness must be reconceived to take this unity into account.
>
> CAREL, 2008: 13–14

This view that energy and consciousness are inseparable is echoed by Gill Edwards, whose notion of *Conscious Medicine* (2010) influenced the title of my theatre research. For Edwards, 'the human body can be seen as a visible and structured energy system, which interacts with structured "invisible energies" such as thoughts and emotions, as well as with the universal energy field' (Edwards, 2010: 9). Edwards' aspirations for conscious medicine resonate to some extent with those of conscious theatre practice, both being: 'energy-conscious – releasing blockages or limitations, shifting negative beliefs, resolving inner conflicts, discharging past traumas, or helping energy flow more freely' (Edwards, 2010: xxii). I suggest that Edward's aims might not be out of place in the practice of any contemporary, devised or physical theatre company; a workshop undertaken with Glasgow-based 'Company of Wolves', perhaps providing a case in point (2015).

As explored in the following chapter, the connection between energy and consciousness is not new in its application to theatre-making. Diverse performance pioneers have established practices that work with the body's 'inner energy', central to many global training methods. At times I will refer to contemplative practices as 'energy practices,' which tap into 'universal energy,' also known as Chi, qi, ki, prana, mana or vital force' (Edwards, 2010: 28). However, as Susan Mower cautions, 'a multiple of conflicting theories surround the explanation as to whether a singular, universal life-force exists and what this could be attributed to – a divine entity for instance, or yogic principles' (Mower, 2010: 194). This enquiry supports investigations around the latter over the former, analysing ways in which yogic principles might contribute to contemporary and historical performance praxis. Carel points to studies that 'claim that the experience of illness can promote personal growth through awareness and transformational change,' and that 'others note that for some chronically ill people illness becomes a tool of self-discovery and a fundamental source of later self-development' (Carel, 2008: 77). This research aligns itself with these claims. It argues for the centrality of 'energy' to discussions of the body in performance, as inextricably linked to the ideas of self-realisation inherent in the 'conscious theatre practice' model.

5   Outline of Chapters

Chapter 2 expands upon the conceptual contexts around yoga and meditation that underpin theatre practices resonating with this study. It includes Nicolas Núñez' *Anthropocosmic Theatre* (1996); Phillip Zarrilli's *Psychophysical Acting* (2009) and Richard Shusterman's *Somaesthetics* (2008, 2012), as much for the embodiment of their respective energy practices as for their theoretical insights. Through their work, an analysis of the conjoined term 'bodymind' comes into play, a concept that dissolves mind and body dualities and becomes integral to holistic training systems. Although the work of Japanese Noh Theatre creator Motokiyo Zeami influenced all three theorists, the scope of this far-reaching Japanese aesthetic extends beyond the conceptual frameworks of this book. Rather, the section focuses on the yogic ideas and practices that contributed to systems developed by Konstantin Stanislavski and Jerzy Grotowski. Further explorations of the spiritual and the holy include Peter Brook's theatre-making processes. The praxis of these influential theatre-making theorists resonates with CTP, situating my practice in the wider field.

The thrust of Chapter 3 is methodology. It examines practice as research and autoethnography; from embodied knowledge to self-reflexivity. It explores the methods that guided the research, beginning with a justification of PaR as the appropriate methodological approach. This line of enquiry continues through somatic knowledge gathering. Autoethnography is a simultaneous research thread, dealing with personal narrative and self-enquiry. In Chapter 4, an analysis is presented of the ways in which experiments in consciousness impacted upon the design of the research. It was crucial to 'really walk the walk, not just talk the talk' in order to filter out the practices that were less useful to this enquiry (Shusterman, 2012: 4). Consequently, I deepened my understanding of why specific disciplines are essential to it. Actor training programmes with Philip Zarrilli (2016), Nicolás Núñez (2015) and Company of Wolves (2016) informed thinking around energy and arts-making; as did workshops with Deborah Templeton (Yoga and Creativity, 2014) and Lee Worley (Mudra Space Awareness, 2016). The intensity of deep engagement with Bikram Yoga and Vipassana meditation were most transformative. These experiences became embodied methodologies that provided research 'data'.

Chapter 5 introduces the 'three 'C's' research model, a comparative framework for thinking through the creative processes on each production: casting; collaborating; and craft (writing, directing, performing). If the principles, as well as the rigorous practices of Bikram Yoga and Vipassana meditation purport to form the cornerstone of the art of living, this enquiry asks how these concepts might be adapted and translated into a blueprint for the art of theatre-making. This is tested throughout the section, interrogating the practical elements of the work through this bespoke model. The three C's framework enables ethereal concepts to be 'rooted in doing, in actions, in breathing' as Brask and Meyer-Dinkgräfe suggest of 'shifts in consciousness' (2010: vii). Elements of the making of the work are compared and contrasted against it. Moreover, the work of other theatre-makers is explored, analysing the positioning of my performance practice in relation to theirs.

Each one of the three practical works is followed by an evaluation, drawing upon qualitative research methods including questionnaires and discussions. CTP involves listening to and learning from others. Theatre-making peers provided feedback, both in a focus group setting and in consultancy roles, throughout the creative processes. Theatre critics' reviews are also consulted, utilising discourse analysis as a further evaluation tool. Informative and useful critique of the work(s) was drawn from these discursive media strategies. The interpretation of the data generated through each theatre project influenced and shaped the design of the next. This reflexive approach enabled the cyclical process of 'planning, acting, observing, reflecting and re-planning' outlined in Kemmis and McTaggart's model of critical action research (Kemmis and McTaggart, 2008: 276). In turn, this field of analysis contributed to ideas around the development of Black Star Projects; a new, socially engaged theatre company that draws upon yogic practice as a self-realisation process.

In the book's Conclusion, I recap the research questions and intentions; and consider the highlights, along with the limitations and antagonisms of working with conscious theatre practice throughout the project. Research findings are applied to the development of the Black Star Projects' manifesto. Moreover, a discussion of ethics and the working practices of ensemble contribute to the social aims at the heart of the company's creative practice. As an adjunct to theatre, the setting up of the BodyMind Studio as a Community Interest Company has afforded the opportunity to work with those on society's margins, to make positive changes in their lives through the embodiment of yoga, and potentially theatre. I discuss ideas around making new work; with those attending the studio as potential theatre collaborators. A new concept of yoga for addiction: Y12SR – the Yoga of 12-Step Recovery, is introduced along with TCTSY – Trauma Centre Trauma Sensitive Yoga.

In summary of this multi-layered project, sharing my experience for the benefit of other practitioners, it oscillates between: (1.) personal transformation through contemplative performance practice; (2.) the making of the theatre work(s) and (3.) the tensions and negotiations around public presentations of the productions. It occupies a feminist, intersectional position that is implicit in the work. It uses autoethnographic methods, from yogic practice to reflexive analysis of autobiographical writing and performance. Anecdotal theory and phenomenology are drawn upon. Self-realisation as an ongoing process drives the research through the challenges of collaboration with 'other(s)'; in their actual and/or semi-fictionalised marginality, and their 'otherness' to the aims of the project. They were inside and outside of the research; as were the staff at the venues, the essential spaces where the works were seen; and the audience(s), occupying yet another relationship with, and to, the productions. This theatre study challenges and tests the potential for social and/or cultural change through experiencing the work.

FIGURE 2   Tom McGovern performing in *Tommy's Song*
SOURCE: PHOTOGRAPHY LESLIE BLACK, 2015

I flipped.
I pulled ma fist back and smashed him in the mouth.
His false teeth split.
Blood spurted onto ma ma's good carpet.
He staggered fae the blow and grabbed the back o a chair.
I hit him again. And again.
He bashed his heid aff the table and ended up on the flair.
I goat this rush.
This flashback tae him crackin me ow'er the heid wi a chair leg.
I wiz aboot fourteen.
I remember trying to get away fae um.
He widnae stoap.
The pain wiz so bad a wid o jumped oot the windae to get away.
It wiz like we wur back there.
Only this time it wiz me that widnae stoap.
Sinkin the boot in.
I wiz like a wild beast.
Kickin an stampin! An kickin! An stampin!

PRENDERGAST, 2015

CHAPTER 2

Bodymind

Yoga, Meditation and Theatre Practice

The actor's bodymind is the vehicle for the audience's experience.

ZARRILLI, 2009: 77

∴

This chapter examines ways in which yoga and meditation can contribute to the principles and processes of theatre practice. It consults published works in which theorists and/or theatre-makers, past and present, draw upon ideas around energy in relation to performance: conceptually; physically; and arguably, spiritually. Energy practices that resonate with this projects' interest in self-realisation processes in theatre-making are fused together with disparate elements of theoretical and epistemological knowledge around yoga and meditation, to form a newly interpreted holism of performance praxis.

Multiple lines of enquiry are inherent in the 'conscious theatre practice' at the heart of the research. Consequently, Bikram Yoga and Vipassana meditation specifically, are expanded upon as a pre-cursor to the discussion of theatre practitioners who use(d) energy practices in their creative processes. Defining these practices as 'conscious' theatre practices, I apply my own term (CTP) to the work of artists whose methods connect to my research in illuminating ways. Simultaneously, spaces and challenges are identified for the discovery of new knowledge around how these apparently distinct disciplines might be drawn upon in theatre. This opens a route by which gaps can be established and methodologies can be shaped.

In the call for proposals for the 2016 Performance and Mindfulness Symposium, the Centre for Psychophysical Performance Research at Huddersfield University suggests that ever since Stanislavsky, Eastern philosophies and meditation practices have held an enduring allure for practitioners of Western theatre. However, the growing body of research around mindfulness in clinical and educational contexts is not being matched in performance fields. There are 'few studies explicitly examining the role of mindfulness and meditation in theatre and performance' (Mindfulness and Performance, 2016).

© KONINKLIJKE BRILL NV, LEIDEN, 2022 | DOI:10.1163/9789004467927_003

This project contributes to the aforementioned gap in knowledge, through an interrogation of yoga and meditation as contemplative performance practices.

Utilising a thematic approach, this chapter begins with an expansion of the term 'bodymind'. The purpose of this is twofold. First, it explores the academic literature that points to the historic moment when mind and body became separate, impacting knowledge production in Western philosophical circles. Second, the term is explored in relation to emotional and energetic 'psychophysical' systems, as a crucial point of reference for CTP practitioners. Segueing into the following section, a selection of literature around yoga and meditation philosophies and practices in their own right is discussed. As this field is infinite, the chapter hones-in upon those works that resonate with self-realisation concepts and/or systems believed to enhance energy. Both disciplines are discussed more fully in later chapters, as they become increasingly important to rehearsal processes. Yoga and meditation are ancient systems of self-cultivation. As the literature reveals, yoga's role was interwoven with traditional Indian drama and has been an influence on Western theatre for the past one hundred years. It is from this point of departure that the final section of this chapter begins.

Turning to Conscious Theatre Practice, the section narrows the field to the five theatre-makers whose work is of particular interest. Following a discussion of key spiritual concepts inherent in the principles of yoga and meditation, the section explores Indian drama and the Hindu religious-philosophic base from which it originally emerged. This provides context for the subsequent exploration of literature around Stanislavsky's fascination with Eastern disciplines and the impact of Yogi Ramacharaka on his work. The director's palpable influence is then compared and contrasted with Grotowski's working principles. Brook's notion of Holy theatre is also examined. Zarrilli and Núñez have also worked with psychophysical energy systems in their respective workshops (which I had the privilege to attended), demonstrating the lineage of ancient philosophies and practices on contemporary theatre.

1   Bodymind

This section explores the concept of 'bodymind', in which mind and body are perceived as a single entity; the entire human organism. It begins with a discussion of the historical circumstances that brought about the dualism of mind and body that prevails in the West today. This dichotomy has ramifications for the research in a number of ways. The philosophical tradition of privileging mind over body affects the ways in which knowledge gathering is perceived within academia. It is consequently argued that practice-as-research (PaR) poses a challenge to existing educational paradigms (Nelson, 2009). Moreover, through the lens of alternative medicine, the case is presented that mind and body are inextricably linked in health and well-being. Harmonious energy flow is further promoted through the embodied philosophy of Richard Shusterman, for whom bodymind is a central concern of his *Somaesthetics* (2008, 2012). The section ends with Michael Khan's comparative study of two approaches for eliminating energy blockages (1985). Wilhelm Reich's Orgone Energy and the Vipassana of Theravada Buddhists reveal the ways in which these apparently opposing systems share some common goals.

Robin Nelson suggests the division of mind and body goes back to classical Athens, where it was first introduced by Plato (Nelson, 2009). Moreover, Nelson posits that Plato's philosophy opened a schism between theory and practice which, by the late seventeenth century, prioritised knowledge over 'reasoning, belief and illusion' as 'the origins and nature of the universe were de-coupled from myth and religion' (Nelson, 2009: 114). Gill Edwards provides further insights into the ways in which science and religion contributed to this division:

> During the Reformation, when the rational, masculine world of Protestantism suppressed the more feminine world of Catholicism and the Holy Mother [...] Descartes split mind from body and scientists came to an arrangement with the church whereby science would deal with the visible world (including nature and the body), while religion would address the unseen realms (including the mind and mortality).
>
> EDWARDS, 2010: 22

Edwards presents key theoretical insights relating to a defining moment in science and religion, which for Nelson, led to the ' "problem of knowledge": when intellect and objective, rational thought, were prioritised over the carnal desires and emotions in the "lowest part of the soul"'(Nelson, 2009: 114). This divide was further deepened 'by Descartes' retreat in the "cogito" ('I think therefore I am') into the mind as the sole locus of certain knowledge' (Nelson, 2009: 115). This line of thought advances Nelson's argument that Descartes' privileging of *thinking* over doing, cemented the prioritising of theory over practice in the Western intellectual tradition. Forms of 'bodily dissemination of knowledge', of which we can include practice-as-research, therefore challenge academic culture (Nelson, 2009: 115). PaR is thus an approach operating within an inherited skepticism. Consequently, this project adopts systematic methodological rigour and documentation to support the research.

Although Nelson charges Descartes with the 'denigration' of embodied knowledge, he also credits the philosopher's pioneering approach with 'opening up possibilities for establishing new paradigms based upon rigorous questioning' which continue to prevail (Nelson, 2009: 115). In the early 1990s, for example, Simon Jones called for a new epistemology: a practice 'not guaranteed in texts and their translations, but bodies and their transformations' (Jones, 2009: 20). Jones' clarion call for movement in mainstream thinking towards embodied knowledge fits the contemporary concept of the corporeal turn. This paradigm shift challenges the age-old disunion between mind and body.

According to Gay McAuley 'actor training institutions have, somewhat belatedly, begun to recognise that these developments call for a shift in the nature of their own practices' (McAuley, 2000: 121). McAuley cites Philip Zarrilli's training as a system that is challenging the 'dominant psychological paradigm underpinning actor training in the West' (McAuley, 2000: 121). The notion of bodymind is essential to Zarrilli's work with actors. He described it as 'a deeply felt, resonant inhabitation of the subtle psychophysical dimensions of the body and mind at work together as one in the moment' (Zarrilli, 2009: 4). This optimal state of bodymind 'oneness' acknowledges the importance of energy in performance, supporting theories that it is inseparable from consciousness.

Debbie Shapiro augments the debate with an explanation of bodymind as the 'complexity of the energies that make up our entire being, energies that are constantly communicating and flowing between each other; between our thoughts, feelings and the physical maintenance of our physical parts' (Shapiro, 1990: 2). As a practitioner of meditation and psychology, her interests lie predominantly in healing. Shapiro believes that the 'bodymind matrix reflects psychological and somatic harmony: the body is simply a gross manifestation of the subtlety of the mind' (Shapiro, 1990: 3). Moreover, Gill Edwards perceives 'disease as the expression of emotional dis-ease', which would necessarily require a holistic, somatic remedy.

The attainment of somatic harmony is also pertinent for Shusterman, who describes 'Somaesthetics' as 'the critical study and meliorative cultivation of how we experience and use the living body (or soma) as a site of sensory appreciation (aesthesis) and creative self-fashioning' (Shusterman, 2008: 1). Shusterman's use of the term 'meliorative' captures ideas of self-improvement inherent in this embodied philosophy, while 'sensory appreciation' speaks to the sharpening of focus that can be brought about by meditative practices. Both parts of the definition are useful to this research, as a disciplinary framework. The 'soma' for Shusterman is the 'living, feeling, sentient' body linked to the study of somatic consciousness, somatic cultivation and somatic understanding (Shusterman, 2008: 1). Even the latter part of his description, 'creative self-fashioning' speaks to the importance of aesthetics in performance.

Yoga and meditation fall within Shusterman's ideal of somatic training, which aims to 'instill better bodymind harmony, proper demeanor, and superior skill for appropriate action' (Shusterman, 2012: 34). It could be argued that the development of these same attributes enhances theatrical performance. Although Shusterman is not a theatre practitioner *per se*, he asserts that somaesthetics can be 'applied to theatre through an analysis of the somatic styles of movement and posture of actors on stage' (Shusterman, 2012: 8). Somaesthetics is concerned with perception, consciousness and feeling, which are also the interests of the performer. Comprising theory and practice, Somaesthetics provides an appropriate critical underpinning for this research.

Shusterman uses the term 'body-mind' in order to 'aptly express their essential union', as Edwards, Shapiro and Zarrilli do, while simultaneously enabling a pragmatic 'distinguishing between mental and physical aspects of behaviour' (2012: 27). This apparent contradiction dissipates with Shusterman's explanation that a mind and body distinction 'leaves room ... for the project of increasing their experiential unity' (2012: 27). Attaining experiential unity of mind and body is a goal common to all the bodymind theorists and practitioners included in this section. Moreover, a commitment to the 'key role of meditative, spiritual somatic disciplines' in somaesthetics (Shusterman, 2012: 16) and the approaches to practice 'that awaken experience through the subtle, inner bodymind,' in Zarrilli's psychophysical acting (2009: 59), render both frameworks fundamental to investigations around CTP.

It is worth noting antagonism towards bodymind, however. Although the conjoining of body with mind may appear plausible at the surface level, in Victor Ramirez Ladron de Guevara's discussion, 'the term "body" is a contested concept' (Ladron de Guevara, 2011: 21). Many theories around the body have emerged in response to Descartes' separation of mind and body, known as Cartesian dualism (Ladron de Guevara, 2011: 23). Ladron de Guevara points out how psychologists, including Freud (1977) and Lacan (1980), wrote *about* the body, as did philosophers including Derrida (1990), Bourdieu (1990) and Foucalt (1991); and for feminist writers, including Irigaray (1985) and Kristeva (1995), the body became crucial to their theories (Ladron de Guevara, 2011:23). Nonetheless, the Cartesian legacy continues to permeate understandings of the body in science, and consequently medicine.

Ladron de Guevara asserts that Maurice Merleau-Ponty's concept of phenomenology in which 'the mind is not detached from the body's senses ... has had a profound effect on a wide-range of performance studies scholars who have used a phenomenological approach to engage with diverse disciplines'

(Ladron de Guevara, 2011: 26). Zarrilli is cited among those who have utilised Merleau-Ponty's work as a lens through which to analyse acting processes. For Ladron de Guevara, however, these phenomenological methods 'are still contested by many' (Ladron de Guevara, 2011: 24). Amy Cook argues that 'our language reflects (and thus rehearses and repeats) the Cartesian split of heart, mind and body' (Cook, 2013: 83). I suggest that yoga and meditation are crucial to their essential re-union.

2   Philosophical Contexts of Yoga and Meditation

This section provides an overview of the literature pertaining to Bikram Yoga and Vipassana meditation. Its inclusion at this particular juncture provides requisite background information on the specific disciplines this research draws upon to inform new ways of working in theatre. As the following chapter explores the *practices* of theatre-makers influenced by non-Western training systems, it is appropriate here to establish the *principles* of Bikram Yoga (Bikram) and Vipassana meditation (Vipassana). As both schools of thought take their place within a lineage stretching back thousands of years, this discussion draws upon literature connected to the broader concepts of yoga and meditation. Brief historical context is provided to situate both practices within their contemporary materialisations.

Parallels can be drawn between the role of the director of a theatrical production, or theatre training regime, and the leader of a yoga or meditation system. This section compares the two overall teachers of the Bikram and Vipassana techniques, Bikram Choudhury and Satya Narayan Goenka, revealing vast differences in their approach, and striking similarities in their ideologies. Although the concern of this research is with their practices, not their personal lives or personalities, it is nonetheless useful to introduce some basic facts regarding the ways in which each teacher discovered their 'calling'. Building upon the themes of knowing one's true Self, introduced in the preceding chapter, key principles shared by the philosophical bases from which these practices emerged are explored. These ancient codes of conduct continue to inform the development of the theatre company manifesto under development, which will be analysed in the concluding chapter.

From the earliest incarnations of yoga, as the discussion below attests, it could be argued that yoga is in itself a form of practice-as-research. Historically, those committed to it were akin to researchers, questioning and challenging sources of knowledge and power. Stephen Cope asserts that 'the wisdom of classical yoga has its roots in the social and spiritual crucible of what is now

India, during the sixth, fifth and fourth centuries BCE' (Cope, 2006: xxvii). It was a time of social and religious upheaval, a time of enquiry. Cope states that 'thousands of seekers and wandering philosophers and ascetics examined the meaning of life, and the possibilities of being human' (Cope, 2006: xxvii). Through their study of life and their experiments involving their own bodies and minds, 'a set of reliable principles and practices emerged ... this tradition became known as yoga – a word that literally means "to yoke" or to bring into union – and its practitioners as "yogis" ' (Cope, 2006: xxvii).

Those undertaking PaR in performance are also experimenting with their own bodies and minds to create principles and practices. The Black Star Projects manifesto is developing in this way, bridging the gap perhaps, between theatre practitioner and 'yogi'. This term is used with some caution here, acknowledging that within contemporary translations, a yogi may simply refer to any student attending a class, belying the more purist origins of the word.

Contrary to looser, latter-day definitions of the term, the authentic yogi, or 'guru', is regarded in India as a spiritual master. Bikram Choudhury, yoga teacher and hot yoga creator, formerly possessed such yogic credentials. Born in Calcutta, in the Indian state of Bengal, Choudhury began practicing yoga at the age of three. He was educated at the Ramakrishna Mission in Deoghar, one of India's great *ashrams,* or yoga schools. Ram Krishna was the guru of Swami Vivekenanda, described by Choudhury as 'the first Indian yogi to bring the message of Self-realization to the United States, in 1893' (Choudhury, 2007: 27). Choudhury dedicates his life's work to his own guru, Bishnu Charan Gosh. The brother of Paramahansa Yogananda, author of *Autobiography of a Yogi* (1946), Choudhury describes Bishnu Gosh as 'the greatest physical culturist to emerge in the last 500 years' (Choudhury, 2007: 22). Choudhury reveres this 'sacred' lineage, remaining committed to the ideal of yoga as a spiritual practice, despite creating a global business empire and achieving celebrity status in the US; until spectacularly falling from grace in recent years as allegations of sexual abuse and bullying emerged.

By way of contrast, the late S. N. Goenka was a spiritual master who avoided the spotlight. William Hart states of the Vipassana meditation teacher that:

> despite his magnetic presence, Mr. Goenka has no wish to be a guru who turns his disciples into automatons [...] he shuns all expressions of devotion to him, instead directing his students to be devoted to the technique, to the truth that they find within themselves.
>
> HART, 1988: 2

Choudhury also demands devotion to his technique, but Goenka's enduring belief, in diametric opposition to capitalist pursuits, is that 'meditation must never become a business, to maintain its purity' (Hart, 1988: 2). As with Bikram Yoga studios and courses, Vipassana meditation centres are peppered all over the globe. However, Vipassana runs on a not-for-profit basis. Courses are donation based, with each student's *dana* (donation) enabling a future student to attend a course. Goenka never received pay for his teaching, nor do any of his authorised assistant teachers. Goenka 'distributes the technique of Vipassana purely as a service to humanity, to help those who are in need' (Hart, 1988: 2). Despite major operational differences, both teachings, drawn respectively from Hindu and Buddhist faiths, are ideologically aligned with the notion of Self, and therefore this theatre study.

As with Choudhury, Goenka occupies a position within a lineage of Vipassana teachers dating back through the centuries. Goenka was taught the technique by Sayagyi U Ba Khin of Burma, who was in turn taught by Saya U Thet, one of Burma's prominent meditation teachers in the first half of the century and former pupil of Ledi Sayadaw, 'a famous Burmese scholar-monk of the late nineteenth and early twentieth centuries' (Hart, 1988: 8). Goenka was born into a Hindu family in Burma. He became a businessman. In reversal to the path taken by Choudhury, who began helping people for free in India but later created a fortune, Goenka began with enterprise but turned away from it as his Vipassana practice deepened. He first met U Ba Khin in 1955 when attending meditation in search of a cure for his chronic migraine headaches.

Choudhury began developing his yogic system after a weight-lifting accident left him with a crushed knee and doctors said he would never walk again. Both masters were drawn into their respective practices due to their own physical suffering. Like Choudhury, Goenka began teaching in India, bringing the Vipassana technique back to its country of origin, after being authorised by U Ba Khin in 1969. Goenka cites Buddha via the Pali *Sutta Pitaka*, the most ancient and accurate record of Gautama Buddha's experiences. Choudhury cites from Patanjali's Sanskrit *Yoga Sutras*. Pali and Sanskrit are both ancient languages of India, with the reach of Pali extending to Theravadin Buddhist countries. The relevance of both teachings to this study is couched within inherent ideas of self-realisation and bodymind harmony.

Zarrilli points out that from its first beginnings, yoga 'developed as a practical pathway towards the transformation of consciousness (and thereby self) and spiritual release (*moksa*) through renunciation by withdrawal from the world and the cycles of rebirth' (Zarrilli, 2009: 65). However, yoga philosophy has always been embraced and adapted by non-renunciants as well, (that is) those who keep both feet firmly in the spatio-temporal world' (Zarrilli,

2009:66). Zarrilli argues that for performers, yogic practice does not signal a withdrawal from everyday life: 'as the practitioner engages in yoga-based psychophysical practices, the ego becomes quiet and the emotions calm' (Zarrilli, 2009: 66). One is therefore better prepared to perform positively, in life and on stage.

In CTP the practices of yoga and meditation facilitate the observation of societal problems with a humanitarian perspective. Embodying Zarrilli's assertion that practitioners are 'better able to act within their respective socio-cultural domain while still in the world,' CTP's concern is with human welfare and dignity (Zarrilli, 2009: 66). Through CTP, higher states of consciousness are (potentially) arrived at, through somatic training systems that encourage compassion and empathy in the theatre practitioner. Choudhury asserts that 'by striving for balance, for union – for yoga – you can create a marriage within you to heal the sickness that exists all around you' (Choudhury, 2007: 274). The belief that by changing ourselves we can change society, inherent in Vipassana and Bikram, forms the basis of CTP. Self-regulation pertaining to each discipline can be compared by consulting the original, key sources; Buddha and Patanjali, respectively.

The five Vipassana meditation precepts:
to abstain from killing living creatures
to abstain from taking what is not given
to abstain from sexual misconduct
to abstain from wrong speech
to abstain from intoxicants, which are causes of intemperate behaviour
  HART, 1987: 80

The five Yoga *Yamas*:
Ahimsa: non-violence, non-harming, non-injury
Satya: truthfulness, honesty
Asteya: non-stealing, abstention from theft
Brahmacharya: self-restraint, right use of energy, remembering the divine
Aparigraha: non-possessiveness, non-holding through senses, non-greed,
  non-grasping, non-indulgence, non-acquisitiveness
  JNANESHVARA (n.d.)

These ideal behaviours and their potential application to working theatre practices contribute to the Black Star Projects manifesto and to the discussion of ethics in the concluding chapter of this book. These codes of conduct for 'life practice' serve as reminders that yoga does not simply relate to the *asanas* (postures) performed. Donna Farhi explains this common misconception as 'understandable given our obsession with form and our desire to have some kind of concrete evidence of attainment' (Farhi, 2004: 93). *Asanas*, although only a small part of the practice of yoga, were considered crucial, as a strong, flexible, alert body was required to prepare one for meditation. For Farhi, 'to do such practices as well as to fulfill our duties in the world would take enormous energy, energy that would not be available if we suffered ill health or disease' (Farhi, 2004: 94). In contemporary times the postures have become discon- nected from the wider philosophical concerns of which they form an impor- tant part. CTP would seek to reconnect the *asanas,* through theatre processes, with wider social aims. Farhi states that:

> When we realise that what we are advancing toward is not some physi- cal form but an inward recognition of the truth of who we are, then we will not feel ourselves to be failing if we cannot attain difficult postures – "advanced" practice is any movement that brings us closer to this recog- nition of our true self.
>
> FARHI 2004: 94

In order to realise certain realities of self, the role of meditative practices is tantamount to dissolution of ego. Choudhury states that 'the "self" we think we are, the one spelled with a lowercase s, is just a creation of our minds, the ego' (Choudhury, 2007: 5). Yoga helps to 'break down and fight through that ego to get to the right Self' (Choudhury, 2007: 5). This view of ego as a creation of our mind chimes with Vipassana's teachings of the perils of an attachment to a separate 'I'. It is suggested that once one understands the true nature of Self, in line with the laws of nature, or *dhamma*, it becomes clear that this 'self', this beloved 'I' that the human being gives such importance to, is an illusion that can be 'dissolved' though Buddhist meditation, according to Shusterman:

> in this strategy, the self's apparent permanence and individuality is – through focused body consciousness – mindfully dissolved into a porous, messy welter of different elements (liquids, solids and gases) whose tran- sitory and changing collaboration gives rise to the temporary, fragile con- struct we identify as the bodily self and falsely oppose to the rest of the world from which it is temporally constructed and without whose mate- rials and energies it could never be.
>
> SHUSTERMAN, 2012: 89

This idea is contentious to Herbert Muller, who disagrees: 'to say ... that a man is made up of certain chemical elements is a satisfactory description only for those who intend to use him as a fertilizer' (Muller, 1943: 107, cited in Sheets-Johnstone, 2011: 347). With insights from embodied experience, I would argue that what seems complex, or even spurious, when approached intellectually, makes sense experientially. Deep insight is gained when one's faculties sharpen through meditation; to the point of becoming keenly aware of sensations of air, heat, cold, pulsing, vibrating, lightness, heaviness, perspiration and sometimes pain, that continually manifest in the body.

Hart explains that 'the Universe exists for each of us only when we experience it with body and mind' (Hart, 1987: 6). In Vipassana this 'mind-matter phenomenon' is gradually conceived through practice. The ego dissolves, as the prioritising of that which is 'I', 'my' and 'mine' gives way to strategies for the common good of all mankind. This research tests the extent to which such strategies might work within a theatre company. Shusterman's understanding of Buddha's teachings is that 'such self-knowledge is ... a release from ultimately depressing illusions of the self's substantial permanence that make us take our individual selves with too much of the wrong kind of seriousness and selfishness' (Shusterman, 2012: 89). In theatre, egos can become inflated.

It could also be argued, however, that ego is necessary. As theatre director Anne Bogart proclaims:

> you can only thrill yourself. Being a director, you have to have, simultaneously, huge ego and no ego. Huge ego is the audacity to say 'what delights me and tickles me will delight other people, and if I lose touch with that delight, I'm lost ... At the same time you do have to listen to the audience. And that's painful and necessary.
>
> BOGART, 2001

Reflecting upon personal experience with Bogart's ego standpoint, it could be further suggested that having no ego is tantamount to a humility that enables one to listen to everybody on the production, giving full consideration to all ideas. Huge ego could also refer to inhabiting a leadership role in which one deems oneself guardian of the overall artistic vision of the work. With no ego, one might be reticent about promoting one's work or crafting one's persona in such a way as to attract funding or collaborators. This 'self-marketing' requires the self to be perceived with some sense of importance, as opposed to someone of no importance, perhaps. However, this 'necessary evil' need not permeate the production itself. This research tests whether the undertaking of contemplative performance practice for company members harnesses some collective consciousness resulting in 'oneness', the essence of collaboration, rather than separateness. The principles of yoga and meditation can be further drawn upon to this end, as outlined in the following section.

> **The five causes of suffering, or *kleshas*:**
> *Avidha*: Ignorance of our eternal nature.
> *Asmitta*: seeing oneself as separate and divided from the rest of the world.
> *Raga*: Attraction and attachment to permanent things.
> *Dvesha*: Aversion to the unpleasant.
> *Abbinivesha*: clinging to life because we fail to perceive the seamless continuity of consciousness, which cannot be broken by death.
>
>   Patanjali's Yoga-Sutra 2.3, cited in FARHI, 2004: 58

Suffering, attachment and aversion, and failure to understand the birth-life-death cycle are also the concerns of Vipassana, through three concepts:

> *Anicca*: the impermanence of everything, the ceaseless change of all matter and energy. Nothing is solid, nothing endures.
> *Dukkha*: Suffering: the attempt to grasp and hold that which flickers and vanishes leads to inevitable, ceaseless suffering.
> *Annata*: no soul, no essence, no ego, no I. If nothing is permanent, if everything arises and passes away, there can be no I, with its implication of continuity.
>
>   cited in KHAN, 1985: 120

Performance too, arises and passes away. As a temporal event, a theatre performance has no core continuum. Gay McAuley notes, 'performance is always in process, never a finished product' (McAuley, 2000: 124). Even on a production with an enduring run, each show is different. The audience is not the same, the actors give slightly different performances, and most pertinent to this research, the energy between actor and audience is different. McAuley states that 'energy does not simply emanate from the performer but is produced through the relationship between performer and spectator, and this can only occur when both are present in the same physical space' (McAuley, 2000: 124). Every performance is subject to *annata*. The production might be grasped and held to an extent through documentation, but the energy of each particular show has arisen and passed away. For McAuley this is part of theatre's appeal:

> knowledge of the essential uniqueness of each performance is another factor in the creation of the special energy that marks live performance,

for it fosters in both spectators and performers a certain kind of awareness of the present moment, also a certain kind of alertness because
what is missed is permanently missed.

MCAULEY, 2000: 124

Perhaps by definition, heightened awareness of the *present moment* can only
be fleeting. It can be enhanced, however. Shusterman claims that the 'diligent
practitioner' engaged in self-reflective, meditative practices will experience
'enhanced mental focus, strength of will, spiritual peace, psychic happiness,
and somatic well-being (including great pleasure)' (Shusterman, 2012: 84–85).
This list of benefits is reminiscent of the increased energy flow and pleasurable sensations that have been reported in the Vipassana taught by U Ba Khin
and the psychobiology of Wilhelm Reich. In an article that attempts to link
Theravada Buddhism with Reich's controversial 'orgone' therapy, Michael Khan
argues that both systems would cultivate better energy *flow* through removal
of energy *blocks*. He notes that 'Reich's therapy aims at giving patients, probably for the first time in their lives, access to all of the bodily sensations, even
the very subtle ones', and this is also what is experienced through Vipassana
(Khan, 1985: 123).

Both techniques use breath to achieve their aims. In Khan's discussion, it
is suggested that for Reich's patients in the 1940s, 'where there had been an
unfeeling, rigid body, there appeared the awesome pulsing and vibrating of life,
as the patient experienced what Reich came to call the flow of "orgone energy"
through the body' (Khan, 1985: 122). This pulsing, vibrating flow of energy, this
sense of 'aliveness' common to both Vipassana and Reichian therapy, taps into
the broader aims of the actor training systems that will be discussed in the
following section. Khan's claim that 'twenty-five centuries before Reich, the
Theravada (Buddhists) had discovered something very like orgone energy'
contributes to this investigation into how ancient energy practices might be
used today to improve life; and performance (Khan, 1985: 124).

Antagonism exists however, between aspects of Khan's findings and those
of this research. Writing thirty years ago, and focusing on the Vipassana teachings of U Ba Khin, as opposed to those of Goenka as this enquiry does, casts
disparities. In his comparison of both systems, Khan states that 'the Theravada
would lead us toward a state of quiet, a state in which the wisdom is so profound that there is no tension, only a peaceful monostate' (Khan 1985: 126).
It could be argued, however, that Vipassana's current teaching not only fully
acknowledges tension, but also purports to be a pathway for eliminating it.
As Hart points out, 'Goenka is a pragmatic person, in touch with the ordinary
realities of life and able to deal with them incisively, but in every situation, he

maintains an extraordinary calmness of mind (Hart, 1987: 1). Therefore, Khan's argument that 'as opposed to the still, silent Buddhists seeking the end of all suffering, Reich counseled a fully engaged life, its joys interspersed with inevitable disappointments and losses appearing and vanishing in the universal rhythm' denies Vipassana's contemporary agency (Khan, 1985: 126).

Vipassana's premise is that there will always be disappointment and misery as long as there is expectation and attachment. This technique could hardly claim to offer 'freedom from suffering' if suffering did not exist (Hart, 1987, Foreword). Nonetheless, Khan's conclusion that 'two such disparate sources give rise to a common perspective,' is relevant to this research in the concern of each with energy pertaining to the human bodymind (Khan, 1985: 127). It asks if Vipassana, in its compatibility with yoga, is a technique that could be sustained as part of a theatre company's ongoing CTP processes. Eastern energy systems have certainly influenced theatre processes in the past.

3   Conscious Theatre Practitioners

Traditionally, Indian theatre grew from sources inherent in the great Hindu epics and stories, including the *Mahabharata*, of which the *Bhagavad Gita* is a part. The dance-dramas and plays of the genre feature characters and stories from this sacred canon. Stories are passed down orally throughout the generations, preserving the essence of the messages contained therein. These narratives provide a vital creative source in performing arts. Through Farley Richmond, Darius Swann and Phillip Zarrilli's exploration of traditional Indian theatre, we understand Hinduism as integral to Indian performance literature. The theatre aesthetics of the genre share accepted philosophical and religious beliefs (Richmond et al., 1990: 7). Similarly to Buddhist meditation, the authors note that 'the foremost of these assumptions is that this life is characterised by *maya*, or illusion, and is part of an endless cycle of birth, death and rebirth' (Richmond et al., 1990: 7). The Hindu must find a way to break free from the fetters of life, to be released from this continuous cycle of rebirth.

Three approaches are accepted as routes to liberation: 'the way of action, the way of knowledge, and the way of devotion', with each pathway contributing to the rich fabric of Indian theatre (Richmond et al., 1990: 7). All three paths are referenced in the *Bhagavad Gita*. Devotion is held in highest esteem, although there is slippage between all three. Richmond et al. state that 'in the practice of classical yoga' for example, 'devotion to Isvara and the development of an appropriate devotional attitude are necessary prerequisites for taking up the path' (Richmond et al., 1990: 7). Depending on the branch of Hinduism,

Isvara might infer the highest reality, supreme soul, God, King, or even husband: whatever or whoever is the object of one's devotion.

Furthermore, in ritual performance, some specific purpose is always served:

> the fulfillment of a vow, the granting of a boon, the transformation of an individual, a family, a village, or some other discreet entity from one state of being to another, from illness to health or from a state of unrest and fear to one of repose and confidence.
>
> RICHMOND ET AL., 1990: 10

As transformation is key to this research, it links particularly well with the notions of change from illness to wellness; from *dis-ease* to harmonious, fearless living, outlined above. Perhaps Indian theatre could be defined as the earliest incarnation of CTP, in its endeavour to transform the consciousness and energy of people and places. McAuley acknowledges 'the "nervous force" of the exceptional performer' as a contributory factor 'to the energy peculiar to a theatre performance' (McAuley, 2000: 124). Contemporaneous with this notion, Zarrilli discusses an "energetics" of performance' (Zarrilli, 2009: 2). Meyer-Dinkgräfe also speaks of a special 'force' that must be tapped into to enable 'inspired acting,' by which he means the subconscious (Meyer-Dinkgräfe, 2005: 40). An exploration of Stanislavski's fascination with yoga demonstrates his shared understandings of the subconscious as a source of inspiration.

4   Konstantin Stanislavski

By the beginning of the 1900s, an interest in Eastern religions and spiritualism was sweeping through Russian society. It was from this culture that Stanislavski's curiosity grew. During a trip to Finland in 1906, the director began to include concepts belonging to Eastern mysticism and yogic practices into his System. According to Sharon Carnike, it was Stanislavski's son's tutor, who first introduced him to two books by Yogi Ramacharaka, asking him: 'why invent exercises yourself, and why look for words to name that which has already been named?' (Carnicke 2009: 170). So began Stanislavski's engagement with the titles *Hatha Yoga; or The Yogi Philosophy of Physical Well-Being*, (Ramacharaka, 2007) and *Raja Yoga or Mental Development* (Ramacharaka, 2008). However, as Andrew White explains, this particular 'Yogi' was actually an American named William Walker Atkinson, a former lawyer who relocated to Chicago at the turn of the twentieth century. Using the pen name Yogi Ramacharaka, Atkinson published a series of literature on Hinduism and yoga. Under the auspices of the Yogi Publication Society of Chicago, he was also editor of *New Thought* magazine (White, 2014: 295). Atkinson's collection of books, which includes *Bhagavad Gita* commentaries and translations, are still in print having earned the author international recognition (White, 2014: 295).

Atkinson drew upon various branches of yoga, claiming an eclecticism in regard to his own yogic practices. The exercises Stanislavski's actors were working with came from these books. His System would be tried and tested as 'laboratory work', demonstrating an aspiration to 'join mysticism and science holistically' (White, 2014: 290). This was a holism that was unavailable to Stanislavski via the rationalism of Western thought. He began conducting practical experiments drawn directly from yoga in rehearsals, with actors of the First Studio of the Moscow Art Theatre. Zarrilli suggests that 'the most important gift and legacy left by Stanislavski was the notion that theatre-making is best when it is practiced as an ever-growing process of constant practical enquiry and reflection in the studio' (Zarrilli, 2009: 5). Stanislavski fully understood yoga as a system that goes beyond the physical aspects of the body, seeking a richer engagement with the discipline for his actors. As White asserts, he adapted 'specific yogic practices in order to help actors transcend the limitations of the physical senses and tap into higher levels of creative consciousness and, ultimately, inspiration' (2014: 287). Stanislavski searched for conscious techniques that would aid the actor in harnessing the unconscious (Meyer-Dinkgräfe, 2005: 60).

Interested in both the subconscious (internalized in every person) and the superconscious (that which transcends the individual), Stanislavski appropriates Ramacharaka's notions of the sun and superconscious planes for his actor training methods (White, 2014: 300). By holding the superconscious in such high esteem, White further suggests that Stanislavski 'affords it a yogi's reverence; for, in yoga, the superconscious refers to an inspired state ... for the yogi, the object of meditation is God; for Stanislavski, the object of meditation is the role' (White, 2014: 301). The ardent performer might recognise this notion of their role being 'God-like': omnipresent; all-consuming; taking priority over everything else. For Meyer-Dinkgräfe, 'instances of higher states of consciousness in drama often create a very impressive and moving impact on the audience and possibly also for the actor relating such experiences' (Meyer-Dinkgräfe, 2005: 40). By way of example, Meyer-Dinkgräfe cites Richards' description of actor Ray Reinhardt's shift in consciousness, in which he was 'no longer acting actively, although things were happening: my arms moved independently, there was no effort required; my body was loose and very light. It was the closest I've ever come in a waking state to a mystical experience'

(Richards, 1977: 43). Similar experiences have manifested during my own intensive yoga and meditation practices.

For Sharon Carnicke, Reinhardt's experience might represent the moment when 'the actor, like the yogi, engulfed by the creative state of mind, undergoes something akin to when mind, body and soul unite in communion, not only with each other but with others on stage and those present in the audience' (Carnike, 2009: 167). Jill Dolan would describe such an event as a *Utopian performative,* a moment in which audience are lifted 'slightly above the present, into a hopeful feeling of what the world might be like if every moment of our lives were as emotionally voluminous, generous, aesthetically striking, and intersubjectively intense' (Dolan, 2005: 5). Dolan's language, couched in notions of emotional intensity and generosity, of being present in the moment and elevated in some way through performance, encapsulates the aims of CTP.

Dolan's term may also describe Stanislavski's aims for System, which for Carnike 'presupposes an indissoluble link between mind and body' (Carnike, 2009: 168). Theatre practitioners, as Dolan suggests, 'know the magic, utopic moments that happen after weeks of rehearsals, of experimenting with people across a range of "what ifs" until we settle on the best choices' (Dolan, 2005: 15). Finding those 'best choices' is the challenge. Yoga can be used as a tool in achieving it. Stanislavski recognised the benefit of such fine-tuning of the human organism to performance. It appears, however, that the yogic influence was in danger of being lost from the canon of literature around Stanislavski. Carnike explains that 'both Russian and American acting lore, for different reasons, erased Yoga from Stanislavsky's work and privileged psychology' (Carnike, 2009: 168). In the translations of his work, which was subject to both editing and censorship, details became diluted or omitted altogether. In reference to *prana,* for example, Elizabeth Hapgood who translated *An Actor Prepares* (1936), left out certain phrases and descriptions, which according to White, 'obfuscates Stanislavsky's belief about the use of such energy to establish unspoken communication with one's partner and the audience' (White, 2014: 294) Moreover, the soviet version, published in 1938 completely omits the term.

Such 'abridgment' as White suggests, as well as the 'the absence of scholarly notes' contribute to the circumstances in which yoga was 'obscured' in Stanislavsky's acting manuals (White, 2014: 302). As a consequence of Soviet censorship, the 'yogic undertones' in Stanislavsky's censored texts meant that yoga could only be found 'between the lines' (Carnike, 2009: 168), rather than in any explicit reference to the practice. Carnike points out that if the Russians 'had merely cut all references without comment, the Yoga in the System might have disappeared entirely from the official publications and languished in unopened archives' (Carnike, 2009: 168). Carnike and White have undoubtedly contributed to the revelation of yoga in Stanislavsky's work being returned to the forefront. For White, 'further research on the spiritual elements of Stanislavsky's work not only expands Westerners perspectives of the System but revives some of its fundamental elements that have remained dormant over the past century' (White, 2014:302). Stanislavsky's work takes on new agency with an understanding of his spirituality, breathing new life into his teachings for our time (White, 2014: 302).

5   Nicolás Núñez

Nicolás Núñez, creator of *Anthropocosmic Theatre* (1996), reminds us that as theatre practitioners, we evolve through the lineage of Stanislavski and Grotowski, among others, stating that:

> in declaring the 'here and now' and establishing the idea of 'as if' as a mechanism for action on the stage, Stanislavski was not inventing anything new; the huge significance of these two propositions which revolutionised theatre lies in the fact that they form the cornerstone of the majority of religious and philosophical conceptions known to us.
>
>   NÚÑEZ, 1997:35

From working together at the Old Vic Theatre, Núñez cites actor Peter O'Toole's understanding of Stanislavski's teachings as the ability 'to keep yourself in the here and now with total mindfulness, and to do what you have to do, not pretend to be doing it' (Núñez, 1997: 35). Núñez credits O'Toole with performing 'the path from the internal offering of our being "here and now" to an energy which lets us float on the platform of the moment' (Núñez, 1997: 42). For Núñez, this is a notion common to many religious and sacred rituals. He suggests that these principles were not invented by Stanislavsky, but rather 'reawakened' in theatre as the Russian director 'promoted the spread of this consciousness,' hence becoming 'a kind of prophet in contemporary theatre' (Núñez : 1997: 35). Núñez, like Zarrilli, reminds us of the importance of Stanislavski's practical explorations. He worked with his formulas until the end of his life, when studio work took priority over public performances.

   Núñez' credits Stanislavsky with laying 'the touchstone which brought the 'essential content back to western theatre' (Núñez, 1997: Intro). It might be surmised, from Deborah Middleton's description of Núñez own work as the 'raising and focusing of energy, and in a journey of self-knowledge,' that the 'essential content' to which Núñez refers, also involves some union of body, mind and spirit (Middleton, 1997: xiii). Middleton recognises, through Núñez' paratheatrical activity, an 'attempt to inhabit one's own experience' that resembles yoga' (Núñez, 1997: xiii). As yoga encourages a focusing of energy that brings the aspirant's attention to the present moment, inhabiting one's own experience might translate as being in a state of mindfulness. This consciousness that Núñez suggests was initiated into theatre processes by Stanislavsky, chimes with his own processes of leading the human being to 'discover' their Self. Núñez' belief that we are searching for 'a kind of secular/sacred discipline that gives us the means to contact ourselves' is a key critical premise underpinning this chapter.

6   Peter Brook

Núñez' secular/sacred concept could be encapsulated within Peter Brook's notion of *holy theatre* as a 'need for a true contact with a sacred invisibility through theatre,' or a spirituality perhaps, while acknowledging that this need can no longer be filled by churches in a secular society (Brook, 1968: 49, 60). The energy practices utilised in CTP are perhaps one means by which we can 'contact ourselves' and deepen self-realisation processes; out with the realms of fear-based organised religion, with its respective promises and threats of 'heaven' and 'hell'. However, the notion of the theatre as a healing or spiritual space cannot be taken for granted. William Weiss suggests that 'doing theatre is an activity that is no more spiritually advanced than dentistry,' before adding the caveat that 'the theatre is not a vehicle for spiritual ideas except if this is what you are looking for' (Weiss, 2010: 137). For Weiss, both theatre and spirituality are potential pathways to happiness, both attempting 'to reconcile what *is* to what ought to be.' (Weiss, 2010: 137). In regard to locating the spiritual within theatre, the mantra 'seek and thou shall find' might apply.

According to Brook, however, the spiritual inhabits the realm of the unseen. It only becomes visible in certain circumstances. He suggests that these special conditions 'can relate to certain states or to certain understanding(s)', which might take a lifetime to achieve (Brook, 1968: 56). For Brook, art brings us closer to this comprehension. He states that 'a holy theatre not only presents the invisible, but also offers conditions that make its perception possible' (Brook, 1968: 56). Brook cites the work of Jerzy Grotowski, among others, as an example of holy theatre.

7   Jerzy Grotowski

Brook describes Grotowski's project as a 'small company led by a visionary, that also has a sacred aim' (Brook, 1968: 59). Brook suggests that in Grotowski's world, the performer studies himself as a discipline, exploring every part of himself and allowing a role to 'penetrate' him. All resistance eventually drops through rigorous rehearsal and the actor eventually exposes himself, until the act of performance becomes 'an act of sacrifice, of sacrificing what most men prefer to hide – this sacrifice is his gift to the spectator' (Brook, 1968: 60). Brook likens this revelation between performer and spectator to the relation between a worshipper and a priest (Brook, 1968: 60). Grotowski describes this method himself as 'a technique of the "trance" and of the integration of all the actor's psychic and bodily powers which emerge from the most intimate layers of his being and his instinct, springing forth in a sort of "translumination"' (Grotowski, 1968: 16).

For Meyer-Dinkgräfe, Grotowski's translumination relates to the notion of presence, which is akin to 'acting in a higher state of consciousness' (Meyer-Dinkgräfe, 2005: 82). Grotowski developed this concept in line with 'poor theatre', in which everything is concentrated on the "ripening" of the actor' (Grotowski, 1968: 16). In a discussion of Grotowski's actor training, Meyer-Dinkgräfe cites Jennifer Kumiega's understanding of it, as a method leading to a 'state where the actor transcends incompleteness and the "mind-body split": the "division between thought and feeling, body and soul, consciousness and the unconscious' (Meyer-Dinkgräfe, 2005: 83). This state of translumination could also be aligned with yogic experience.

Like Stanislavski, Grotowski had been fascinated with Hindu philosophy, which he had studied since childhood. Lisa Wolford points out that although 'Grotowski acknowledges that in early phases of developing the Laboratory Theatre's physical training, he and his collaborators experimented with Hatha yoga techniques,' he did not apply them directly to performance (Wolford, 1996: 23). Despite using the term *asanas* in his training system, Grotowski was not necessarily utilising the sequence of postures known to yoga as *asanas*. His borrowing from yogic systems appears to have been used mainly to inform his *Statement of Principles* (Grotowski, 1968: 255). This text, crafted for internal use within Grotowski's company, the Theatre Laboratory, would also be given to actors undertaking a trial period. Grotowski's principles have subsequently informed the Black Star Projects manifesto, which will be deconstructed in the manifesto's corresponding chapter.

Grotowski created the Theatre Laboratory in Poland in 1959, continuing Stanislavski's notion of rehearsal process as 'laboratory work'. Perhaps the company name was in homage to Stanislavski, who Grotowski cites as his 'personal ideal' (Grotowski, 2002: 16). Grotowski declares that he was 'brought up on Stanislavski; his persistent study, his systematic renewal of the methods of observation, and his dialectical relationship to his own earlier work' (Grotowski, 2002: 16). As Stanislavski's most intense research into yoga took place in the early decades of the twentieth century, it could be suggested that Stanislavski's 'dialectical relationship', as described by Grotowski, was with the study of yoga.

Stanislavsky's influence upon Grotowski is clear in his assertion that 'Stanislavski asked the key methodological questions,' although their respective systems produced divergent results (Grotowski, 2002: 16). Grotowski states of the director that, 'sometimes we reach opposite conclusions' (Grotowski, 2002: 16). Nonetheless, Stanislavski's work on 'physical actions' is among the actor-training methods most important to Grotowski's purposes. As John Gillett explains, 'the process of creating a physical score of actions, which are responses to impulses, was explored by Stanislavski in his Method of Physical Action, and later by Grotowski in his montages of actors' experiences' (Gillett, 2007: 103). Grotowski's training aims were less concerned with adding to the actor's knowledge than subtracting from the actor's resistance. Rather than teaching a range of acting tools, Grotowski's concern was with eradicating internal intransigence; described by Grotowski as the 'organisms' resistance to this psychic process' (Grotowski, 2002: 16). Reminiscent perhaps of both Vipassana meditation and Reich's concern with the removal of energy blocks, Grotowski states of his technique that it is a *'via negativa* – not a collection of skills but an eradication of blocks' (Grotowski, 2002: 17). Chiming with Núñez' anthropocosmic theatre, these blocks and resistances prevent the actor from revealing his or her *true* Self.

Núñez' believes that the main purpose of methods of actor training should be to help the human being 'to master his instrument, which in this case happens to be his own organism, with all its stakes, internal and external' (Núñez, 1997: 38). This is a step towards development and knowledge: towards personal evolution. Núñez' explains that 'to discover that every single part of our body and our emotions is connected to, or rather interplaying with, the cosmos, is to realise that when we study our body, we are also studying part of the cosmos' (Núñez, 1968: 38). This recognition of the human as being a part of nature, of the Universe, is also the premise of Vipassana meditation. Núñez cautions that 'not all acting systems understand this' (Núñez, 1968: 38). Vipassana's message that 'by observing ourselves however, we can come to know reality directly and can learn to deal with it in a positive, creative way' is embraced by Black Star Projects (Hart, 1978: 6). CTP is an acting system that *does* understand that to be human is to part of the cosmos. Guided by the law of nature, by *dharma*, the idea of theatre providing something special, or sacred, is a potentially exciting premise for the practice-led element of this research.

FIGURE 3   Lou Prendergast, Laura Fahey and Anna Lecky performing in *AWKWARD* * *– A Life
              in Twenty-Six Postures*
              SOURCE: PHOTOGRAPHY BY SWALLOW THEATRE, 2016

Meditation brings self-realisation. I wasn't cut out for call centres and
death knocks. I was attracting the wrong people because I felt wrong
about myself. Superficial sex and drugs and rock 'n' roll were no longer
for me. If I couldn't be loved and respected, I wouldn't be giving my body
away. Meditation teaches compassion, not passion. I chose celibacy.

PRENDERGAST, 2016

CHAPTER 3

Research Approaches

From Embodied Knowledge to Self-Reflexivity

> Working towards an ethnographic consciousness ...
>
> ARTHUR BOCHNER, 2000: 760

∴

Several broad research methodologies informed this theatre project, including Practice-as-Research, Autoethnography and Immersive Contemplative Practice (ICP), which can also be considered as fieldwork. ICP is the term I use to describe the part of the research that involves intensive yoga and meditation experiments, in contexts that were specific to those respective disciplines. ICP is crucial to the project as it explores the ways in which energy practices can contribute original knowledge to the contemporary theatre-making field. Specifically, the research examines the efficacy of Bikram Yoga and Vipassana meditation upon theatre-making. Personal experiences with both practices contributed to research questions around the way in which:

1. 'energy practices' that create some shift in consciousness inform the creative processes of a 'conscious theatre practice' in which the work is derived from lived experience.

2. the creative outputs of a 'conscious theatre practice' (in which work is drawn from lived experience and influenced by energy practices) contribute to processes of socio-cultural transformation.

3. research methods aligned with theatre practice can evaluate the degree to which 'conscious theatre practice' might contribute to a shift in consciousness.

In Chapter 1, Practice-as-Research (PaR) was established as the most appropriate approach for exploring creative processes as research methods. PaR is embodied knowledge that the researcher comes to know through doing. The 'practice' in this study is the creative processes involved in the making of the performance work(s). Another key methodology is autoethnography, which involves putting *the self* at the centre of the research process. Described by Ellis and Bochner as 'an autobiographical genre of writing and research that

© KONINKLIJKE BRILL NV, LEIDEN, 2022 | DOI:10.1163/9789004467927_004

displays multiple layers of consciousness,' it resonates keenly with this project's concerns (Ellis and Bochner, 2000: 39). These methods are explored more fully in their respective sections below. This chapter also sets up an enquiry around embodied knowledge and altered consciousness(es) gained though immersive yoga and meditation, which contributed new insights to theatre work.

1 Practice as Research

As this project examines yoga and meditation as potential pathways to harmonious, ethical and enhanced creative processes in theatre, it meets Baz Kershaw's principal defining feature of contemporary performance practice as 'a radical diversity of approaches producing an incongruous field' (Kershaw, 2009: 115). The practice-led researcher, according to Haseman and Mafe, is constantly 'making decisions and moving forwards and backwards ... to cope with the "messy" research project (Haseman and Mafe, 2009: 217). Here, the aspiration towards CTP is the *raison d'etre* for the study, while the methodological approaches contributed systematic rigour, and the emergence of a new research framework.

Haseman and Mafe assert that 'traditional research approaches seem too linear, too predictable and too ordered to capture the messiness and dynamism of the process of inquiry that lies at the heart of their creative production' (Haseman and Mafe, 2010: 211). The theatrical works at the heart of this research were presented at yearly intervals, but despite their measured timing, the knowledge generated through practice has not always followed a linear path. Congruous with the research overall, various approaches and methodologies *simultaneously* informed and expanded the potential for deeper understandings of the project. ICP cast new light on conceptual frameworks; creating theatrical performances informed the writing of conference papers; presenting at conferences sparked new thinking around rehearsal processes; collaborating with others prompted the necessity to rethink the working manifesto; the desire to teach physical training led to the completion of professional training; other scholar's writing about my productions, assimilated them into the canon of academic literature (and media discourse) from which my research investigations first began.

For Kershaw, 'the "as" (in PaR) functions to problematise conventional notions of theatre and performance practice ... (making) a claim that the theatre or performance event itself may be a form of research' (Kershaw, 2010: 106–107). Under the auspices of PaR as the overarching research methodology for theatre interrogations, other lines of enquiry coexist within more specific frameworks. At the core of this research there is an investigation of Self. In the context of this enquiry, theatre and performance practice is autobiographical, and therefore the research method is autoethnographic.

Considering the former first, autobiographical performance is defined by Emma Govan, Helen Nicholson and Katie Normington as 'a distinct mode of working with an emphasis on a self-reflexive, creative methodology,' a description that has deep resonances with this theatre research (Govan et al., 2007: 62). Here, research around ways of *doing* and ways of *being* in theatre, are entangled with self-investigation. A reflexive approach, as outlined by Haseman and Mafe, 'defines a position where the researcher can refer to and reflect upon themselves and so be able to give an account of their own position of enunciation' (Haseman and Mafe, 2010: 219). I suggest that self-reflexivity is inherent in the concept of self-realisation and is therefore an entirely useful approach in this project.

Lived experience is also harnessed as a methodological approach across the practical elements of the research. The final work, *AWKWARD: A Life in Twenty-Six Postures*, is perhaps the epitome of Govan et al's notion of autobiographical performance as 'the use of personal interests and narratives as source material (that) leads to a complex creative process that reflects upon real life data to shape a performance piece' (Govan et al., 2007: 60). The middle work, *Tommy's Song*, was also based upon real life data, although this was not made explicit to the audience. Govan et al. note that some companies 'employ personal experience as a vehicle to explore sociopolitical situations (Govan et al., 2007: 60).' This criterion fits the first work, *Blood Lines*. Methodologically, the artworks manifested from the phenomenology of conscious experience.

2   Autoethnography

For Nelson, 'phenomenology has emerged as an influential conceptual framework contemporaneously with the rise of practice-as-research ... it emphasises, among other things, a life practice of becoming (as distinct from being), and the embodiment of thought rather than the Cartesian discreet mind' (Nelson, 2009: 121). Through the prism of embodied knowledge derived from phenomenology, a framework emerges that is pivotal to epistemological concerns around the self's shifting consciousness, increased spiritual awareness and potential self-realisation. Nelson's notion of *becoming* is therefore appropriate to this study. It is perhaps a paradox that, as Haseman and Mafe point out, 'most established research strategies are carefully structured to exclude the researcher, based on the belief that the researcher stands to infect the subjective "truth" and universal applicability of research findings;' while this study's concern with self-realisation opens it up to the universal "truths" of being human (Haseman and Mafe, 2010: 212).

Tami Spry asserts that knowledge is articulated through what she terms, a ' "Performative-I" disposition, where the researcher critically reflects upon what and where the body knows [...] embodiment is the theoretical and methodological core of autoethnography and performance, and as such is integral to the performative-I disposition' (Spry, 2011: 53). This disposition, or propensity for critical reflection, echoes Bochner and Ellis' standpoint that 'often our accounts of ourselves are unflattering and imperfect, but human and believable,' and the text becomes an 'agent' of self-understanding (Ellis and Bochner 2000: 748). Both the journal entries and the autobiographical scripts attached to this project align with an autoethnographic research method.

Julia Varley states that,

> theatre technique is embodied, it is thought in action, intelligence of the feet, it cannot be studied at a desk, but must be assimilated and defended day by day with years of practice. In a technological era, perhaps theatre is anachronistic, but I want to defend it precisely because it maintains the necessity of an embodied knowledge which is reached through self-discipline and self-learning.
>
> VARLEY, 2013: 183

Varley's acknowledgement of self-discipline and self-learning as embodied knowledge gives credence to the method of employing yoga and meditation as part of the rehearsal processes of all three productions, to lesser and greater degrees. Spry points to embodied knowledge as being 'gained by paying close somatic attention to how and what our body feels when interacting with others in context' (Spry, 2011: 64). Here, energy practices become methodologies.

Beyond my own productions, I respectfully acknowledge the connections between theatre and consciousness that were deepened through the undertaking of psychophysical training with a host of conscious theatre practitioners, some of whom were introduced as key theorists in Chapter 2. These embodied encounters include Deborah Middleton's Yoga and Creativity workshop (September 2014); Ewan Downie and Anna Porubcansky's Company of Wolves Winter Training (January 2015); Nicolás Núñez' Acting as a Personal Rite workshop (March 2015); Lee Worley's Mudra Space Awareness workshop (June 2016) and Phillip Zarrilli's Beginner's Intensive (July 2016). Those workshops, some of which could be considered 'laboratory work' in the Stanislavski and

Grotowski traditions, contributed tacit knowledge through the use of energy practices in my emerging performance consciousness.

3   Immersive Contemplative Practice (ICP)

As outlined in Chapter 1, this theatre study has two parts: 'creating a conscious theatre practice' addressed through the creation of CTP; and 'self-realisation process', explored through yoga teacher training and meditation courses that I include as methodology. They could be described as experiments in consciousness. Higher states of consciousness (Meyer-Dinkgräfe, 2005) reached through these immersive contexts inspired both creative and personal development, shaping the concept of CTP. The third work is the only theatrical production that brings yogic practice into its script and physical score, but the embodied knowledge garnered through intensive Bikram Yoga and Vipassana meditation experiences impacted all three productions.

In chronological order, across the lifespan of this expanded project, I experienced: a 10-day Vipassana meditation course (February 2014) followed by a production (*Blood Lines*, July 2014), followed by a second Vipassana course (Dec 2014) and a second production (*Tommy's Song*, May 2015) followed by a third Vipassana (July 2015), then nine weeks of Bikram Yoga teacher training (October– December 2015) followed by a third production (*Awkward*, July 2016). There is scant mention of *theatrical performance* in the journal entries kept during the yoga training and meditation retreats; rather, they evidence an often emotionally and physically painful path towards personal, spiritual and creative epiphanies.

Shifts in my consciousness inspired a vision that manifested during Vipassana to work with my family on *Blood Lines*. The insights and ethical considerations of creating a work based on a real person's life events in *Tommy's Song*, were guided by the empathetic and compassionate aims of contemplative practice. The revelations and vulnerabilities that were exposed in *Awkward* arose from an evolved self-esteem, which facilitated the telling of one's truths without fear of judgment. Consequently, these verbatim journal entries warrant a stand-alone chapter in this book, occupying an in-between space.

The ICP chapter forms an interstice between the research methodologies explored before it, and the theatre practice examined after it. It belongs to neither chapter while resonating keenly with both. The theoretical underpinnings of consciousness, somatic harmony, bodymind connection and ego were brought to life during this intensive practice. The insecurities and vulnerabilities exposed through the first-person narrative formed the raw materials of a kind of anecdotal theory (Gallop, 2002). ICP experiences foreshadow the theatre-making that followed; in respect of seeing a project through to the end; learning through doing; tuning into an inner strength; trusting one's intuition; taking risks and pushing one's capabilities in the pursuit of optimum results. Collectively, these processes informed CTP and shaped the Black Star Projects manifesto.

4   ICP as Fieldwork

Aligning ICP with the academic concept of 'fieldwork' would place me as both participant and observer. Barbara Kawulich presents various definitions of the participant-observation method. Many do not fit the purposes of this study, as they include a separation between the researcher and the cultural group. For example, Kawulich outlines Schensul, Schensul and LeCompte's perception of participant-observation as a method that can ease relationships with 'informants', which does not apply here (Kawulich, 2005: 4). As the sole 'subject' of the research, and simultaneously part of a group (of other Vipassana meditators on a course; of other Bikram Yoga practitioners attending teacher training), traditional participant-observation methods do not appropriately describe methods undertaken in this particular study.

Gold's notion of 'complete participant' in which the researcher 'takes an insider role, is fully part of the setting' is closer to the method utilised, although his assertion that the researcher usually observes covertly is not accurate (Gold, 1958: 220). In both the Vipassana and Bikram scenarios, I told teachers that I was undertaking research. In Soyini Madison's discussion of Performative-I, she notes Spry's assertion that 'by embracing the performative-I, she experienced a "methodological shift" in her positionality from participant-observer to performative-I subject(ive) researcher' (Madison, 2011: 198). Applying a methodological shift to this enquiry softens the research boundaries somewhat.

Nonetheless, Kawulich's assertion that journal notes are 'the primary way of capturing the data that is collected from participant observations' is appropriate to this study. Capturing 'data' can include what is being observed, activities undertaken and regular journal entries, all of which applies. Furthermore, Dewalt, Dewalt and Wayland attest that these notes can serve as both analysis and data. Kawulich cites their assertion that 'the notes provide an accurate description of what is observed and are the product of the observation process [...] observations are not data unless they are recorded into field notes' (Kawulich, 2005: 16). In my 'fieldwork', systematic journal entries were a reminder that research was my purpose 'in the field', which kept me grounded.

Kawulich also refers to Wolcott's advice around conducting fieldwork. He perceives the process of taking and writing up notes as critical to the success of the fieldwork. He recommends note taking as a *daily* practice, which was not always possible in the circumstances of my respective 'fields', although I was able to keep entries relatively up to date. Kawulich further quotes Wolcott's view that note taking 'provides a connection between what he/she is experiencing and how he/she is translating that experience into a form that can be communicated to others' (Kawulich, 2005: 14). The written articulation of experiences 'in the field' helped me cope with the intensity of the ICP. Walcott also articulates the benefits of capturing 'reflections on and about one's mood, personal reactions and random thoughts' which relates well to the methods employed here (Kawulich, 2005: 14). In a discussion around personal narrative, Arthur Bochner describes its appeal as 'the desire to make sense and preserve coherence over the course of our lives' (Bochner, 2000: 746). As creative expression, this writing method was also cathartic. Fieldwork can also include conversations, and it was through befriending Bikram Yoga teacher trainees, Anna Leckey and Laura Fahey at mealtimes, and before and after lectures, that they subsequently came to collaborate on the work, *Awkward*. This serendipitous meeting of (body)minds might also be considered *Dharma*, in the Vedic Science model of consciousness described by Meyer-Dinkgräfe (2005).

5 Journal Entry Critique

In traditional ethnographic research, diary entries (mine are presented in the next chapter) form the 'data' of the research. Karen O'Reilly asserts that the analysis of data is ongoing. Each time I read my notes, and the further away I am from the experiences I captured; the more objectively I can 'read' them. Karen O'Reilly discusses an ethnographic technique of being 'descriptive about the setting; about feelings of strangeness on arriving' and of writing in the first person (O'Reilly, 2005: 214). My journal entries share these characteristics. This technique lends veracity to the ethnographer's account; that they were really there. In terms of self-reflexivity, it is also pertinent to acknowledge the 'tentative, provisional nature of one's interpretation of events' which I acknowledge in the final chapter. (O'Reilly, 2005: 216–217).

Hammersley and Atkinson caution that the ethnographer's voice is not necessarily the voice of authority, which is an ethical consideration:

> Reflexivity carries an important message in the field of ethics, as it does in relation to other aspects of ethnography [...] the ethical problems

surrounding ethnographic research are, in fact, very similar to those that are relevant to other human activities [...] what and how much to disclose of what one knows, believes, feels, etc. can be an issue for anyone at any time.

HAMMERSLEY and ATKINSON, 2007: 228

At the time of my Bikram Yoga Teacher Training, allegations accusing Bikram Choudhury of sexually abusing female yoga students and employing bullying tactics in his relations with staff had not yet fully come to light. However, I note from my journal entries that I was sensing these behaviours. I describe my feelings around how Bikram responded to me performing 'the dialogue' of a posture for his perusal/approval, as all trainees are required to do:

I wonder if there was something demeaning in all this – my teaching style reduced to 'sexy' and 'romantic' with a 'trail of boys waiting to come to classes' ... I was made to feel something lesser than my real self. I was made smaller, but then allowed to become more again, with his help – like being created by someone else. There are interesting gender politics implications here

PRENDERGAST, 2015

O'Reilly considers a diary on a research project as 'a place where you can log the many things you thought did not seem relevant at the time of hearing about, seeing or thinking about them, yet may well turn out to be relevant at some later stage' (O'Reilly, 2005: 170). The thoughts I logged foreshadowed revelations that emerged later. Many Bikram Yoga teachers, male and female, chose not to believe them. It is perhaps easier to remain in denial, than to consider that there might be something unethical in the promotion of Bikram. This prompted much serious thought on my part. The way to navigate this problem is to separate the practice of Bikram Yoga, which can be life-changing, from the behaviours of the man who created this particular yoga sequence. Many Bikram Yoga studios have since removed his name from their studios. Teachers may now describe the sequence as the '26 and 2': the new moniker for the twenty-six postures and two breathing exercising that the Bikram method entails. More recently, it is referred to as Original Hot Yoga.

The journal entries also include thoughts around Bikram's (suspected by me) childhood trauma, as part of a yoga troupe created by his punitive guru, Bishnu Gosh. Given that Bikram was at the mercy of his guru from a very early age, one can only wonder at the adverse childhood experiences he might have suffered. However, my support is always for the survivors of alleged abuse. Continuing to share the practice he invented does not suggest any tolerance of, or complicity with his alleged crimes. The power dynamics have changed. The Bikram empire has crumbled as a consequence of his own wrongdoing. Here, we see the yogic concept of Karma upheld. I suggest we might also apply yogic concepts of compassion towards this individual.

O'Reilly describes how the ethnographer Malinowski separated facts from feelings by keeping two separate journals during his fieldwork. It is evident from my own entries that facts and feelings are intertwined. In a project with an emphasis around Self, this is more appropriate than for the ethnographer for whom other people form the subject(s) of their study. O'Reilly describes a diary that can 'enable the reflexive approach encouraged by contemporary philosophical approaches to social sciences, by making you think constantly about your own role in the research process, your own history and biography, and how you make decisions' (O'Reilly, 2005: 170). My diary entries on Vipassana meditation experiences were written up immediately after the silent part of the course had ended. The Vipassana process involves a final day when participants can talk, read, write, share and contact the outside world by phone and/or other digital communication. The concentration and focus of the mind by that point afforded the flow of memories captured in my entries.

Diary entries for the first Vipassana course are written in chronological order, following the progress of the course. O'Reilly writes of ethnography as a method that requires 'confronting your relation with others'. In my case, the entries evidence ways in which the experience led me to confront my relationship with myself, which was often a painful but necessary element of the practice. (O'Reilly, 2005: 223). On the second course, I also endeavoured to follow the method of 'conveying the context of the situation and my place in it [...] in line with being 'rigorous, increasingly skeptical, and avoiding complacency and blind faith' although my entries are not broken down into individual days (O'Reilly, 2005: 223). Having only been released from a life-saving, 16-day hospital stay shortly before that particular Vipassana, my reflections are more generalised, pertaining to the experience overall.

Journal entries relating to the final experience demonstrate a deeper reconciliation with Self. Despite Tami Spry's assertion that 'the process of critical reflection is seldom linear' as it is 'located in the intersections of lived experience and larger social issues', I note some personal evolution across the three experiences (Spry, 2011: 152). It is evident that on the third Vipassana I was more in tune with the natural rhythms of nature, and with animals in particular.

I suggest that this was enhanced due to the physical distancing from the 'social world', occupying that liminal space between 'retreat' and reality, between internal and external contexts. Thus, immersive contemplative practice forms an interstice in this book, located between the methods and approaches, and the analysis of the creative processes.

CHAPTER 4

Immersive Contemplative Practice

Vipassana Meditation Courses and Bikram Yoga Teacher Training

1   Vipassana

Vipassana 1: 5–16th February 2014, Kolhapur, Maharashtra, India – Day 0
I leave Goa at 5am by taxi to Panjim. Here, I wait in the dark in a rough bus park for my coach to Kolhapur. There are no officials around; clumps of men eye me curiously. I feel frightened. The scene loses its sinister sense as the sun comes up. The men are just waiting, as I am waiting, for buses or for people coming off buses, to take to other places.

The fat, white Paulo Travels coach rolls in late, which is common, and I'm shown to an upstairs 'sleeper' bunk with room for lying down only. I can't do the whole trip lying on my back and sneak down to sit on a seat. Other non-Indians have boarded the bus and I assume they are going to Vipassana. But as I wait for my ludicrously large suitcase to be brought from the hold, the others disappear. I am left alone to find the final destination. Dragging the case across the dusty bus park in the fierce heat, I'm heading towards some taxis. The driver knows the location but is demanding 1000 rupees for a fare that should cost 600. I'm not up for a fight. I get to the centre and he gets his money. Job done.

A small reception building is crammed with people, filling in forms and standing in queues, completing the registration process in constituent parts: take the blue form and hand it to the lady at the counter; pay your deposit for the laundry over there; take your number tag to the man dealing with accommodation. It is typically Indian in its laboriousness but I'm in good spirits.

I try to make eye contact with the girl I'd seen on the bus, but she looks away. I decide she's unfriendly. Russian. And cold and unfriendly. Anytime I looked at her I managed to find some new reason to confirm this belief. But I caught myself. And suddenly I knew. She was going to be my roommate. What better test to start me off than to pair me with the very person I had been thinking unfounded negative thoughts about. As I'm unpacking in the small, basic room, in she comes. She knows very little English. We don't even exchange names before rushing over to the dining hall for further instructions.

We're asked if we promise to abide by the rules for the whole 10 days: not to kill, steal, lie, be sexually active and above all else, maintain 'noble silence'. This means no talking to each other, no hand gestures, no eye contact. There is to be no communication except with the two 'helpers' who we can whisper questions to, if absolutely necessary. I agreed. I hand over my mobile phones, laptop and reading and writing materials, as instructed. And so it begins.

Tea and snacks are followed by meditation. It is led by two assistant teachers and supplemented by 'discourse' from Mr. S.M. Goenka, the overall Vipassana teacher, on DVD. Another short meditation follows the discourse and at 9pm we're told to 'take rest.' This becomes the evening pattern for the duration. I fall asleep quickly on my concrete slab bed with the thin mattress, grateful for my own feather pillow, fluffy blanket and pretty new cotton bedspread.

Thurs Feb 6th – Day 1

At 4am I wake to a gong being banged outside my room. My roommate and I shuffle around in the semi-darkness, somehow negotiating our respective turns at the sink and in the toilet, without actually looking at each other. It is strange. Like living with someone you're not talking to. Fifteen minutes later a brass bell is being furiously tinkled, signifying that it's time to leave the accommodation and head up the hill to the meditation hall. This first session, from 4.30–6.30am is a killer. Sitting cross-legged on the floor has never been a comfortable position for me, and now, with inflamed joints, the pressure on the hip and knee joints is palpable. And painful.

Breakfast is from 6.30–7am, followed by an hour of rest. My roommate jumps into bed. I do some yoga, attempting to stretch my joints and increase my flexibility. A mandatory 'group sitting' takes place from 8–9am. Then another two hours of meditation. Lunch is from 11–11.30am with another rest period until the 1pm meditation. From 2.15 until 3.30pm we do more meditation, followed by a five-minute break. Meditation again until tea and snacks at 5pm. By 9pm I am exhausted. Ten hours of sitting cross-legged with the eyes closed is already putting a strain on the mind and body.

Fri 7th Feb – Day 2

We continue with the 'Anna Panna' breathing technique. This involves concentrating very hard on the breath coming in and going out. One should maintain the natural breathing rhythm and avoid breathing deeply, unless the breath cannot be felt at the entrance to the nostrils or inside the nose, in which case it is ok to take a few deep breaths in order to feel the breath in these areas.

Relentless concentration on breath is difficult to maintain and requires careful focus. It is explained that many emotions will arise and pass. These will include anger, hatred, sadness, etc. and should be allowed to come to come to the surface and evaporate. Half-way through the day I feel a flash of anger. Uh-oh.

During the 7–8pm group sitting I become aware of a change in the air. Women and men are separated into two sides of the hall, each gender with their own separate entrances, residential quarters and dining halls. I glance slyly at the male species from time to time. How are they coping? I know from yoga that men are often tighter in the legs than women. I see that some of them now have backrests. Many of the women have extra cushions on top of their original cushion pad. I do too, but these are not helping my knees, which feel ready to burst open. We are taught to observe our pain and tension without reacting. We are to remain 'equanimous'.

Concentrating hard, with eyes closed, I become increasingly aware of a stillness in the hall. Still ... but expectant somehow. I feel as though the energy is rising; or becoming more intense to the point of some inevitable crescendo; I sense that something has to give; to pierce through some collective silent power that is building in the twilight. I feel it coming. I don't know what 'it' is, but I know it's coming. And here it is. A sob! Not from me. Someone is crying, behind me and to the left. It is a beautiful, inevitable release. It is one of the boys. 'One of the boys is crying! What a shame!' I thought. And as these thoughts are forming, the centres of both my upturned palms have begun to pulse. And as they continue to pump away, tears are running down my face. But I am not sad. These are tears of compassion. I am experiencing pure empathy. And it feels absolutely exquisite.

Saturday 8th Feb – Day 3

Let the crying commence. Those initial tears for someone else last night have given way to my own woes. Like a little sad sack, I'm slumped on my cushion. I have surrendered to the physical pain and emotions that are surfacing. I don't take my five minutes break after every hour – what's the point? What relief does five minutes bring! I don't do my yoga at morning and lunch break – the pain is getting worse, not better! I cry for my poor mum, again, dead by the age of 53 from such an aggressive cancer. I cry for all the unhappy moments I can recall from childhood, adolescence and adulthood. I cry because I have a disease. And I cry because I understand that I have created it myself.

At lunchtime I go teary-eyed to my teachers, begging to be allowed to sit in a different position. 'I'll be leaving here on crutches,' I warn. They assured me I will not. At the next session a table has been set up for me against the back wall. It isn't ideal because it raises me off the floor above the rest of the students and puts me on a level with the teachers, whom I am now facing. I feel rather exposed. But at least this seated position gives respite to the knees and hips, which are now inflamed. The teachers advise me somberly that it isn't going to be easy. They say the deep Saṅkhāras I have created in my life are now coming out through the meditation. That is why I am experiencing so much discomfort. A Saṅkhāras is a build-up of negative emotions in the body. Goenka asks 'if someone says something that hurts you, how long do you keep that thought?' If you let it go after a couple of hours, then it is like drawing a line on water – the hurt it soon disappears. If the thought and the hurt stay with you until the end of the day, it is like a line that has been drawn in the sand, that the wind will eventually blow over. However, if you hold onto hurt for months or years, or if many layers of hurt have been experienced, then this is like scoring a deep line into a rock. These deep Saṅkhāras take longer to erase. The teachers explain that my Saṅkhāras are in my joints and were made from anger. They assure me they will disappear. 'Keep meditating and the disease will go.'

Sunday 9th Feb – Day 4
I get a grip. I feel better and I'm able to apply the theory that our thoughts are of two types: cravings and aversion. We like something and want more of it or we don't like something and don't want it or want it to stop. We also think in the past – 'so and so hurt me' – or in the future, 'if so and so does that again, I'll just ...'

Now I'm being trained to think in the moment. And here, finally is the technique to make that possible. After three days of anna panna breathing, we're finally being taught Vipassana. The technique involves concentrating very hard on the sensations in and on the body. It begins by focusing on the small area below the nostrils down to the top lip. What can we feel there? Are there any changes in temperature? Pulses, twinges or itching? At first, I can only feel the breath coming in and out of my nose. But after several hours of meditation with this focus, I begin to get it.

In the afternoon we are played a recording of Goenka. He takes us through the Vipassana technique, inviting us to 'look' inside our own body. It is deeply hypnotic and emotional. Images flash up in the darkness of my mind, including a beating heart. I perceive this to be my own. By the end of the day, I swear I can actually feel the minute hairs on my top lip. I am grateful for my table seat. I'm able to concentrate on what is being suggested, as opposed to struggling not to react to the pain in my left hip and both knees. The remainder of the course will hopefully be easier now.

Monday 10th Feb – Day 5

Half-way through and it's all good. Well, as 'good' as a regime as strict as this one can be. By now we are free to use the 'cells' for meditation, at times other than the group sittings, which are compulsory in the meditation hall. These compact, windowless spaces are around 6ft by 4ft, arranged in a circle around a central pagoda with a golden spire. But once inside, with the door closed, one could easily be in a prison. Some foreign jail. My imagination runs riot as I first step inside. A shot of fear darts through me. Movies like Midnight Express jump to mind, and more recent ones about Abu Ghraib and scenes of torture. I sit on the cushion and face the wall, as instructed.

Powerful meditation ensues. I like my cell. It is the only private space available. Even the toilet is not private enough. With its thin walls and close proximity to my roommate's bed. Here in the cell, I am truly alone. It is not soundproof though. Audible sobs, coughs or sneezes from faraway cells break the silence from time to time. I have the option of lying flat. This doesn't feel right, and I resume my cross-legged battles, but having the option is a small victory of freedom. And I do confess, that at 4.30am the next day, I shuffle up the hill wrapped in my blanket and sleep in my cell.

Tuesday 11th Feb – Day 6

Not a good day. The pain in my left hip is becoming unbearable. We're not allowed to stretch out our legs in the meditation hall! This is frustrating for me as I am in agony. The Vipassana technique now involves scanning every inch of the body, with one's mind, and surveying every sensation, good or bad, i.e., pleasurable or unpleasant, equanimously. Pain is a 'gross' sensation, representing aversion. But we must remain equanimous, neither wanting this sensation of pain to cease or to continue, but rather, just observing it. 'Subtle' sensations, which are also plentiful by now, represent ones' cravings. These too, must be observed without reaction – neither wishing for them to continue or trying to create them (which doesn't work), nor wishing them to cease.

At the beginning of every session Goenka's voice is played, advising us to 'start again. Start again. Start with a calm and quiet mind; an equanimous mind.' It's easy enough to start with an equanimous mind, but the pain in my hip and knees now kicks in after just a few minutes of meditating. I find myself moving continuously during the group sittings, when I am not allowed to sit on my table. Those around me seem still and solid. I feel I'm distracting them. Driven by pain and the desire to find a position that doesn't hurt quite as much, I squirm and rustle around, moving every couple of minutes, 20–30 times an hour. It is maddening! And extremely tiring.

I remember the blog I read from the woman who did this same course at this same centre; how she describes sitting there with tears rolling down her cheeks because of the pain. And here I am, tears rolling down my cheeks, because of the pain. Although, I can't really tell by now whether the physical pain is sparked by emotional pain, or the other way round. Either way, there is nothing left to do but cry. It has been made clear that I should endeavor to sit cross-legged at every opportunity until I can no longer remain equanimous towards the pain. During each of the one-hour group sessions that happen three times each day, I must sit on my usual spot on the floor in the middle of the second row. This has become my vision of hell. Each time I get up it's with stiff, locked joints. It's impossible to rise gracefully or walk away without limping. It's bloody embarrassing, hobbling off with an awkward gait.

Wednesday 12th Feb – Day 7
Yet again, a brighter day follows a dreadful one. I wake with strong determination. I practice yoga at every opportunity during breaks. I'm going to sit properly if it kills me. I'm going to rise above the agony, which has now spread from my left hip to my left knee. I observe this pain. Where does it start? Where does it tail off? Where is it exactly? The name of my disease points to the connective tissues, but I feel the pain inside the bone. I practice holding the position until it becomes excruciatingly painful. I push at this all day.

My goal is to remain cross-legged and motionless with eyes closed for a whole hour. I haven't achieved this yet. But I'm getting there. I observe the pain and try not to react to it, over and over again; each time waiting longer before I'm forced to move. And when I do move, I try not to move again for the duration of the session. I sneak a look at the large digital clock behind me once I've moved and note that I've held the posture for 30 minutes, or 37 minutes, or whatever. I can do this. I can bear it. I can learn to bear the pain.

Towards the end of the day, I'm stumbling away from meditation sessions with a happy heart. Something is happening. My mind and body are opening up to some invisible force and I'm experiencing whole body sensations. At the discourse session I usually find a spot against the wall and use it for support, but tonight I've broken away from the wall. I sat cross-legged with no support for a full hour!

My eyes were open, obviously, as I was watching the DVD, but I've somehow transcended the pain in my hip and knee joints. It's always there, nagging away, but I've practiced equanimity and achieved samadhi. This is one of the main principles of Vipassana, it means mastery over the mind through deep meditation. I have really achieved something special today: some transformation in the body-mind.

Thursday 13th Feb – Day 8

As I stir from sleep, I stretch my legs. Pain shoots down my left hip. There's a noise, like a crunch. It occurs to me that something in the joint has shifted – into place? Or out of place? I get up and wash at the sink and check my reflection. A negative thought hits me like a punch: how ugly I am! This has been an occasional but recurring thought throughout my life. I didn't expect to have it here. What the hell's happened to me? I looked ravaged, as if I've aged ten years overnight.

I troop up the hill wrapped in a blanket, to my cell. I sit on the cushion and close my eyes to meditate. Woah! A succession of bright images click and change rapidly, one after the other, click! Click! Click! It's as if my mind can no longer hold a single thought still. It's horrible. I snap my eyes open again. Hmm. That's not nice. I'm scared. I try again. It doesn't happen this time. I'm relieved. But it worries me. Am I losing my mind? At breakfast I'm not hungry. This is unusual. Lunch, the last meal of the day, is at 11am. There's nothing else until the 5pm snack. By 6.30am the next day I'm always ready to eat. Not today.

At the first group sitting my hips are so sore. So very, very sore. All yesterday's efforts have not helped me today. My knees are visibly swollen on the inside. My hip is so tender I can't even rest my hand on my left knee. The weight of my hand brings excruciating pain. I try to remain equanimous. I hold my hand lightly on my leg. That doesn't work. I placed it in my lap ... aow! I can't stand it! What sort of 'technique' is this? Why should meditation be so brutal? If I dislocate my hip, these teachers will not be by my hospital bedside. And my insurance won't pay out. What would the medical profession make of my 'healing' quest: 'You made a decision to deliberately and willfully force your weakened, inflamed, diseased lower joints into agonising positions, which you held for around 100 hours, in spite of the pain'? Suddenly it doesn't seem sensible. I need to take responsibility for my own body. I'm not going to sit cross-legged today. I'm not even going to try. I've fallen out with the 'technique'. I can't even close my eyes.

At lunch break I'm wandering back to my room, eyes downcast, feeling despondent. I casually raise my eyes towards something that caught my attention on the wall to my left ... and look into the eyes of a large, vicious monkey! In a split second he leaps towards me, baring his damaging teeth – No! I scream and turn away. I've seen the documentary A Chimpanzee Tore My Face Off. Twice. In a split-second adrenalin has kicked in and I'm considering how to get it off me as it's ripping my flesh!

Then, to my utter surprise, it runs straight past me. I'm shaken. Some Indian ladies ahead of me hear my scream and see the monkey running off. I've shattered the noble silence of that sacred ground with a shriek of terror. The monkey's gone. But I'm in bits. Deeply shaken. I want to be held, to cry on someone's shoulder, to be assured that everything is going to be okay. No such 'someone' exists in my life. Nor have they for many years. And at this moment I'm keenly aware of it. Another black thought strikes. Why me? Paranoia sets in. There were other people around. Why did the monkey run at me? I know why. It sensed that I was sad, or bad! It smelled my rotten core. With that thought came a realisation: I was depressed. Goenka had warned that days eight and nine would bring up 'some deep complexes of the mind' and perhaps I'm getting to the heart of mine: that deep down I believe that I am unloved and unattractive?

During the group sitting I can't close my eyes. I've lost faith. The teachers beckon me to come forward. They know something is wrong. 'You can't meditate?' they ask. 'There is a block? You are spending too much time in the cell,' they say gravely. 'You have become introverted.' I am to go to my room and 'take full body rest'. I lie in 'dead body pose' with my palms upturned, as instructed. Ah, savasana, I'm familiar with this posture from yoga. It's comforting to adopt a familiar pose – and to be alone in my room. I'm grateful for the teachers' attention. Good. I'm actually under someone's care.

Friday 14th Feb – Day 9
Day Nine is a winner. I'm only changing position a couple of times within the hour now. I'm able to focus well and I'm enjoying some deep meditation sessions. At times I'm still meditating after the hour is up and other people have got up and left the hall. Stopping meditating is like coming out of a peaceful sleep, while simultaneously being acutely aware. This is a rich and rewarding experience. I was right to trust the centre and to trust the technique. I feel quite in awe of this change within myself. I feel like something special is happening to me.

Tomorrow it will be time to talk. I'm not even sure I want to talk anymore. Goenka said in his discourse that we've just undergone a deep, surgical operation and that tomorrow, he'll teach us a new meditation; a compassionate and loving meditation that will 'put balm on the wound.'

Saturday 15th Feb – Day 10
During the group sitting from 8–9am, Goenka's warm, gravelly voice takes us through a 'meta', a meditation that's made up of a series of statements, including 'may I share my peace, my harmony, my merits and my dhamma with all beings' and 'may I be compassionate and loving towards all beings.' For the first time I sit cross-legged without moving or opening my eyes once for the whole hour. Yay! I've done it. The pain is there, but I'm so deeply connected with my meditation that I'm finally capable of not reacting to my physical body. It's a real achievement. I'm happy that I've reached this point before my departure. A feeling of overwhelming emotion is rising in me towards the end of the meditation. It's over.

I rush out of the hall. I need to cry loudly. I can't contain my tears. I run to a tree, away from the path the others will be following down to the residential quarters to break their silence. I'm not ready. My shoulders are shaking with emotion. I scarcely know what I'm crying about! I'm certainly not unhappy. I feel as though I've been turned inside out; prized open, almost. And yet, I've been comforted by the powerful 'balm on the wound', as they said I would. I walk towards my fellow students to join the excited chatter. With tears still flowing, I get someone to translate to my Russian roommate, who looks concerned, that I'm crying because I'm happy, not sad.

For the rest of the day, a sense of euphoria prevails. Getting to know everyone is really interesting. There's a strong sense of camaraderie among us: what a profound and special experience we strangers have just endured together. And we did it! How amazing. We did it.

Sunday 16th Feb – Day 11
I don't feel completely ready to leave. I love the terrain round about me and know that it's going to be difficult to retain this warmth I feel in my chest – a sort of radiating harmony – when I'm back in the 'real' world. I'm tearful as we stand in line to get our passports back. We say our goodbyes and file into cars bound for onward destinations. And very soon, I'm in the city.

How I want to be alone! For three hours now I've been waiting in Kolhapur for my bus to Goa. Waiting inside and outside a small travel agent shop on a chaotic dusty junction. The blaring horns and blazing sun are incongruous with the strange peace I feel inside. I want to meditate. Now I actually want to sit down and close my eyes. I want to process what I've just been through.

What happened back there on that sacred land? I opened. Body and mind opened outwards to face an invisible force. Sometimes it held me. I felt suspended in space and time. But aware. Always aware. And at the end, I 'rose above' the pain, when fortunate enough to go so deep into the meditation that I could transcend unpleasant physical sensations. I guess that was the point of the exercise.

I travel by bus from Kolhapur to Panjim, Panjim to Margao, Margao to Chaudi and by taxi from Chaudi to Agonda. I'm shown to the room that will be home for the next nine days, far from the maddening crowd. And I sleep.

Vipassana 2: 20–31st December 2014, Sheringham, England
On day one I had my first face-to-face chat with the teacher, Jane. I told her I felt instantly comforted as soon as I stepped onto the site; that I experienced the first feeling of peacefulness that I'd had in a long time, during the first meditation, and that I was relieved to hear Goenka's words about 'taking refuge in Dhamma.' She told me, 'it doesn't matter if you feel comfort; that will change again. The point is to feel comfortable with whatever is – to feel comfortable with the reality of the present moment.' I told her that although I was going through physical trauma, my bigger problems were all emotional; that I was astounded by the lack of support from my family throughout my hospital experience. She told me 'you're not here to change your emotions; you're not here to change your disease; you're not here to change your family. You're here to be comfortable with the reality of the present moment, whatever that reality is. Just be comfortable with it.' Okay. I'm beginning to understand. I added that it was nice to get some brief respite though. And she agreed; but reminded me that nothing ever stays the same.

Jane warned me that the negative emotions I was experiencing could get much worse. Expect the unexpected. I knew already there was no linear path on Vipassana. The bad days always come back to bite you. But I nonetheless enjoyed some extremely pleasant sensations early into the course, including a beautiful moment when I was floating among the twinkling stars in a navy-blue Universe. It reminded me of having been in the duty-free shop at the airport and crying to the Ed Sheeran song that was playing: 'kiss me under the light of a thousand stars,' the sentimentality of the words sparking tears that I hid by trying on designer sunglasses. It had been a sad moment. But this one inside my mind was truly peaceful and positive.

And yes, of course, the bad days came. It was a relief to cry. It took about three days, so frozen had I been. I flashed back to the hospital 'procedures' I had undergone and observed my own terror during them, despite being sedated at the time. My tears were big, rolling salty waves, like the ocean, washing everything away. Purifying things. I felt connected to nature in a way that I hadn't understood before. As Mr. Goenka says, 'anicca, anicca, anicca; arising and passing away, arising and passing away.' This is the characteristic of everything in the Universe, including the human body. Nature will run its course. My understanding had jumped considerably since my last course. There is nothing personal in this impermanence – no 'me' or 'I'. The monkey that ran at me on the first course didn't 'know I was bad'! The monkey was just being true to its monkey nature, threatened by a human who looked it in the eye.

As the course progressed, I of course became increasingly sensitive to the passing nature of the sensations in my body. But this was sometimes excruciating, if the sensation involved heart palpitations, for example, or tensing up of muscles, because still the fear of the 'screaming cramp' I'd experienced earlier was lurking. I would experience changes in temperature with bouts of sweating or feeling very cold. These are all symptoms of panic attacks, although I didn't know at the time that was what I was going through. The recurring thought 'is this a sensation that will pass, or is this a symptom and it's me who is going to pass?' would likely have fueled the physical symptoms – or did the physical symptoms come before the thought? There is no denying that in the 'oneness' of the bodymind there is no distinction. Thoughts and sensations are linked. I know this experientially. An 'irrational fear of death' is a classic panic attack symptom, further fueled by the steroids, which brought about physical and psychological sensations.

The meditation sessions in the middle of the day were most difficult, with a sense of being 'blasted' – the very word the doctors had used – from the inside out, as if someone had switched on the air conditioning in my respiratory system. This is a most unpleasant feeling. It made it almost impossible for me to keep my mouth closed during meditation, although I worked hard to do so. At other times I simply gave in to breathing the 'coldness' back out through my mouth and waited for the sensation to pass, which it did. In amongst this, I would experience moments of wonderful peace. During these times, when I felt myself to be in a deep meditation, I could breathe easily with mouth closed and felt a still warmth and sense of well-being around my heart and lungs.

The break times, especially over extended lunch times when not meditating, were more challenging. It was frosty and the drop in temperature would cause my muscles to tense and my fingers to lock into stiff and painful positions. This can be a symptom of Raynaud's syndrome, and I was never quite sure how worried to be about these frightening physical changes. I just had to wait for them to pass, believing in the impermanence of the Universe. And eventually they did. It was very frightening.

On an emotional level, however, everything got sorted out. The scenarios that were so upsetting at the beginning, full of blame and self-pity, gave way to entirely new perspectives and seeing things from the other person's point of view. I understood myself to have been looking for my family to fulfill my emotional needs – to be demanding this from them – and setting myself up for all kinds of hurt when it didn't happen. This self-realisation of myself as demanding was an important break-through in my own emotional maturity. And I began to enjoy feeling less attached to my family. It is not their job to fulfill me emotionally. This must come from within. I can stop chasing their love when I find my own reserves of self-love.

I saw the email I had written to my son, sister and daughter asking for their help after coming out of hospital, as narcissistic. And yet I did not feel guilty; it was a desperate plea, which could only be ugly. That was the reality of the present moment for me and I had to stoop as low as that in order to come through the other side. The fact that the family was unable or unwilling to respond to such a direct plea for help says as much about their situation as it did about mine, and I am able to feel compassionate towards them. I began to recognise the verbal abuse and generations of negativity within the family, causing the unhealthy dynamics and habit patterns, of behaviours we have fallen into with each other.

Knots began to unravel as I saw a clear path through the problems with less attachment to each relationship. And being less attached would also protect me from them and their problems, which I always fully took on board before. I am losing my guilt. I am becoming free. This is what Goenka refers to as being 'liberated from the bondage of misery'. He says we do not need to accept people's 'presents' of abuse or negativity. We can refuse to accept these gifts if they do not serve us. It shouldn't be a case of 'I'm a Vipassana meditator now – you can cut me like a vegetable.' No. It's not a passive state, this particular art of living.

I experienced what felt at the time like stunning insights into my PhD research. I came to know exactly what my research was about. I defined a 'conscious theatre practice' and saw a series of diagrams laid out before me that I simply had to draw into a book as soon as a left the site. I 'saw' the space my theatre practice would run from, with yoga studio/rehearsal space, meditation room, kitchen, bathroom, showers and café. I 'saw' the grey towels and the Black Star logos. The word 'conduit' came to me, which was unusual because

I wasn't sure what it meant. Although of course my subconscious did. I looked it up as soon as I had Wi-Fi, on the train towards London, and saw that it meant I was a kind of funnel through which a force was blowing. This made perfect sense to me: the force of Vipassana – to see things as they really are; as well as the force of nature and the Universe. I realised that working at an intellectual level was only getting me so far and that I had become stuck – until I began working at an experiential level, when everything became clear. Of course, I still have to make things clear, for PhD purposes, for those who are not working at an experiential level. For this, I must concentrate on practice to articulate the ideas I am exploring around.

Vipassana 3: July 13–24th July 2015, Churu, Rajasthan, India

This was by far the most enjoyable of the three Vipassana courses. It was the gentlest, the calmest, with far less intense ups and downs. I felt almost disappointed that my meditation sensations were feeble by comparison to the last course, but this is exactly what Goenka refers to when he speaks of 'playing a game of sensations' i.e., craving pleasurable sensations. To do so is to miss the point of Annica – that everything is changing, changing, changing. So I caught myself and accepted this different experience, which was a little boring at times, and felt slightly superficial, as though I was 'coasting' through it. What I observed is that my life since the last course has been less dramatic. I have neither the physical trauma – having just come out of hospital last time – nor the emotional trauma – having fallen out with all close friends and family members prior to the previous course. There was nothing deep to deal with. I was able to remain balanced and equanimous.

And by comparison to the first course, when I was in such pain physically, when sitting in the cross-legged position, I have come on leaps and bounds. I got through the course without asking for a chair. However, I was not forced to sit cross-legged and changed my position often, to knees bent in front of me, gripping them with my hands and arms. This in turn caused painful tension in the shoulders and spine, but the teacher, Mr. Choudhary, was also less strict about maintaining the one posture for a full hour, and so I was able to change position. As well as a more relaxed teacher, we did not have any female 'helpers' to keep on top of us at our residential quarters. This meant that the bell to wake up was audible but not right outside ones' door. As the bell-ringer was male, and could not enter a female area, neither was he checking up on us when we were in our rooms.

There were only four women and it was very peaceful. I particularly enjoyed the breaks where I was able to sit outside (when the sun wasn't too fierce) and observe the nature and wildlife at this lovely centre: all sorts of beautiful flowers, birds and animals, and how they all interacted with each other. I bonded with a sweet stray dog that lived on the land of the centre and was fed scraps from the kitchen. And the peacock! A very proud male would strut around right outside the meditation hall, showing off his beautiful plume to three females. It amazed me that he would choose a spot where humans are constantly coming and going, although he would quickly move away as humans were approaching.

But once we were inside, he would take up his position directly in front of the low windows and begin his ritual. The peacock has a very loud call, like a cross between a cat and a baby. This appeared to rise in volume in line with the audio recording of Goenka's chanting – as through the peacock was competing. The whole scene was quite comical. This wonderful site is where Goenka himself lived for many years. Did the peacock know? Did the peacock catch the 'good vibrations' in Goenka's voice? I certainly did.

The chanting always helped me meditate and on day 10, when we did the Meta, I finally experienced the powerful meditation that I had wanted. True to form, the session ended in tears of joy, as with the previous two courses (but without the heart palpitations of the previous course, which had left me light-headed and feeling as though I might faint). It was a lovely, lovely experience. Having this time to myself, after such a busy period at home, and after a theatre conference, was simply priceless. I will return to the Churu site.

2   Bikram Yoga Teacher Training

Sunday 4th Oct 2015, Khao Lak, Phuket, Thailand
In the minibus with a few of my fellow Bikram teacher trainees, who are very sweet, I felt freaked out for no reason other than my own insecurities. What was I was doing here among these bendy, nubile, flexible, championship competing, young yogis? Me: old, stiff Grandma. This feeling grew as we waited at the airport for our lift to the hotel and my peers began showing off their best yoga postures in the Arrivals hall, attracting much attention. When they tried to encourage me to 'do a posture' for a video I became a little defensive and told the person pointing a camera in my face to 'go away'.

The hotel foyer is vast and calm. It's everything one ever imagined a posh hotel in Thailand to be. My room is gorgeous. I am very lucky and grateful to be doing this expensive thing. This room will be my haven, no matter what.

Other fears are just about health really. I may get ill. I'm expecting to be broken – to get shouted at, to feel upset, to experience injury and pain; to feel that
I don't 'fit in' etc. All my usual fears, which nobody else here appears to have;
except one French woman who confessed to also feeling scared and emotional
and wondering whether she is 'strange' because everyone else seems so damn
positive.

Orientation. Lots of do's and don'ts. But I'm okay with adhering to a strict
code of discipline. I think. We are a group of 128 – small compared to former
Teacher Training (TT) sessions. I imagine that's a good thing. More personal
attention – but then again, no hiding place. But there's no point in trying to
hide. I'm going to be totally exposed here. My age, physical weakness; illness
maybe even. It's all going to be on show. But I'm feeling very happy right now
at 17.30 – one and a half hours before the 'welcome party'. Being in my room
alone is glorious. Finding that extra £2000 to be home alone was the best decision I made. I'm thinking of the others, with their roommates, some of whom
may want to sleep while the roommate wants to do something noisy ... wow.
How will they all work it out? I sense trouble ahead.

Body? Can we handle these nine weeks of torture? I've been in the vast
hot room. I found it instantly oppressive because there is no daylight. It's
like an aircraft hangar, but without the opening. It will be better when the
lights are on though. It's spacious at least. But I might feel horrible in there
at times.

I promised myself I'd have the Standing Series of the dialogue learned
by training beginning tomorrow. But I'm not quite there. If I learn Standing
Separate Leg Head to Knee tonight, and Tree and Toe tomorrow – it's done.
I'm on target. The challenge then will be to revise them all again, to the point
where I can deliver any of them without warning. The only way that can happen is by saying them out loud, over and over, and over again. I can do that. It's
just like learning lines for a theatre performance.

Nice buffet dinner. Caught a glimpse of Bikram. A little man with a bad
comb-over at the back – just shave it Bikram. He seemed perfectly fine. No
weird vibes or pretenses. His daughter is extremely pretty with a great figure.
She also seems nice. Standing Separate Head to Knee is learned. Tick.

Monday 5th October
It's time to go for the first yoga class. I'm anxious. I don't want to be the worst
person in the room. But if I am, I am.

I wasn't. Neither was I having the hardest time physically. I was having
a difficult time, with my heart thundering in my chest and a dehydration

headache, but I didn't panic. The girl beside me had to be lifted from the floor by two people, one on either side of her, and carted out of the room. She told me later she went all tingly and was paralyzed. A few people threw up. Some outside the room … some inside. All the horror stories I've heard are true. But nobody died. Nobody ever has. Which is comforting. We were in the room for around two hours. Bikram likes to talk – and to sing. And to give corrections. He shows off a lot. But I can't help liking him. So far, I like him.

Tuesday 6th October
First morning class – taught by Bikram's daughter, Laju. It was quite gentle. Heart wasn't racing nearly as bad. She was very sweet.

Enjoyed Bikram's first lecture. Very interesting. But he does show off and name drop a lot. He's worse than Tom Jones on the TV show 'The Voice'.

Bikram's 5pm class was quite tough. He's started giving people hell now.

The second part of todays' lecture involved the trainees reciting the first posture, Half Moon, for Bikram. Their dialogue was well learned, but some of the delivery was lacking connection. He gave everybody really good feedback. I might try mine tomorrow. I would have done it today, had Adam – one of the staff – not convinced me it had to be all three parts, including Back Bending and Hands to Feet pose. He was just kidding me. Still, it was good to let others go first to see what Bikram wants.

Wed 7th
Good class/bad class/Bollywood movie

Thur 8th
So very, very tired. Bad day. Little bit paranoid. Catching weird vibes from people but they were probably emanating from me. Needed a good sleep.

Fri 9th
I enjoyed morning practice for the first time this morning. I was still stiff, but not quite as sore. Was able to hold Standing Bow, calmly, and do Triangle – not a strong one, but was able to just about hold it on the slippy carpet. Sore hips though. Enjoyed talks by the staff – Laju and Anne – about their experience. Both cried when talking about Bikram, as though they empathise with him, maybe? I'm not quite sure what the emotion was about. It seemed real anyway. It was interesting. I'm looking forward to the class I'm about to do. With Bikram.

Good, strong class. I was at the front and worked hard not to be pulled up for anything by Bikram. They told us no lecture tonight. I'm so happy! And there was a Thai singing duo in the dining hall. It was a lovely atmosphere. People were dancing. I would have loved to have stayed longer. But I could feel my heart beating a bit fast and slight cramps in my hands. I thought I better come and lie down. The room is a real resting place for me. Heaven.

Sat 10th
Didn't feel particularly refreshed when I woke up, despite the early night. This morning's class was a real struggle. I started off okay but realised pretty quickly how sore and stiff I was. Had to miss the first set of Camel. I stood up on my knees but was shaking. Not nice. I skipped a set of Rabbit too. I couldn't curl in; pain shooting off my spine when I tried. This is what happens when I've missed yoga for a few weeks – so why should it happen when I'm practicing twice a day! I suppose there are different reasons for being stiff. Stiffness is a symptom of lupus, and the disease battles with the yoga.

I haven't felt well today. It's been a day of recovery, rather than a day of feeling good. Hopefully tomorrow, with NO yoga class, I'll have better energy. I had a massage, which was great. I'll definitely go back to that guy. He really knows what he's doing. But ever since I ate, I've had this elevated heart rate – as though my body has to work too hard to digest the food.

WILL I MAKE IT THROUGH THIS?

One week down, eight to go …

Sunday 11th Oct
Pleasant, productive day: early morning beach chat with Owen; supermarket shopping in Khao Lak; a foot scrub; helping Bobbi learn Half Moon; hair coloured. Have learned the standing series! Not bad for the end of week 1.

Monday 12th Oct
Bikram's wife, Rajashree is teaching this morning. I'm looking forward to it.

Actually, it was really tough. She said she'd go gentle because she hadn't been well herself, but what that meant was that she slowed everything down. This became torturous. We seemed to take forever to complete Prana Yama deep breathing and it really wore me out. The room was too hot, but at least she asked for the doors to be opened. She looked pretty hot and flushed herself. But she's delightful. Chalk and cheese from Bikram. She spoke a lot about the body and the body-mind connection. I'm looking forward to her lectures.

Bikram's class was bloody awful. The room felt disgustingly hot, humid and oppressive – before we even started. He was in a really bad mood and just moaned and moaned at people. There was no fun in it. I realised he was making me stressed: nervous, even. I would be holding a posture and then he'd start on someone, and my strength would wane. His negativity was killing my energy. Eventually I felt nauseous and had to lie out a couple of postures in the floor series, considering leaving the room. But I didn't have the energy for that either. At the end he told us he didn't enjoy teaching us. The feeling was mutual.

In the evening we watched old TV shows from Bikram's days with the yogi troupe he was part of in Calcutta. We saw supernatural feats being performed. Elephants standing on people, people having steam rollers run over their chest, people bending bars with their throat and eyeball; as well as particularly bendy people, doing abnormal things with their bodies. Bikram's guru, Bishnu Gosh, was being interviewed. When asked how dangerous the stunts were, he told the presenter – almost ... proudly? – that his son had died doing a stunt. Wouldn't that be the moment to stop?

Bikram appears to be of this same mindset ... as though that comes with the territory, maybe? I don't really understand. I'd like to talk to him personally.

I'm very keen to understand how these supernatural feats are possible. He says it's about having total control over mind and body – to be able to relax sufficiently to allow this to happen without causing damage. I hope Bikram explains this fully and I come to understand these links with consciousness. The people doing the stunts would have to be 'brought back' by their colleagues, who would rub them furiously until they began to move or open their eyes. But they didn't look well, even after they'd jumped to their feet. It seemed so ... exploitative? Performance and consciousness just took on a new dimension: performance and (temporary) unconsciousness.

Tuesday 13th Oct

Felt brighter in Rajashree's class today. Still got very sore hips. And not much strength in my arms or legs. It was little cooler than yesterday. I enjoyed it.

Evening class. A nice surprise – Manali, who runs the training, taught the class. It was good to have a break from Bikram. I really enjoyed her teaching. It was very upbeat. I did well in the class, without missing any postures. She played a great Indian tune at the end too.

After the class I went back to my massage guy. It was even better once he knew I did yoga. It was like a proper sports massage. It was very painful round about my hips, which have been sore for days, but he definitely released tension in that area. He's going to be one of the people who helps me through this.

Wednesday 14th October
Great class with Rajashree this morning.

Today it was my turn to deliver Half Moon pose for Bikram's judgment. I knew it well and felt confident, but as I began my delivery, he stopped me. Just like Simon Cowell on the X-Factor. He told me it was too dramatic. He told me to do it again, more 'normal'. Trying hard to be 'un-dramatic' it was coming out a bit flat. He stopped me again. I knew that I had the support of the 'audience' (my fellow students) and when I told Bikram I was trying to find the balance between 'dramatic' and 'normal', they cheered and clapped. He told me I was 'too sweet' and that I had to be 'more bitch' because people who come to class are sometimes sick and they don't want to do the posture and you have to make them do the posture, so that they can get better. He then began to digress and started talking about how I was changing his yoga into sexy yoga and that all the boys would come to my class. I wanted to cut this line of chat short. I said, 'I'll have you know I'm a Grandma!' I wanted to be taken seriously. Boys indeed. My fellow students were really enjoying the entertainment by this point.

Bikram was annoying me, and yet I wanted to give him what he wanted, in the same way as I would a Director on a production. If he wanted me to be tough, I'd be tough. I began to deliver the dialogue in a much louder and more assertive way. My peers loved it. The more they cheered and clapped, the tougher I got. It became fun. I was performing. When I got to the incongruous line 'like a flower petal blooming' I changed the cadence of my voice – deliberately returning to my former style of delivery that Bikram had called 'dramatic' – just to get a laugh. It was a special on-stage moment. It was effortless. When I finished, Bikram said: 'Good!' and then 'very good!' Then he turned to the audience and said: 'see how I changed what she was doing? See how I helped her?' It had to be his success and not mine.

And I wonder if there was something demeaning in all this – my teaching style reduced to 'sexy' and 'romantic' with a 'trail of boys waiting to come to classes' ... I was made to feel something lesser than my real self. I was made smaller, but then allowed to become more again, with his help – like being created by someone else. There are interesting gender politics implications here. I had already worked out through his comments to everybody else, that Bikram prefers a harder style of dialogue delivery. But the way I delivered it, when he did finally approve of it, felt artificially aggressive to me – not the way I necessarily want to teach – although I do want to get that balance.

He had said to people in the past that he was getting bored, he had said to people 'sing it! – do anything! Just don't be boring', but when I tried to deliver it with feeling, he called it 'too dramatic'.

I was lucky to have great feedback from the other students though – who said they loved all the incarnations of my dialogue. Some said he shouldn't have stopped me and that if they ever come to my class, they want me to use my 'dramatic' style. Someone else said they loved my style and that I 'really have something'. The staff mentioned it to me too – one said that I need to 'take that power back to Glasgow – it needs it!' another said it was 'entertaining' and that Bikram likes that, and yet another, a female, seemed to latch onto the 'sexy' comments and said something about being a 'horny bastard'. I wasn't sure who she was referring to and wasn't happy anyway. I wanted to nip this in the bud. There was nothing sexual going on. And it's dangerous the way these labels get slapped on people. 'Who's a horny bastard?' I asked her, unsmiling. She didn't answer. Another student asked me if I was an educator and said that Bikram was way off with his 'romantic' chat. I was relieved about this. He suggested it was maybe what Bikram himself was thinking, but that wasn't what was coming across. Good. It amazed me that even at almost 50-years-old, this sort of stuff still surfaces.

Great class with Bikram in the evening. The talk by Bikram on the Mahabharata in the evening was also very relevant to my research.

Thursday 15th
Good class with Rajashree in the morning – stiff but encouraged to take it slow. Great class with Bikram – was more flexible and encouraged to push!

Friday 16th Oct
Weird day.

Laju took the morning class. I enjoy her upbeat style and positive, bubbly personality. I was sore and stiff again. Such sore hips, and around the sit-bones. It was very painful, but again, I was able to take it slow and easy.

Lecture with Rajashree which touched on yoga science and philosophy, and emotions – it was really interesting. Then everyone had to introduce himself or herself and tell a bit about their selves. This quickly became highly emotional. I realised that everyone is feeling messed-up in one way or another, but I think this outpouring may have permeated evening class …

It was Rajashree teaching, not Bikram – and perhaps a change of energy might have shaken us out of what had gone before. My body was particularly sore for an evening class. I've got sore finger joints, for example, which I haven't had for a year. And a sore knee. And a burning right shoulder. Symptoms that have been controlled by medication are very much still there.

Lupus, and whether I should tell I've got it, was kind of on my mind during the class, as well as a sense of sadness, a little bit. Maybe because of the emotional pain the group was expressing.

Then Bikram came in and wanted to say something before he left. He told us to beware of a guy – one of us – who I couldn't see in the room. A guy he had liked previously, who also came from Calcutta, but was now calling 'a snake' and I think there was some implication that he was here on false pretenses or something ... I don't know. It was horrible anyway. I feel upset. I don't want to stand up and talk about myself tonight.

It's 9.30pm. Sign-in for the lecture is now open. I don't want to go. I'm really tired with very sore hips. Is it going to be a heavy couple of hours of sad stories? I'm not sure I can bear that pain either.

It was okay. We heard stories around someone's mum getting murdered; someone having a hysterectomy because their mum died of cancer of the womb; someone who couldn't leave the house because of her phobias, etc. But it didn't affect me too badly. I actually really like this group of people. I'm lucky to be in this group that is small enough for trust to build between us.

Thankfully there's only one class in the morning. What a heavy week!

We had a teacher called Ben today, an Ozzie guy with a Bikram retreat in Tasmania, which sounds great. I enjoyed his teaching – nice and straight-forward. Good energy without barking at us. Very encouraging. I was sore though. I was also in the back row and didn't have even a glimpse of myself in the mirror. I was slightly paranoid because Adam was behind me, and the staff do tell you they're watching you. I couldn't touch my face in Pada-Hastasana.

I went for a massage. It was painful but he got into all the areas that are problematic – as if he knew which postures I'm having trouble with. He's intuitive. I stayed in my room for the rest of the day. Except for a trip to the shop where I bought an ice-lolly and cartons of juice. I just ate crap and relaxed. No more dialogue. No more exercising. Just watching movies lying on my bed. I felt like my body was seizing up and my joints were aching. I didn't go to dinner. It was heaven, not having to be anywhere.

Sunday 18th Oct
Looked at some PhD books – practice-as-research mostly. Looked through my Bikram Yoga binder and flicked through the anatomy book. It's going to

be a busy week with dialogue at the posture clinics and anatomy at the lectures, which we'll be tested on. I've been revising dialogue up until Standing Head to Knee, as that's what we'll be reciting this week, but I'd also like to push on and get past Cobra and onto the next one. Revised dialogue up until Eagle.

Monday 19th Oct
Anne was teaching. I love her. She's probably my favourite so far. But I was emotional. Hearing her Caribbean accent made me long for Harry. I suppose I'm still not quite over my separation from him. You'd think I would be. I haven't seen my father for 35 years. It's strange because Bikram reminds me of him too. So charismatic. So quick-tempered, but also so able to laugh fast, and heartily – and to morph smoothly from one mood to the other. Both ostentatious characters. Both show-offs. Both with barks worse than their bites, I suspect – but also capable of badness.

I didn't get off to a very good start with people this morning before class, having spent most of the weekend alone. I'm a weirdo. I'm having the thought that nobody thinks I have anything to offer – as someone to know. I don't think it's about my own self-worth because I know that I do have something to offer, but I feel that they don't think I have something to offer. This makes me want to stay away from people – and yet, I know that it's me who is being weird and not other people. I cried quietly in class.

It was a good class. It wasn't my strongest or most flexible, but it was far better than the end of last week: not nearly as painful to do Pada-Hastasana (although I didn't lock my knees) or Separate Leg Stretching (on the floor). Rabbit was still a problem with those pains shooting off my spine when I tried to walk my knees forward. I'll be braver in this posture in the later classes.

Posture clinic: delivered Back Bending/Pada-Hastasana. All good. The feedback was that I should be louder, and I was maybe a bit slower than some students would be comfortable with. (That was more about me trying to remember my lines).

Tuesday 20th
Good classes. Nice and crisp and clean and the teachers just got on with it. Didn't get to deliver Awkward at posture clinic with Adam. Felt a bit gutted, would have liked to get it over with, but was just very tired, I think. Sore hips.
Wednesday 21st

Quite enjoyed the morning class because I had energy, although the teaching was all a bit wordy. Didn't enjoy the evening class at all. I left the room to go to the toilet and also sat out postures. It was a drag. Heavy energy and drawn-out dialogue.

Posture clinic: jumped up and did Awkward before anybody else. All good, but I was moving about a bit. That's probably what I'm going to do when I'm teaching though. I was asked by staff to work with a student who was struggling, because I was 'really good with my delivery and I understand the postures'. It was great to hear this – a boost to my confidence.

Thursday 22nd
Good classes! My joints are not nearly as sore. I did a good Rabbit today.

I suffered later. I was falling asleep in the posture clinic and had terrible left hip and back pain. I took a pain killer. It wasn't a good idea. I got up and delivered Eagle and messed it up a little bit – even though I knew it perfectly. I got away with it though because I was laughing and so were the demonstrators. So it became fun. They said some nice things – that 'I'd make a nice teacher and that the smile really helped'. Deepak said, 'my people' were going to love me and I said, 'only them?' and he said, 'well let's start with them'. I think it was probably a compliment, but I wondered if he meant I wouldn't be considered any good outside of my own town. This upset me a bit. By the time I got back to my room I was exhausted but unable to sleep. I had an elevated heart rate and was having anxious thoughts.

Friday 23rd
I took it very easy at morning class. I was fearful of having palpitations again. I missed out the second set of Camel, Rabbit and Stretching. The teacher was excellent. She did a good job of trying to keep us galvanized. I told her next time I'd give her more energy.

I felt sleepy and unwell at the lecture. I was sweating even though the air con was on. My back hurt. Grace did a bit of bodywork on me – loosening up stuff. I felt better after it.

Evening class. Manali was teaching. I didn't feel good, very emotional from the start and low energy. I was upset after seeing a picture of the pancreas in the lecture. I was thinking of my mum's pancreatic cancer. I was crying a lot during the standing series. By the floor series I had to leave the class. I went outside and cried and cried. It was strange, crying really hard. Jenny offered a sympathetic hand on my shoulder. Anne came out, she said 'let it our darlin'' in her lovely Caribbean accent. I was okay after 5mins and went back in and finished the class. Strange day.

Saturday 24th

Morning class with Nancy. People were complaining that she didn't know what she was doing, didn't know the dialogue, etc. but I enjoyed the gentler pace.

Sunday 25th

Not feeling that great about my health. We'll see how it goes this week.

Monday 26th October

At Rajashree's evening class I felt strong and happy and able to hold the postures for longer than usual.

The evening lecture comprised the last part of everyone sharing their stories. I spoke about having lupus and how it wasn't a sad story because, with Bikram yoga at the heart of it, I have found meditation and learned to be more self-accepting and have found out more about nutrition and diet and become more ecologically aware; and I spoke about how it gives me strength and is an alternative at times to taking medication. I can use it as a way to manage my symptoms. I also said that the programme might be a little intense for me and that if anyone sees me falling – please come running. Without going into all the details, as other people have, about nearly dying, I made the point that illness and disease can be an opportunity for personal transformation. I said that all of this will make me a stronger teacher.

At this moment I feel great, physically. One can never second-guess it. What will tomorrow – day two of week four – bring?

Tuesday 27th Oct

Woke up sweating with a burning throat. I think I have an infection and I think I should go to the hospital this weekend and not leave it until the 8th.

Wednesday 28 Oct

Rajashree's posture clinic was interesting, going through every single pose and explaining it. At the evening class she was 'on the floor' among us again, making adjustments. I enjoyed the class.

At night we had a lecture and then posture clinic. I had a cup of coffee at dinner. After the lecture I suddenly realised I was going to have to deliver Standing Head to Knee. My heart began pounding. I was thirsty and almost dizzy. It was very unpleasant. I couldn't calm down. I got up and did it and it was okay – a good laugh even.

Thursday 29 Oct

The first class with Jill was good. I like her style. Then Rajashree's posture clinics, where we finished the standing series. I wanted to show her my Triangle but was too tired. I didn't want to show a posture on stage. Also, it looked tiring for people to be stretched and pulled into the right form of the pose. They looked almost dizzy afterwards.

By Rajashree's class in the evening, I was very tired. My energy was low in the standing series and I had to sit down a couple of times. I got through it.

I really, really, didn't want to go out of my room again at night. I was so tired. I went to dinner late and was napping during the last lecture. It was a shame to miss it. It sounded interesting but I couldn't keep my eyes open.

Friday 30th Oct

Great nights' sleep.

Sat 31st

Morning class; massage; bed early.

Sunday 1st November

Lovely day off in Phuket – hospital first, then the mall!

Monday 2nd

Lovely class in the morning. Bikram back after two weeks in the evening. It was tough. It really wiped me out. Bikram was tired too, with jet lag, so we watched a documentary about Yogananda, which I loved.

Tuesday 3rd

I found Bikram's class less difficult than the day before. In the evening he just talked, mostly about how yoga was 'everything'. It was okay.

Wed 4th

Class was stronger again. The lecture wasn't as interesting – 'pig, dog, goat' story. And I was nodding off, which was uncomfortable.

Thu 5th

The first late-night Bollywood movie. Only until 1.30pm but it was tough. I was falling asleep during it, but at least staff were allowing people to sleep.

Fri 6th

Didn't push myself in morning class. Posture clinic was oppressive. Blanked after reciting a few lines of Standing Separate Head to Knee, but gained pace and momentum by the end and did well. Tired and low energy today. Enjoyed Bikram's lecture at night. It felt quite intimate. He's a charismatic storyteller.

Sat 7th

Class was great. Make-up class was also nice. Didn't work very hard.

Sun 8th

Learning postures most of the day. Tomorrow is the beginning of week 6. Only four to go. I'd like to sort a few things out about myself in these four weeks, to finish on an even higher high. I've written a list and pinned it on my mirror.

Sun 15th

It was a strange week. Some things happened that disturbed me. One day in the lecture, when I was sitting in the front row, Nancy approached me and said, 'you're always in the front, go find another friend.' It felt hurtful and I wondered 'why me?' as everyone has their favourite spots, in the lecture hall and in the yoga studio.

On Friday morning, we had Ulysses. I had been dreading his arrival a little bit. It was a very hard class. Many people didn't enjoy it. I was worried he might teach the afternoon class too, and I was so tired from the morning, so I went in the back row. Bikram taught the class, but I didn't have a strong one. The next morning, Manali called me to move in front of the podium. I found it a bit embarrassing, as though I was one of the ones who try to hide. I guess that's exactly what I had done, the day before – but only once! There are people who hide every day! I felt I was being picked on. Was I becoming paranoid? Then a fellow student walked past me and said 'Manali is picking on you? Why?' I said, 'I have no idea,' and she said, 'me neither – you're good!' I suppose it was a supportive comment but showed that people are watching my practice.

I felt slightly better after speaking to Alicia. She also got moved in the lecture hall. If I thought they were moving me because they didn't like me, that certainly wasn't the case for Alicia, as she is related to Bikram. Her theory is that they pick on the ones who they think can take it. Fair enough. I can take it. Just like I took the injustice of make-up class. There was no make-up class this week. All those students with all their misdemeanors were let off from the punishment I had to endure – without committing a misdemeanor. So what. Good for them.

If the staff believe I'm being a wallflower with my practice, or becoming attached to any particular person or place, then I'll change it up myself, rather than wait until they change things for me. It's time to demonstrate my strength. No matter what row I'm in tomorrow, I'll go in front of the podium. Even if it's Ulysses, I'll face the problem and not try to hide from it.

Other exciting developments are: the chance to teach a mock class at the Patong studio on the Monday or Tuesday after graduation – I have booked three nights at the Phuket Graceland resort, to be close to the studio; the chance to teach in Delhi for a while directly after Patong, on December 9th. Pavalli from the Delhi studio is coming to TT on Tuesday. I can't wait to meet her/him? I have only two postures still to learn – Spine Twisting and Blowing in Firm. I'll then need to start reciting them all from beginning to end, and adding the left side and additional dialogue. It seems like an impossible task – but of course, it isn't. I'll do it.

I had a bad posture clinic where I blanked, followed the next night by a great posture delivery, where I excelled.

Sunday, Nov 22
Week 7 was a good week. Lots of meditation and strong classes. Was feeling the love. Good class in front row in front of Bikram on the Friday. Feel strong.

Sunday, Nov 29
Week 8, not so good. Started off strong on Monday morning class with Lyn, but felt exhausted after it and didn't really recover for a few days. Finished posture clinic by Tuesday, which was great. Everyone was elated. By the weekend I wanted to give myself space and time to learn the dialogue alone. Went away by myself to Ka Khao Kho today to recite the whole Bikram Yoga sequence, but have only got as far as learning Pranayama deep breathing.

I feel unhappy. It's ridiculous, I'm here in this beautiful place, but I think I'm lonely. Off to Delhi next, which I'm not even sure I'm going to enjoy.

Final Week
Snapped out of my mini depression. As I do. I graduated as a Bikram Yoga teacher on December the 5th. For all my aches and pains, and at times emotional turmoil, I finished teacher training on a high. I never missed a single class.

FIGURE 4   Lou Prendergast with Bikram Choudhury, 5th December 2015
             SOURCE: PHOTOGRAPHY BY BIKRAM YOGA TEACHER TRAINING OFFICIAL
             PHOTOGRAPHER

CHAPTER 5

Three C's Research Model

Conscious Craft, Conscious Casting, Conscious Collaborations

> The way to learn is to **do**.
> BIKRAM CHOUDHURY, 2007: 15

∴

I created the concept of conscious theatre practice (CTP), which describes theatre processes aligned with aspirations towards higher states of consciousness. The next phase of the research involved the formulation of a framework for analysing and deconstructing the theatrical productions. To this end, I designed the 'Three C's Research Model'. It evolved as the lens through which to peer at the practice; to study the creative processes of each production. Conscious craft: writing, directing and performance; conscious casting; and conscious collaborations are aspects of arts-making that I wanted to measure against my new notion of Conscious Theatre Practice.

Broad research questions prevailed while the Three 'C's model invited more specific lines of enquiry, evidenced below as a twelve-point set of ideal criteria that came into play in varying degrees on each production. Through the work, this model became an early draft of a working manifesto for Black Star Projects. In the format below, however, it served as a paradigm for testing and questioning the validity of CTP across the rehearsal processes on each play. The successes, failures and antagonisms of this model, in practice, are revealed in the next chapter where it is applied to the three plays.

The model aims to encapsulate all the theoretical frameworks and methodological approaches under investigation. It became the way to finally hone in on what it was that I wanted to know: what would a Conscious Theatre Practice really look like? What could I learn across the three productions that I was making, by testing these three C's? And what lessons could this new and original knowledge contribute to how Black Star Projects might actually work as a theatre company, beyond the research?

© KONINKLIJKE BRILL NV, LEIDEN, 2022 | DOI:10.1163/9789004467927_006

1   The Three C's Research Model

1.1   *Conscious Craft*

– Present 'real-life' stories from marginalised sections of society (writing/directing)

In practice this could mean writing stories from my own life and/or recounting verbatim text from interaction with the lives of others; or incorporating historical events, leading to socially engaged and/or historically informed work.

– Keep audience close (directing/staging)

In practice this relates to staging the work in ways that enable more of the audience to be closer to more of the performers, dissolving 'us and them' barriers and creating union – stronger human connections.

– Undertake daily yoga and meditation to exercise our bodies, increase our attention and focus, and shift our consciousness and energy (performing – *bodymind training*)

In practice this would involve the company, or members of the company undertaking yoga and/or meditation sessions daily, as part of the rehearsal process

– Apply a strong and determined work ethic, as we learn to do in yoga and meditation (writing/directing/performing)

In practice this means seeing the project through, pushing through the challenges and the difficulties that arise during theatre practice – with its highs, lows, moments of fatigue and flashes of inspiration – to arrive at resolution.

– Strive to push our potential for self-realisation through yoga and meditation (writing/directing/performing)

In practice this means challenging oneself, finding an inner confidence that transcends the yoga mat or meditation cushion and brings embodied wisdom to the production. It means facing our weaknesses and learning to be truthful with ourselves and working through our fear-based limitations.

1.2   *Conscious Casting*

– Work with actors with some authentic relation to the work

In practice this means casting performers who are part of the social issues we are engaging with, or, working with professional actors who bear some similarities to the character beyond the superficiality of physical appearance.

– Choose company members intuitively, because they 'feel' right

In practice this means one-to-one auditions with performers in an attempt to 'tune into' their energy and sense their interest in/resistance to CTP

– Enable less advantaged/experienced practitioners to work with the company to enhance their skills

In practice this means welcoming trainee theatre-making personnel onto the production and/or working with performers who are not trained actors

1.3 *Conscious Collaborations*
– Encourage honest conversations
In practice this means ensuring that every company member feels comfortable enough to speak honestly and openly without negative consequences
– Be kind and supportive, modelling empathy and compassion
In practice this means being equanimous rather than reactionary, as we learn in Vipassana meditation, mitigating emotions that arise in rehearsals that are triggered by stress and pressure
– Adopt ethical guidelines for treating company members fairly
In practice this means budgeting correctly and paying fees that meet industry standard rates of pay, and honouring breaks and working hours, etc.
– Encourage company members to contribute creatively
In practice this means respecting suggestions from anyone involved, while not necessarily implementing them. Even in more devised ways of working, the Director still has the final say

2 Higher States of Theatre Consciousness

All three productions encourage empathy in the human suffering embedded in (often) dark narrative content, seeking compassion for not only the victims but also for the villain(s) of the piece(s). A theatre practice based upon the principles of yoga and meditation would not be congruous with solipsism, however. Through processes of self-realisation, one evolves as a human being, acknowledging and learning from past mistakes. Traits such as dwelling in the past, harbouring negativity and indulging in any blame mentality are the anathema to CTP. Finding compassion for those who commit heinous acts is perhaps a spiritual, or utopian aspiration that can potentially be realised through theatre. As Jill Dolan notes, 'utopian performatives exceed the content of a play or performance; spectators might draw a utopian performative from even the most dystopian theatrical universe' (Dolan, 2005:8). Humour is a further inherent quality of CTP, common to all three productions. Conscious of the audience's need for the relief of tension, the work aims to embolden the audience to laugh, necessarily shifting the energy from dark to lighter states.

The productions are based upon personal narratives, each with varying degrees of autobiography. *Blood Lines* deals with my early childhood, focusing mainly on my father. In *Tommy's Song* the autobiography was hidden. I wrote myself into the play as one of the characters that the protagonist engages with. *AWKWARD – A Life in Twenty-Six Postures* was the purest in terms of its autobiographical content, centring on my own life and children. Each project shifts between the personal and the socio-political, raising questions of life and love, but also power and justice. The potential folly of the autobiographical practitioner is to slide into self-absorption. CTP is ever vigilant therefore, of aspiring towards work that speaks to the range of universal emotions that the audience can relate to and engage with meaningfully.

Each production is analysed for the unique insights pertaining to whichever 'C' best matches the ideas under exploration. Working in chronological order, an analysis of *Blood Lines* begins with research into Conscious Casting; from initial inspiration through to the challenges of working with non-actors. The discussion broadens to consider notions of devising, narrative and ensemble. *Tommy's Song*, the only work that I did not perform myself, is read through the Conscious Craft lens, raising questions around truth, media discourse and masculinities; through writing, directing and performance. In the discussion of *AWKWARD*, the focus centres on Conscious Collaborations.

The first two plays took place in Glasgow: *Blood Lines* (2014) was presented as a four-night run at the (now defunct) Arches theatre, and *Tommy's Song* (2015) had a six-day run at Òran Mór as part of the lunchtime theatre programme, 'A Play, A Pie and A Pint'. The final work, *AWKWARD – A Life in Twenty-Six Postures* (2016), was presented at the Swallow Theatre in Whithorn, as a one-off preview performance. Although one production followed the other sequentially, a host of energy-based workshops, meditation retreats and a yoga teacher-training programme took place in and around the productions, as well as during the actual rehearsal processes. I would suggest therefore that this research has amounted to a lateral process: always progressing overall, but not necessarily in a straight line.

Lateral thinking, according to Edward de Bono who coined the phrase in the late 1960s, is 'closely related to insight, creativity and humour' (de Bono, 1970: 9). Its relevance to this section resonates with the use of those same processes during the theatre-making trials, tribulations and (arguably) triumphs, unpacked below. By necessity, this analysis follows a logical narrative. Its structure is aligned with vertical thinking, described by de Bono as 'moving forward by sequential steps each of which must be justified', befitting the demands of academic discourse (de Bono, 1970: 11). For De Bono however, lateral thinking is enhanced by vertical thinking. He suggests that 'vertical thinking is used to dig the same hole deeper' while 'lateral thinking is used to dig a hole in a different place' (de Bono, 1970: 12). One foot did not necessarily follow the other throughout my research; many holes were being systematically dug in different places, and eventually the dots were joined.

De Bono reminds us that both thought processes are complementary: 'lateral thinking is generative while vertical thinking is selective' (de Bono, 1970: 12). Selection is pivotal in the analysis and articulation of practice, just as the text of this book must, by design, 'be clear and "tell a story"' (Murray, 2011: 69). The story it tells is not neat, however. Madison suggests that 'like good theory, performance is a blur of meaning, language, and a bit of pain' further complicating any straightforward critique, perhaps (Madison, 2011: 245, quoted in Spry, 2011: 179). Lessons were learned out of sequence. During *Blood Lines* for example, the Three 'C's research model was forming in my mind as a methodological framework; but had not yet travelled 'down the back of my arms, and finally down to my fingertips' and onto the page, to re-quote Decroux (cited in Mower, 2010: 195). Although there was a research question floating above *Blood Lines*, the interconnections between yoga and meditation, and theatre practice, grew exponentially as the benefits of the former upon the latter became clearer in line with the expansion of my own consciousness through practice, or 'doing'.

Any insight, creativity and humour that emerged during the collaborative processes described below, likened by de Bono to lateral thinking, was tempered with Soyini's blurred meanings and language and pain. With a passion for practice and a commitment to rigorous and systematic research methodology, however, the Three 'C's model became the pivotal 'hook on which to hang' the explorations. It invites a comprehensive and comparative analysis of multiple facets of theatre-making practice and processes, physical and ideological, spiritual and secular. The antithesis to step-by-step logic perhaps, this more lateral, more ethereal research process aspires towards epistemologies from both conventional, and cosmic planes.

CTP emerged from theatre making processes; yoga and meditation; consciousness; self-realisation; and alternative health and healing. Each of these influenced its formulation. CTP could be imagined as a transdisciplinary concept that could be rolled out beyond theatre. As Daniel Henry explains:

> Transdisciplinarity claims that disciplines cannot individually address the complex problems that emerge in society today [...] these problems cannot be dissected into areas that are 'scientific', 'cultural', 'political', or 'societal' since they are, from an ecological point of view, interrelated.
>
> HENRY, 2009: 153

The notion of *Dharma* inherent in self-realisation is perhaps located at the intersection of spirituality and ecology, evident in Maharishi Mahesh Yogi's description of it as 'that invincible power of nature which upholds existence (which) forms the very basis of cosmic life (and) supports all that is helpful for evolution and discourages all that is opposed to it' (cited earlier in Dinkgräfe, 2005: 31, 32). I suggest these descriptions of transdisciplinarity and *Dharma* share inherent aspirations towards higher states of consciousness; described by Meyer-Dinkgräfe via the Indian Vedic Science model of consciousness. My understandings of this complex concept grew from research around the medical condition Lupus, and the alternative healing view that *dis-ease* is the physical manifestation of thoughts and emotions. Our consciousness encompasses all parts of us: body, mind, and spirit. A key step on the ongoing path towards healing myself is *knowing* myself. Yogic practice deepens this process, while autoethnography supports the research processes related to it.

Gill Edwards believes that as we 'shift towards a higher level of consciousness and release the limiting beliefs and traumas of the past – healing from *any* disease becomes not only possible, but more and more probable (Edwards, 2010: 18).' Edwards argues that once we understand the wider picture, we can accept the possibility of true healing as opposed to the temporary relief of symptoms; from the doctor or specialist who focuses on just one part of the body, receiving only a fragmented view of the problem. A person is not 'read' as a whole in Western medical systems. Edwards discusses a state of 'ego-consciousness' that she describes as 'fixed, constricted, limited and isolated (Edwards, 2010: 31).' I would argue that the same could be said of theatre making that is driven by ego-consciousness. An aspect of this research asks what might happen to theatre if it supported ways of *being* on the planet that contributed towards some higher collective consciousness, a higher humanity.

Edwards describes a consciousness central to her concept of conscious medicine, as being 'like an energetic wave shifting into the wave-like consciousness of our higher-self, which is more free-flowing, expansive and connected to others' (Edwards, 2010: 31). As an autobiographical theatre-maker and researcher, for whom intense participation in yoga and meditation formed a key phase of the research, the ideologies of these ancient Eastern disciplines certainly impacted my flow of creativity. I began to consider elements of meditation precepts: abstaining from killing, stealing, inappropriate sexual activity; lying and abusing intoxicants; and yogic codes of restraint (*Yamas*) involving our relationship with the external world and other people: non-harming, truthfulness, non-grasping; and practices of self-training that deal with our personal, inner world (*Niyamas*): purity of body and mind, contentment, self-study, reflection and surrender, cited in Patanjali's *Yoga Sutras*. The making of the work my tests how these ideologies might apply to creative processes; alternative ways of *being* and of *doing* in theatre; of *becoming*.

From readings of the *Yoga Sutras* and the other theorists introduced in Chapter 2; coupled with the embodied knowledge of immersive contemplative practice; and the (lived) experiences of working in the arts, laterally as an emerging theatre-maker, CTP evolved as a potential new theatre paradigm. It questions how one might go about casting company members while holding higher states of consciousness in mind; how the craft of performing, of writing and of directing might be undertaken under the auspices of higher states of consciousness, and how collaborations with others might be enhanced via shared understandings around higher states of consciousness.

PART 2

Practice

∴

Blood Lines (2014)

United in Diversity: 'But Who Could Resist You Dad?'

Blood Lines was an amalgamation of a trilogy of previously presented short plays: *Waiting for My Daddy* (Ankur/Citizens Theatre, 2012), *Whatever Happened to Harry?* (Arches LIVE 2012) and *Fifty Shades of Black* (Ankur/Citizens Theatre, 2013). All three works referenced my fragmented relationship with my late father, Harry Prendergast, a Jamaican migrant to the UK in the 1950s. The latter work received support from (now defunct) black and minority ethnic (BAME) theatre organisation, Ankur Productions. It was presented as the final expression of work via the development programme, the Ankur HaHa. The plays' themes were opportune to Glasgow's 2014 Commonwealth Games.

Encouraged by the Artistic Director of the (now defunct) Arches Theatre, I submitted a successful proposal to Creative Scotland. I was commissioned to create work for the '20 for 14' Commonwealth Games initiative. *Blood Lines* became part of the official Cultural Programme. I dropped the previously implicit relationship to the *Fifty Shades of Grey* novel (James, 2012) that underpinned *Fifty Shades of Black*, when developing Blood *Lines*, following Creative Scotland (CS) guidance around 'new work responding to, or reflecting upon, the unique cultural, social, political and historical contexts of the Commonwealth' (CS, 2014).

1 Conscious Casting: *Blood Lines*

It was during my first Vipassana meditation course in Kolhapur, India, three months before rehearsals for *Blood Lines* began, that conscious connections with theatre began to form. Vipassana *Bhavana,* defined in the glossary of *Pali* terms as 'the systematic development of insight through the meditation technique of observing the reality of oneself by observing sensations within the body', means 'to see things as they really are' (Hart 1987: 89). Thoughts around presenting the truth in my forthcoming production began to manifest. Collaborating with family members intrinsic to the *Blood Lines* narrative would lend authenticity to the production. It would extend notions of telling stories 'as they really are', straight from our own mouths. This was conscious casting in

© KONINKLIJKE BRILL NV, LEIDEN, 2022 | DOI:10.1163/9789004467927_007

action. Directorial decisions were emerging from an altered consciousness: a meditative state of creative inspiration (Meyer-Dinkgräfe, 2005).

Arriving at this very particular 'state', which is different from the flow of ideas one experiences in ordinary consciousness, is for me, only ever achieved during these radical retreats from society. The process could be thought of as a *pre*-theatre-making methodology, working at a level of consciousness. Meyer-Dinkgräfe suggests that if one chooses to believe artists' first-person accounts of inspiration, 'it becomes obvious that they represent states of consciousness that are certainly not common, or everyday' (Meyer-Dinkgräfe, 2005: 20). In my experience, these altered states cannot be guaranteed, even by repeating the circumstances in which they arose. I concur that intensive meditation opens a pathway to inspired thinking. Potentially. Unsullied by language or writing, creativity arose from an embodied, tacit knowledge, arrived at through the lived experience of several days of silent meditation. I valued the power of this inspiration, over and above rational thinking around the risks posed to the quality of the play. I harnessed this 'epiphany' as a casting methodology. I sourced performers (including myself) who would contribute racial diversity and an atypical aesthetic to the work, prioritising this over acting prowess.

For the philosopher Charles Taylor, the ethics of authenticity are intrinsically bound up with being true to oneself; otherwise, one misses the point of what being human is. He asserts that 'being true to myself means being true to my own originality, and that is something only I can articulate and discover' (Taylor, 1992: 28). Practice-as-research enhances such inquiry, deepening self-discovery through creative exploration. The articulation of one's own originality (through art in my case) helps to define it. Taylor posits that this originality is the foundation that 'gives moral force to the culture of authenticity', and this in turn lends itself well to CTP (Taylor, 1992: 28). My aspiration to cast performers with some authentic relationship to the work marked a break from conventional casting methods, which in Taylor's terms amounts to 'doing your own thing'; and believing in it. For Taylor, realising one's potential is 'the background understanding to the modern ideal of authenticity, and to the goal of self-fulfillment or self-realisation in which it is usually coveted' (Taylor, 1992: 29). CTP facilitates the revelation of my abilities and shortcomings, guided by aspirations towards an enlightened consciousness.

Through Vipassana's insight and augmented intuition, it 'felt right' to cast my family, not necessarily on an intellectual level, but in my body: my gut feeling. My sister and I share a childhood, and although seen through very different eyes, hers one year older than mine, my autobiography is her story too. My Scottish born mother's brother is a Rastafarian; a follower of the Rastafari religion that emerged in Jamaica in the 1930s. By dint of his maturity, with long grey dreadlocks, he too represented a visual 'otherness'. My uncle had been influenced by my father's record collection as a young man. He is a reggae music drummer; performing music gigs his whole adult life. A further Scottish-Caribbean connection manifested through the casting of a Glasgow-based musician of Jamaican origin, who had spent ten years working to support the African and Caribbean diaspora across Scotland. With drums and guitar in place, I cast a keyboard player of Scottish African heritage, who at the time was in the early stages of an actor-training programme. The conscious casting of these individuals gave a rawness and honesty to the work, aligned to the autobiographical expression of some shared truths, through theatre making.

In this tale of black oppression, it was essential to CTP, although I had not yet coined that term, to work with those who had truly faced discrimination in their own lives. Collectively, the cast had first-hand experience; personally and/or via our immediate families, of racism, poverty, disease, learning difficulties and other mental and physical disability, illegitimacy, abandonment and abuse. The cast mirrored the issues we were engaging with, bringing together the narrative and the embodiment of it in a resonant, authentic way. We were 'otherness' personified. We shared an implicit politics; an understanding of how it feels to be treated differently; and a desire for social justice. My father's saying, 'who feels it, knows it,' suited this company of marginalised performers, all of whom knew how it felt to be out with the white dominant group. While the audience could not know the issues facing the performers, other than those touched upon in the play text, gazing upon a group of actors with varying skin tones, from black to white, went some way towards addressing inequalities around race; and age, my uncle was sixty years-old at that time.

The *Blood Lines'* choreographer was also of Caribbean heritage. A student of Indian heritage from Glasgow School of Art and a Romanian Assistant Director, paid for by Ankur Productions, also joined the company, along with a (white) student from the Royal Conservatoire of Scotland who was looking to gain experience working across the Commonwealth shows running at the Arches.

Drawing upon a play that also integrated cultural diversity and concepts of higher states of consciousness to a far greater degree, Meyer-Dinkgräfe's analysis of Peter Brook's epic, *Mahabharata,* becomes useful to this discussion of *Blood Lines*. Of particular interest are Meyer-Dinkgräfe's insights into the production's international cast and its ideas around pure consciousness. Exploring the latter point first, Meyer-Dinkgräfe argues that Brook's work was capable of elevating the consciousness of those who engaged with the production. Commentators, particularly Rustom Bharucha (1993), believed that Brook's *Mahabharata* did not do justice to Indian Society or Hindu philosophy.

In defense of the production however, Meyer-Dinkgräfe states that 'the key method used by Brook to access subtler levels of the mind, such as intuition and especially pure consciousness, is suggestion' (2002: 78). Perhaps the 'suggestion' of higher states of consciousness, or at the very least an aspiration towards the evolution of human potential, is also embedded in *Blood Lines*.

Meyer-Dinkgräfe argues that as the source of Brook's work is the *Mahabharata* itself, engagement with it in any form impacts upon the mind at the level of the ego, intuition and inspiration, given that it is ' "universal" in a very special sense' (Meyer-Dinkgräfe in Bradby and Delgado, 2002: 80). Therefore, although wider philosophical notions contained within the original text are not dramatically presented in Brook's *Mahabharata*, they are nonetheless present. As theatre-making methodologies for *Blood Lines* arose in line with the laws of nature or *Dhamma*, during meditation, could the audience still experience some shift in consciousness where the aforementioned concepts are *not* part of its content? This question is addressed to some extent through Meyer-Dinkgräfe's understanding of the Vedic Science concept of unity in diversity, in which 'ultimate unity exists only on the level of pure consciousness' (2002: 80).

Brook cast performers with a range of ethnic backgrounds and traditions including film, oral storytelling cultures and Japanese Noh theatre, creating an experience aligned with unity in diversity. The idea of diversity as a unifying principle is also at the heart of the European Union's motto, *United in Diversity*, whereby Europeans joined forces 'to work for peace and prosperity, while at the same time being enriched by the continent's many different cultures, traditions and languages' (European Union). This research project is being concluded in the wake of Britain's exit from the European Union. In 2014, however, it was the Commonwealth Games motto of *humanity-equality-destiny* that prompted *Blood Lines,* in response to how those universal values might co-exist with the atrocities of slavery. Slavery was trade carried out by the British Empire, which later became the 'Commonwealth of Nations' formerly under British rule (https://www.royal.uk/commonwealth).

The wave of Commonwealth immigration in Britain's post-war years heralded the influx of the Afro-Caribbean diaspora. The five *Blood Lines* cast members were descendants of those migrants. My sister and I were born in the two years preceding the controversial 'Rivers of Blood' speech, delivered by Conservative politician Enoch Powell in 1968. Powell criticised Commonwealth immigration and anti-discrimination legislation, sparking race riots. Excerpts of his speech formed the pre-set recording and the opening section of *Blood Lines*. Powell's text provided tangible links, both to the Commonwealth and to our own histories, demonstrating the racial context at the time of our infancy. In those postwar years, UK establishments offering lodgings are believed to have warned off undesirable ethnic groups by displaying signs stating 'no Irish, no blacks, no dogs' (Guardian, October 28th, 2015). In an academic paper I presented at the Irish-Caribbean conference in Cork, Ireland, I discussed my earliest memories of family, and the ways in which

> my sister and I, to whom Powell would have referred as piccaninnies (a racist term for black children that ultimately lost the Politician his position), my half Irish, half-black dad, and our pony-proportioned Great Dane dog (called Blackie, ironically) would have been the epitome of all that Powell feared and loathed.
>
> PRENDERGAST, 2016

Blood Lines' semi-autobiographical narrative was the device driving the socio-political-historical questions arising from the staging of the Commonwealth Games in Glasgow 2014, as well as questions around patriarchy and feminism, linked to the dysfunctional, inter-racial family dynamics of our Glasgow household in the late 1960s, early 1970s. As Michael Morris' analysis of *Blood Lines* attests, 'Prendergast draws on Scots-Caribbean experience to inform an interrogation of Scotland's imperial role; though her own ambivalent feelings about her father's "dodgy dealings ... which extended to prostitution" complicate any straightforward postcolonial championing of her father' (Devine, 2015: 41–61). Identity is complicated. Autobiographical theatre contributes to explorations and understandings of 'messy' lived experience; of intersectionality that refutes clear-cut notions or binary positions of who we are.

Dee Heddon perceives the autobiographical form to be a 'useful tool in the struggle for emancipation, equal rights, recognition, debate or simply the means to take (a) place' (Heddon, 2008: 20). Feminism's mantra that the personal is political continues to provide a potent framework through which to examine the connections between private lives and the sociopolitical structures that influence them. I identify as Scottish, but my paternal ancestors were slaves. Morris asserts that bringing the nation's entanglement in Caribbean slavery to the forefront helps 'to disrupt and rethink traditional narratives of Scottish identity' (Morris, 2015: 3). In *Blood Lines* this possibility was expanded, not through academic analysis, but through performance.

Along with the historical and personal narratives interchanging throughout the piece, broader issues of racism embedded within explorations of Empire were given agency through the conscious casting of Scots-Afro-Caribbean performers. The premise of conscious casting as part of CTP methodology refutes race being overlooked; seeking a visibility in an industry where BAME performers are marginalised. In conscious casting racial diversity is embodied.

Returning to the notion of 'who feels it, knows it,' conscious casting aspires to an authentic relationship with race: those who have *felt* racial discrimination, *know* racial discrimination, thereby bringing tacit knowledge to performance. In *Blood Lines* race is further complicated, however, by dint of my mixed-race roots. This confusion is articulated in the script when my sister asks: 'are we black now?' demonstrating an ambiguity around our own racial identity.

2   Narrative

In the first week of rehearsals only the three cast members of Jamaican heritage were present. We began reading various sections of my three former scripts, making decisions about which parts could be included in the new work, and who might deliver which lines. We discussed our parents, our childhoods and the proclivity of many Jamaican men to have second families. Govan et al. explain that performance makers work with narrative devices through the 'selection of events and moments, and the ordering and telling of them' (Govan et al., 2007: 55). Narrative pertains to the sequence of events, which was not linear in *Blood Lines*. Furthermore, the authors state that 'creating an original performance, as opposed to staging a play, inevitably involves drawing upon personal experience or reframing pre-existing material within a collectively designed structure (Govan et al., 2007: 55). In *Blood Lines*, pre-existing material was brought to the rehearsal space along with new material, such as the *Rivers of Blood* speech, and worked through by the group as a whole.

Such processes might fit with Deirdre Heddon and Jane Milling's idea of devising, which concerns collaborative performance processes in which 'all members of the group contribute equally to the creation of the performance or the performance script' (Heddon, 2006: 4). The *Blood Lines* process could not claim to have fully embraced this definition, however. As I go on to discuss in the final chapter, it was not a totally equal or shared process of creation. Nonetheless, parts of the work were certainly devised. As practical research, through making, the work resonates with Govan et al's assertion that devised performance raises questions around the 'positioning of the company in relation to the chosen material' (Govan et al., 2007: 57). This is an appropriate premise for *Blood Lines,* where the universal, egalitarian values inherent to Black Star Projects coalesced with the historical injustices of slavery.

The autobiographical narrative was quickly established in the opening section of the play. As the audience entered the space, the pre-recorded Enoch Powell speech was being played, with the cast inside a stationary vehicle. The action begins with performers jumping out of the car and repeating a few pertinent lines of the speech individually, before introducing ourselves *as ourselves,* and our relation to the immigrant community. Heddon discusses autobiographical performance in terms of its concern with using 'the public arena of performance in order to 'speak out', attempting to make visible denied or marginalised subjects, or to 'talk back', aiming to challenge, contest and problematise dominant representations and assumptions about those sub-jects' (Heddon, 2008: 20). In a political climate of hostility towards immigra-tion, presenting ourselves as real people rather than actors mitigated barriers between spectators and performers. Govan et al. point out that narratives com-prise the storyteller and the person receiving the story, and that 'the sharing of a narrative may attempt to conjoin these groups [...] creating a bond between the storyteller and the rest of the community' (Govan et al., 2007: 57). In *Blood Lines,* this bond might have related to increased empathy for the immigrant community, creating a shift in consciousness.

The oeuvre of Glasgow-based Company, Glass Performance, is also based on working with non-professional performers. The definition of what the company does holds similarities and disparities with my own practice. In the first part of its descriptive statement for example, the company explains that its 'socially engaged performance practice collaborates with real people in the place of fictional characters to tell stories that resonate with audiences of all ages and experience' (Glass Performance website). The description of a socially engaged performance practice resonates with Black Star Projects' aspirations to create social change. However, although non-professionals were cast for *Blood Lines,* a professional actor did perform the *Tommy's Song* script, as I go on to dis-cuss in the following chapter. The autobiographical work of Glass Performance aims to 'create a national platform for Scottish communities and individuals to tell their stories and share their histories in a professional and valued context' (*ibid.*). My practice also facilitates the telling of stories by Scottish communi-ties (*Blood Lines*) and individuals (*Tommy's Song*). However, the subject matter of my work relates closely to my own life (*Awkward*), although these parame-ters will continue to broaden by necessity.

3   Staging

Concomitant with the extensive, cavernous part of the Arches in which I chose to stage *Blood Lines,* I worked with a designer with an ability to think expansively about space. Literally pushing the design outwards and upwards, aligned with CTP's desire to think laterally about the world; bright red rope was stretched across the space in diagonal lines, high above the playing area. The central playing area remained empty; pulled into focus with a massive map of Jamaica, drawn directly onto the concrete ground in white chalk. The names of Jamaican locations were drawn into the map at their correct positions. These places include Glasgow, Edinburgh, Inverness and Aberdeen. The familiarity of Scottish names may have delayed the realisation that the map was not of Scotland. The 'otherness' of the map's shape may have dawned upon the audience over the duration of the work, exponentially deepening understandings of Scottish-Jamaican interconnections. Stephen Mullen argues that Scotland's role in the slave trade has evolved as a 'myth of denial' couched in a heroic historical past expediting the distortion that 'it wisnae us' (Mullen 2009: 5). With Scots-Caribbean actors inhabiitng the Jamaican map, however, Morris notes that 'the geographical and moral distances' between now and then become narrower through this visual narrative device (Devine, 2015: 41–61).

   In a discussion of the use of maps in devising ensemble Forced Entertainment's work, Peggy Phelan attests that 'mapping space and time in this manner transforms history (and travel) into an actively composed set of personal stories and not just a passively experienced set of external events and locations' (Etchells, 1999: 12). As the *Blood Lines* audience faced each other across and through the performance unfolding within, and out with, the boundaries of the map, a more communal sensibility was enabled. Conscious staging seeks alternatives to the distance created between performers and audience through the use of a seating bank, for example, especially for those at the back. There is a risk that the seating bank creates not only spatial, but emotional distance, enabling the spectator to 'zone out'. CTP strives to keep the audience close through breaking those conventions. As Govan et al. state:

> the presentation of a shared story offers not only the potential for the establishment of a bond between the audience and performers, but also an opportunity for the spectators to partake of a creative aesthetic that challenges the patterns established by traditional plays.
>
> GOVAN ET AL, 2007: 58

Space was used in all the ways that it offered: ways that might not have been possible on purpose-built stages. With a Mercedes Benz at one end, and the band's instruments at the other, the gaze of the audience seated at floor level in traverse formation, shifted from the far left to the far right and back again, throughout the show. For Gay McAuley, traverse seating has been

> a recurring feature of various alternative theatre movements of the last thirty years [...] reviving the possibility for spectators to see each other

during the performance, and it can be argued that the spectator/specta-
tor look is important in achieving a vital theatre experience.

MCAULEY, 2000: 268

The *Blood Lines* seating arrangement provided a shift away from the conventional spectating experience of the audience facing forward towards the stage.
Perhaps this physically broader view also facilitated a greater sense of the
sweeping timespan of the narrative, from the 1700s to the present moment.
For Govan et al. 'the stage becomes a flexible playground in which epic presentations of place, time and characterisation embrace the audience as collaborators in an imaginative journey' (Govan et al., 2007: 58). In *Blood Lines* this
collaboration goes beyond the imaginative, inviting the Glasgow audience to
witness our complicity as a nation, in this shameful chapter in the history of
our city; our country; our continent. Govan et al. perceive 'the act of witness-
ing as central to the reception of autobiographical performance,' prompting
an engagement with spectators, whose role becomes active within a two-way
process. This 'dialogue' calls for direct address to the audience, impacting upon
the form of autobiographical theatre, as well as the content. Tim Etchells exemplifies contemporary performances' pursuit of 'witnesses', not just spectators,
as 'an invitation to be here and now, to feel exactly what it is to be in this place
and this time' (Etchells, 1998: 18). I suggest that along with the audience, *Blood
Lines* performers experienced a sense of being 'in-the-same-boat', bringing us
closer, perhaps, to practices associated with ensemble.

4   Ensemble

Contemporaneous with the earlier discussion around devising, I suggest that
the *Blood Lines* process shared *some* elements of ensemble. I go on to discuss
the contradictions and shared aspirations of ensemble in the concluding chapter. CTP resonates with John Britton's assertion that 'practitioners concerned
with developing *ensemble* have repeatedly found their attention drawn to the
need for performers to share a common training' (Britton, 2013: 273). Although
I was not familiar with the word itself at that time, I note retrospectively ways
in which I was striving for its essence. I knew it to be crucial that my sister
and I practice yoga together, as training for the performance. I enrolled my
sister, with her consent, in the Bikram Yoga studio where I was undertaking
daily practice. Britton cites Brook, Grotowski, Núñez and Worley among those
'most obviously informed by encounters with such (meditation based spiritual

and/or bodily) practices', all of whom, along with Zarrilli, are key practitioners explored in this research (Britton, 2013: 282).

As experienced first-hand through Zarrilli's training much later, these techniques seek to enhance attention to the 'here and now'. As the protagonists of the piece of theatre I was creating, my sister and I must prepare our bodymind for 'public consumption'. We attended the yoga studio every day after rehearsals, yielding the results of a grueling but rewarding regime. I *self*-realised during this period that becoming a certified yoga teacher would contribute palpably to a conscious theatre practice. Britton suggests that practitioners encourage 'ensemble-ness' through the enhancement of the senses brought about through psychophysical activity (Britton, 2013: 282). I assimilated notions of ensemble-ness into my understandings of conscious directing: 'director' intermittently interchangeable with 'leader of the ensemble'.

However, for many practical reasons, including not being trained to teach yoga at the time, it was not possible for the whole company to undertake physical training together as an ensemble. The rehearsal period with full cast, including all musicians, was ten short days. There were challenges, in practice, with the casting choices that had made sense conceptually. Bringing the production to fruition within the given time scale required a commitment to an already arduous rehearsal process. It was therefore unreasonable to expect the other three cast members to undertake yoga practice in their own time. I would argue however, that by virtue of my sister and I practicing yoga together daily, a beneficial effect on the whole group was achieved. Bikram calls his practice a ninety-minute moving meditation (Choudhury, 2007: 75). The classes provided space for introspection, observing how the self was feeling, and developing patience, tolerance and empathy. The conscious director aspires towards these optimum qualities of CTP, not least when motivating an untrained cast of actors to go beyond what they believe they are capable of.

I observed my sister unfurling. What we practiced in the heat of the yoga studio fed directly into what took place in rehearsals. I had been practicing for five years, but in three short weeks my sister was also undergoing a transformation. Her posture changed. She straightened up and began to deliver her lines outward and not downward. With shoulders back and head held higher, the words had purpose. She became more willing and able to accept direction. I was urging her to cover a larger area of the stage, to literally travel further, giving more of the audience a decent view. The delivery had intention. My sister was more *present*. Britton describes an optimal state in which 'she cannot be distracted by trying to remember her next line, worrying about whether someone in the audience is having a good time, musing on a conversation she had with a friend at lunchtime' (Britton, 2013: 281). Performance always improves through the repetition of rehearsal, but in CTP this is taken further. Feeling connected in one's bodymind relates somehow to a more holistic confidence: self-realisation in process perhaps.

5   'Fierce and Self-Searching Reflection'

   1. How might 'energy practices' that create some shift in consciousness inform the creative process of a 'conscious theatre practice' in which the work is derived from lived experience?

The relatively undefined research question above has been addressed to a large degree via the Three 'C's research model. We may further evaluate the performance through traditional qualitative methods employed, including questionnaires, discourse analysis via press reviews and focus group discussions with theatre-making peers; all of which amounts to research data, inviting broader analysis of the work.

From questionnaires distributed at the Arches during the 2014 Cultural Programme, 24 respondents answered to: '*what did you think of tonight's performance?*' The question provoked these separate, verbatim responses:

   Excellent; enjoyed it; very good; great performance; superb; moving; entertaining; much about it to recommend; great; really good; informative; fantastic; funny; thoughtful; engaging; provoking; topical; personal; original; interesting; great stories; personal tied to historical; a powerful subject dealt with in a sensitive way; really interesting and pertinent content from an often ignored angle, from an engaging group of performers; genius in parts!
       collated from Arches feedback forms, June 2014

Although there does not appear to be a single negative comment, this data is only reliable to the extent that it forms a small percentage of the number of people who experienced the work, approximately 200 over the four-night performance run. It is not possible to ascertain whether the only people who enjoyed the work were the ones who filled in the questionnaires. Negative feedback can be more useful than positive feedback, which satisfies the ego but is less conducive to constructive critique. For that reason, I include here segments of press reviews. Not academic in nature, media discourse provides a wider barometer with which to measure the work, subjecting it to public, professional critique. Through this discourse, a more revealing analysis of the flaws in the work surfaces, illuminating potential antagonisms within CTP. The following four-star reviews of the performance by theatre critics Joyce MacMillan and Mary Brennan respectively, are demonstrative of successful and less successful aspects of the work:

> fierce and self-searching reflection, embodied in this brave, vivid and sometimes mind-blowing (work) [...] slightly hesitant but searingly important and timely [...] if the presentation of the show is sometimes a little less than smooth, its subject could hardly be more important to the city of Glasgow.
>
> MACMILLAN, 2014

> this really is a gorgeous broth of a piece, albeit not without flaws, but iron out lapses in pace, sharpen up some of the delivery and you have a vibrant, thought-provoking excursion into the shawdowlands of our legacy from the slave and tobacco trade [...] such salty, affectionate humour in *Blood Lines* [...] narrated without rancour or 'poor me' whinging [...] so joyously positive that it makes you want to cheer.
>
> BRENNAN, 2014

A further source of evaluation, arguably the most useful in terms of its influence upon the next phase of theatre research, was the focus group. Four theatre-making peers attended a discussion of *Blood Lines* in the Arches. The format for the discussion involved a PowerPoint presentation of my research questions followed by a description of the rehearsal process, including issues around working with non-professional performers. The theatre-makers were asked to comment on the existing questions or suggest new ones. The talk, which lasted over two hours, was recorded. It produced many pertinent questions, triggering new thinking ahead of *Tommy's Song*, prompting new questions and methods for its production. Below is a condensed transcript, highlighting the salient points and suggestions from that discussion:

> It seems like there may be a clash between CTP processes and professional theatre practice? It's all very inclusive, but might it have been better to say: 'these are the rules'? Or could you have recreated the rules to meet CTP?
>
> The person who took two hours for lunch to go and sort out their council tax demonstrated the realities of life with the people you want to work with. Perhaps they were the epitome of conscious casting, and that's part of it. But perhaps that person needed more/different support in order to fulfill their responsibilities on the production?

Is it about finding people who are not artists and giving them the opportunity to try out this theatre-making methodology, or is it about working with professional actors, who are also flawed human beings, in a way that helps them to break down the structures they've been working with in professional theatre and approach work in a different way?

Is it about devising a casting process that fits the aims of conscious casting that involves spending more time and being able to test, maybe through casting workshops, who would be able to go with those processes?

How much is it about your leadership and how much is about your process – does the creative process include rules and boundaries?

Why not just get professionals to act like authentic people? It would be easier. Whose consciousness do you want to 'shift' the most – the cast or the audience?

Do all the actors have to buy into the yoga/meditation ideologies? How important is that?

What impact did CTP have? Did the production meet the methodology?

You've used yoga to bring breathing to performers, but that's separate from putting the text together. Could generating text have been more collaborative?

Is part of your conscious casting about going back and building the skills of those you are working with; changing your processes to incorporate the Three 'C's model as toolbox from which to work as an alternative process?

Is it important for the audience to know that the people on stage have a personal connection to the story?

Would it be an idea to work with those non-trained actors for a much longer period of time – creating another system of working, for say, six months?

It was hugely important for me to know that it was your story, your family and your extended community. I would have felt hard-done-by if it had been done any other way. I want diversity from theatre.

You could keep trying out different variants of the show, continually testing the processes.

It would be interesting to redo the whole show with professional actors and then measure the success of both – but how do you measure success?

If one of the goals was about being more socially conscious, the work totally achieved that. There was lots of discussion after Blood Lines.

I watched the show with a Canadian and an American. They were experiencing Glasgow during Commonwealth, which was slightly unreal. Through your work they got a different awareness of Glasgow as a city.

There is something valuable in learning something new. I learned things I didn't know, about things that happened in this city. If I go to see a piece and don't feel changed then I wonder what's the point.

Is it about raising awareness or changing behaviour? Entertainment can be the vehicle through which to make change happen.

You can have a real person telling their story as themselves, or you can have a brilliant actor with an amazing voice telling a real story. *Blood Lines* worked most when people told their own stories and didn't work as well when your uncle, for example, was telling other people's stories.

If you know you are going to have less control with your processes on the next work, think ahead to how you can bring your processes, and the already established conventions of the venue, together.

You're getting an assistant director that you didn't choose, so how can you get the new people you are working with to buy into the CTP process? Can you communicate the aims of the project from the beginning? Because once you're 'in', you've already skewed the process, so do it before you start.

FIGURE 5   Lou and Sophie Prendergast performing in *Blood Lines*
SOURCE: PHOTOGRAPHY TIM COURTNEY, 2014

FIGURE 6   Neil Stewart performing in *Blood Lines*
SOURCE: PHOTOGRAPHY TIM COURTNEY, 2014

FIGURE 7   Michael Abubakar performing in *Blood Lines*
SOURCE: PHOTOGRAPHY TIM COURTNEY, 2014

FIGURE 8   Lou and Sophie Prendergast performing in *Blood Lines*
SOURCE: PHOTOGRAPHY TIM COURTNEY, 2014

Tommy's Song (2015)

Imagining Masculinities: 'Kickin' an Stampin!'

The second production, *Tommy's Song*, was produced by Glasgow Lunchtime Theatre and presented at Òran Mór. My script was submitted through National Theatre of Scotland's Breakthrough Writers scheme. Data gathered during the *Blood Lines* research processes prompted an enquiry around working with a professional actor on this next project. The Conscious Craft model opened a space for examining the extent to which CTP's objective of presenting real life stories could be negotiated. The play is autobiographical in the sense that the script draws inspiration from a 'real life' relationship. In many respects it is a hidden autobiography. As this research overall involves creating a conscious theatre practice as part of an ongoing self-realisation process, the work played a significant part in the illumination of *my* ongoing personal transformation.

In its portrayal of a living, sentient being other than myself, I endeavored to be simultaneously honest yet ethical in my representation of this person in line with the principles of CTP; through the character I developed on the page and through the direction I gave the actor on the stage. As the personal is political, the character not only presents a snapshot of a real life, the work also sheds light upon a marginalised section of society: the underclass. The character displays traits that I suggest are resonant of Scottish machismo, and thus I draw upon Katarzyna Kosmala's theories of socially constructed masculinities. Kosmala reminds us that 'masculinities are problematic, fragmented and multiple,' fitting the themes of the work. (Kosmala, 2013: 38). The play is socially engaged, commenting on a socio-economic reality recounted through the delivery of anecdotes from the character's lived experience. The views expressed throughout the script are the characters', not my own. In observing them, however, it may be possible to disrupt them. I 'consciously' chose not to take a didactic approach in this work.

1   Conscious Craft: *Tommy's Song*

The Conscious Craft lens requires a shift in interpretation in its application to *Tommy's Song* given that the narrative being delivered was *not* true to the person recounting it. That person was an actor playing a role. Already then, there is an untruth, the anathema to CTP potentially. The use of verbatim text from a real person's life reinstates its position however, albeit with new challenges associated with directing a professional actor's performance in line with the principles of CTP. Furthermore, in practical terms, ideas around conscious casting met with resistance from producers. Staying true to conscious writing also required sensitive handling in the representation of actual events in the construction of the script. The 'messiness' and struggles emerging through the practice-as-research process deepened my awareness of potential resistances to CTP within certain aspects of professional theatre. This was *my* self-realisation process; it was not necessarily embraced by producers, or permitted to risk disrupting their notion of collaboration, or business as usual, creating tensions between personal and public/commercial aspirations.

2   Writing

I 'bashed out' an early version of the script at the artist's retreat, Cove Park. I was there at the behest of National Theatre of Scotland, which was supporting the Ankur HaHa development programme I was on. Prior to my immersion in the Argyll countryside, I had spent time with the individual who was about to become Tommy, with whom I had a dysfunctional relationship several years before. The interaction sparked a flood of memories and I was struck by the positive changes in myself since that difficult time. CTP respects the power of the natural world, and from its tranquility, a violent urban tale was unleashed. As each real-life scenario, many of which were emotionally painful or perplexing at the time, transitioned from my mind to the page, I felt relief. It was an unburdening; a cathartic creative process that marked a further step in my self-realisation through art; deepening my evolution as a human being.

Mindful of the ethical principles of CTP, I showed the script to the person whose life it involved and received permission to continue to develop it. Originally, I had consulted playwriting books that provided step-by-step guides to creating a character. However, on those quiet, still days at Cove Park, the play poured out of me; *he* poured out of me. This 'character' existed. I could hear his voice and see his facial expressions. He was a living being. I concealed myself in the narrative as a former girlfriend of the protagonist. I was invited to send the script to the literary manager at NTS, with a view to its debut at Glasgow's *A Play, A Pie and A Pint*. On confirmation of its inclusion in Òran Mór's spring season, I reworked the script over several months. It would take ten rewrites to make it work.

The first 'outside eye' came in the form of an anonymous script report through Playwright Studio Scotland's service, which was entirely useful. Furthermore, a dramaturge and NTS project consultant provided objective feedback on new drafts, with the former suggesting I wrote a fourth scene. Every strand, every anecdote that the character recounts had to be brought to a close. It was an arduous process, but one which dramatically improved the play. I was about to commence an even shorter rehearsal period than I had on *Blood Lines*, and as I was again directing the piece myself, it was crucial to begin rehearsals with a more polished piece of work on this occasion, while remaining open to the possibility of further changes. I had learned lessons from *Blood Lines*.

In its aspiration to work with things 'as they really are' as we do in Vipassana meditation, CTP is not commensurate with pure fiction writing. It was occasionally necessary, however. In *Tommy's Song*, a narrative bridge was required to link elements out with their real-life sequence. I imagined a scene that took place in a taxi and added it to the script to resolve a particular dramaturgical issue. Even in those circumstances, I was able to utilise memories of being in a taxi with the character, and of his speech-acts when intoxicated. Govan et al. view memory as an essential element to the development of autobiographical performance, while noting that it may also be tinted: 'the human memory acts as a filter and, as a consequence, what is remembered may not be the truth but an embroidered version of the real' (Govan et al 2007: 63). Non-intentional adornments may contribute dramatic tension and emotional realism; they are psychologically and consciously 'real' even if they do not recount events with absolute accuracy.

3   Casting

Casting actors with some real relation to the work could not be achieved to the extent that it was on *Blood Lines*, when performers were at times playing themselves. For the *Tommy's Song* research, I was nonetheless seeking connections between the actor and the actual person that the work represents. Challenges to CTP became evident in the venue's established protocols around casting. As well as a set of questions designed around my CTP research, I wanted to focus on the 'energy' of the actors invited to audition. I believed this could be best achieved in an actor-director one-to-one. Venue producers, who had contacted actors' agents on the director's behalf, expected to be present during auditions. This was incongruent with the methods I was testing. My insistence on enabling the physical and mental space to talk to actors alone caused some tension. Despite the antagonisms between CTP and the venue, it felt very important to avoid any conflicting energies or agendas in the room. I facilitated the purer focus that a conscious casting process seeks. The one-to-one actor/director audition enabled an intimate zone; more conducive to having conversations about undertaking daily yoga and meditation practice as part of the rehearsal process, more conducive to 'gut feeling'.

Ultimately, I cast an actor who bore the greatest physical resemblance, was raised in the same neighbourhood, and intimated that his life may have taken a similar turn to the characters, had he not been introduced to theatre. I perceived this exchange as demonstrative of the actors' empathy with the character. This was important because CTP's ethical concerns seek to respect the marginalised individuals it re-presents through the work, even where the attitudes/actions of the protagonist are morally reprehensible. Although I was in pursuit of higher quality performance for this second practice-as-research investigation, casting through conventional routes posed risks to CTP. It is challenging to ascertain an actor's true feelings towards a subject within an audition process that would normally prioitise acting skills and/or technical ability, over any empathic attitude towards less advantaged individuals.

The venue works with the Royal Conservatoire of Scotland, offering placements to students on its productions. I was offered an assistant. As I had learned on *Blood Lines*, bright students can contribute fresh energy to a rehearsal process. Being thrown together with an unknown assistant would not be in line with the principles of Conscious Theatre Practice, however. I therefore met with the student in advance, armed with the same set of CTP related questions that were posed to the actor. Once into the rehearsal process, this Assistant Director, as third company member, balanced the tensions that arose between actor and director during intense creative processes. As someone who has been supported through placements and schemes myself in the past, CTP urges a sharing of my knowledge while respecting and learning from theirs.

4   Directing

The research set out to explore an increased use of yoga and meditation as part of the rehearsal process. Applying embodied knowledge from *Blood Lines* on the value of daily yoga practice with my sister, I was determined to incorporate contemplative performance practice into rehearsals on *Tommy's Song*. I was not yet trained to teach yoga myself and we followed a recording of an 8-minute routine by nutritionist and founder of 'Fitlife TV', Drew Canole (Canole, 2014). Daily journals were kept by the actor and assistant director. One statement of conscious craft in the Three 'C's model is that we 'apply a strong and determined *embodied* work ethic, as taught in yoga and meditation, working through our difficulties by doing'. This highly talented actor embodied the role, not only through text but also via singing and dancing, becoming entirely believable as the real person his character emulated.

However, there was resistance at times when challenges arose. Perhaps performers with embodied knowledge of yoga and meditation, gained over the course of a prolonged practice, would be more willing to fully embrace the concepts of CTP. Yoga, which means union, increases unity in the bodymind. In her discussion of resistance, Anne Bogart cites John Dewy thus:

> As the artist cares in a particular way for the phase of experience in which union is achieved, he does not shun moments of resistance and tension [but] rather cultivates them, not for their own sake but because of their potentialities, bringing to living consciousness an experience that is unified and total.
>
> BOGART, 201: 137

In ideal circumstances conscious theatre practice would facilitate consciousness of the self, rather than self-consciousness, using energy practices to strip away insecurities. Performing a solo show was risky for the actor, especially when working with an early-career director. Trust must be earned. Bogart sees overcoming resistance as a 'heroic act that requires courage and a connection to a reason for the action' (Bogart, 2001: 137). She views resistance as a necessary ingredient of the creative process. It was the first time I had not performed my own work, and this created a more objective role for me. I was able to sit back and observe and make decisions from a nonpartisan perspective. Pushing against resistance in an intended spirit of collaboration with the actor contributed ideas and improvements to the work, but not necessarily to the actor/director relationship.

As the venue produced the play, responsibility of budgets and other time-consuming producing tasks were not in the equation. Here, I was able to give directing my full focus. Working up the performance and watching the script burst into life through the skills and capabilities of a highly experienced actor was thrilling at times. Less responsibility was consistent with less control however, posing further challenges to CTP. Producers set up a newspaper interview with the actor, the 'star' of the work rather the creator of the work. The resulting preview piece by Brian Beacom in the Evening Times newspaper, which the actor was not in control of either, refuted CTP's notions of compassion and/or empathy. In the discourse of popular media, the play's complex character was reduced to a 'housing scheme psychopath' further exemplifying antagonisms to CTP within hegemonic structures of power (Beacom, 2015).

In *Imagining Masculinities* (2013), Katarzyna Kosmala's engagement with Foucault's description of discourse as 'the location where power and knowledge intersects' speaks to the constructed masculinities of popular media (Kosmala, 2013: 4). The newspaper article explained how the actor had spent the previous 20 years avoiding 'working class stereotypes' for fear of being typecast. The actor was not the only cultural commentator to perceive the character as a stereotype, evident in journalist Lorna's Irvine's premise that Tommy's 'song is one that is a little over-familiar' (Irvine, 2015). She perhaps did not know that the majority of text in the piece was verbatim: the actual words spoken by a living person sitting in the audience, rather than a fictionalised stereotype. This precipitated new thinking around the principles of CTP and the antagonisms to it through patriarchal systems of power, including media organisations.

According to Bogart, the stereotype can be a friend to the theatrical venture, as a means of challenging accepted definitions. She states that

> when approaching stereotype as an ally, you do not embrace a stereotype in order to hold it rigid; rather, you burn through it, undefining it and allowing human experience to perform its alchemy. You meet one another in an arena of potential transcendence of customary definitions.
>   BOGART, 2001: 104–5

The character Tommy presents an exaggeration of the stereotyped behaviours that he believes to be masculine; a hypermasculinity, capable of disrupting masculinity through its comicality; going too far to be taken at face value. As demonstrated through audience questionnaires, the work sparked conflicting views around social issues, meeting Bogart's premise that the stereotype can be useful in awakening 'opposition and disagreement' (Bogart, 2001: 104–5). Scottish culture and the character himself: 'I'm a guy darlin' – drinkin's what we do,' is complicit in perpetuating masculine stereotypes, unless we consciously 'burn through them,' as Bogart suggests, challenging our 'own assumptions about originality' (Bogart, 2001: 111). Journalist Mary Brennan was able to 'burn through' the stereotype and catch the complexities of the character, stating that

> You almost feel like passing a hat round, to help this kind, thoughtful – seriously skint – Glesca' guy bring home those Christmas goodies. But writer/director Lou Prendergast is wise to the dark, damaged side to

Tommy that, in Jekyll and Hyde mode, cause the charming chancer to
lash out.

BRENNAN, 2015

Referring to categories of men and masculinities, Kosmala suggests that they
'do not exist, and are not perceived as 'true' until they are articulated and val-
idated though discourse' (Kosmala, 2013: 4). Michael Kimmel compounds this
view, asserting that 'manhood does not bubble up to consciousness from our
biological makeup; it is created in culture' (Kimmel, 2001: 273). Kosmala's work
engages with a visual archive that aims to disrupt the reductive readings of
what is understood as manhood related to a heterosexual rubric. This becomes
an interesting premise for my research as the work expressed a less than
straightforward positioning of the character's sexuality through the imagined
scene in which he is caught engaging with homosexual pornography, sparking the violent climax of the play. His father's homophobic jeering pushes
Tommy over the edge. According to Kimmel, 'the fear – sometimes conscious,
sometimes not – that others might perceive us as homosexual propels men to
enact all manner of exaggerated masculine behaviours and attitudes' and this
includes putting women down (Kimmel, 2001: 280).

The character's performative utterances relating to women, including 'an
intelligent burd?' and 'she forgets I'm the gaffer' demonstrate an implied belief
in his male superiority. His subordination of women is often in parenthesis
in the script, almost as an afterthought, invalidating women through their
objectification: 'pain in the arse (sexy but. big tits, nae hips)' and 'Pakistani
burd (beautiful tae)' (Prendergast, 2015). 'Historically and developmentally'
according to Kimmel, 'masculinity has been defined as the flight from women,
the repudiation of femininity' (Kimmel, 2001: 274). Kosmala reminds us that
'masculinity itself (is) commonly understood in terms of the binary categories
of homosexuality and heterosexuality [...] sexual and gender categories and
divisions are indeed very messy, contradictory and temporal,' and these were
consciously left open in the work (Kosmala, 2013: 39). Kosmala suggests that
applying a poststructuralist lens 'allows for moving beyond the binary frame,
or at least contesting and disrupting it' (Kosmala, 2013: 39).

Kosmala points to ways in which 'increasing downsizing and rising unem-
ployment have resulted in occupational insecurity, contract terminations and
a sense of instability across the labour markets' (Kosmala, 2013: 43). These
themes resonate with the play text as Tommy struggles with systems of austerity, including the benefits system, which appear to be designed to work against
individuals who would genuinely rather be earning their own wage. Kosmala's
theories around a crisis of masculinity being aligned with the 'collapsing of the

grand narrative of patriarchy and an increasing phenomenon of powerlessness of certain types of men and masculinity' fits with the character's perceived loss of control as the narrative develops, leading him back to a position of incarceration where his masculinity feels less threatened (Kosmala, 2013: 43). David Collinson and Jeff Hearn analysed ethnographic studies of men in the workplace. They revealed that continuous, paid work is central to masculine identity: 'for many men, employment provides the interrelated economic resources and symbolic benefits of wages/salaries, skills and experience, and positions of power' (Collinson & Hearn, 2001: 146).

Where does this leave the man for whom, for a variety of complex social inequalities, continuous paid work cannot be attained or maintained? If, as Collinson and Hearn attest 'men's gender identities are constructed, compared and evaluated by self and others according to a whole variety of criteria indicating personal "success" in the workplace,' then the character Tommy's sense of masculinity remains elusive. His 'successes' must necessarily be sought through edgier, more marginalised and inherently riskier avenues (Collinson & Hearn, 2001: 146). The directorial challenges in the work involved sweeping the audience along in Tommy's mutation from a kind-at-heart good-guy, benignly stuck in the old-fashioned rhetoric of being 'a man's man', to a series of turning points in which his malevolence becomes palpable, challenging accepted epistemologies of the loveable rouge.

5   Performance

An irony of *Tommy's Song* is that the very person that the character desperately seeks approval from finally falls victim to his rage. Given that his 'wee da' was the one who exposed Tommy to violence in the first place, the beating of his father almost operates as an acceptable code of conduct between them. Kimmel states that 'violence is often the single most evident marker of manhood' (Kimmel, 2001: 278). Despite the line 'I hear the auld yin was oot on his scooter the day efter he got oot the hospital – away roon' the bookies,' there appeared to be ambiguity over whether the father had lived or died. I learned this from conversations with those who had experienced the play. In such a short play, death would have raised the stakes too high. A severe beating, however, left room for the possibility of reconciliation between father and son in the future. CTP seeks hope in dark matters. *Tommy's Song* perhaps shares the themes of self-sabotage and unchecked rage destroying whatever we love the most, that were presented in Mike Leigh's film *Naked* (1993) and Peter Mullan's *Tyrannosaur* (2011). For Kosmala, these works examine nearly masochistic gender-based subordination to the controlling power of hegemonic masculinity within the heteronormative paradigm by having a candid and rather morbid look at underclass issues and the problem of poverty.

KOSMALA, 2013: 43

In my own work, Tommy's attack on the family Christmas tree as he recounts the graphic violence that his father suffered at his hands (and that he suffered at his father's hands in his early years) could also be interpreted as an attack on Capitalism and the commercial pressures of the festive season. As Elvis Presley's 'If I can Dream' builds in volume with the rising ferocity of the aggression, the character imagines himself as powerful, as a king; as his hero: The King of Rock n Roll, appropriating the visual discourse of the boxing ring.

Kosmala suggests of the artworks she discussed that they can 'locate a sense of discomfort in us as viewers and participants through a provocation or a shock,' which might also be true of *Tommy's Song* (Kosmala, 2013: 55).

Vipassana meditation teaches that if a person is being attacked in the street the Vipassana meditator is not passive. He or she attempts to stop the violence like the other onlookers; with the difference that when the fight is broken up the Vipassana meditator gives more attention to the perpetrator than the victim, as they are the person in the most (emotional) pain. In *Tommy's Song*, the research was about exploring the extent to which the audience could feel compassion for the character, and/or empathise with him, despite his wretched acts. There is no doubt that this character would have scored high on the Adverse Childhood Experiences survey.

Music was used for emotive effect in the work, evoking a drunken, gospel-tinged sense of spirituality in one scene, as Tommy believes his dream is about to be realised. For a brief moment, the stage becomes a holy space. Brook cites the theatre of Samuel Beckett among three examples of holy theatre, alongside Jerzy Grotowski and Merce Cunningham, describing Beckett's work as 'perhaps the most intense and personal writing of our time' (Brook, 1968: 58). Brook says of the work's spectators, 'this audience laughs and cries out – and in the end celebrates with Beckett; this audience leaves his plays, his black plays, nourished and enriched, with a lighter heart, full of strange irrational joy' (Brook, 1968: 59). Such responses to their work may be the aspiration of any theatre-maker. All that can be claimed for *Tommy's Song* is that the audience was affected by the play, demonstrative in their laughter, tears, and written articulation of the work's engagement with the social issues inherent in CTP.

6   'Childhood Poverty and Family Dysfunction'

> How might the creative outputs of a 'conscious theatre practice' (in which
> work is drawn from lived experience and influenced by energy practices)
> contribute to processes of socio-cultural transformation?

The above question is the second of the three research questions pertaining to
the project overall. All three questions can be applied to all three projects. It is
useful to evaluate *Tommy's Song* in terms of its potential social impact, however, over and above what has already been explored about writing, directing
and performance through the Conscious Craft lens above. Questionnaires and
media reviews are again taken into consideration when exploring the research,
especially its resonance with the more specific research question: *Do you feel
empathy/compassion for the character Tommy?* From questionnaires given to
audience after the performances and compiled into a single document presented below, the following data can be drawn:

From a total of 111 respondents, 67 were female and 44 were male. People
who were over 50 years old totaled 71, with 40 people under 50. Addressing
the main question, did you feel empathy/compassion for the character, 85
answered 'yes' and 31 answered 'no'; 5 people answered 'yes and no'. The data
demonstrates that more women than men saw the show; that most were over
50 years old and that 76 per cent of respondents felt empathy for the character Tommy. I would suggest from this data that CTP achieved its aims around
empathy and compassion with this production. Many thoughtful comments
were added, demonstrating concerns around what can be done with a character such as Tommy; with one respondent suggesting the play be sent to
Westminster. Increasing awareness of, and provoking responses towards social
issues could also be interpreted as contributing to processes of social transformation. The efficacy of media discourse for academic research is unconventional, but utilised again here to provide a further layer of understanding
around how the work was perceived. As Jill Dolan points out

> scholars, historians, and other thoughtful cultural critics face the contin-
> uing problem of how to capture and archive spectators' responses to per-
> formance. We rely on reviewers and their idiosyncratic reports of what
> they see not only to reconstruct the content and form of a given perfor-
> mance, but also to gain at least a glimmer of how it might have made the
> audience (and the performers, by virtue of their motivating presence)
> *feel.*
>
> DOLAN, 2005: 9

As feelings are important to conscious theatre practice, I consult media discourse via two press reviews. Mary Brennan's description of the work as an 'astutely observed portrait of what childhood poverty and family dysfunction can do to a man like Tommy' (Brennan, 2015) speaks to wider social issues; as does Lorna Irvine's premise that the work raises 'keenly observed points on the cycle of hurt working-class masculinity' (Irvine, 2015). This discourse may not bring us any closer to finding empathy for those less advantaged than ourselves, but media shapes popular opinion and can therefore contribute to socio-cultural transformation, or at least to shifts in consciousness.

A further area for analysis is the daily yoga and meditation journals kept by the actor and the assistant director. It is evident through their entries that the busy, urban location of the rehearsal room posed challenges during the meditation sessions. Only experienced meditators can embrace distraction without it affecting their practice negatively. In terms of yoga, it appears that changes were beginning to take place. A statement concerning one company member's sense that they 'might cry' signals the manifestation of an emotional release, a shift occurring through the practice. This data informed thinking around the final research process. It led to an aspiration to work with performers with a developed yoga practice, who already possessed embodied knowledge of yoga as a moving meditation.

TABLE 1   Tommy's Song Company member's daily yoga and meditation entries

Day	Company member A	Company member B
1	I can definitely see how this practice can be of benefit, to the start of the day in a creative environment. However, the room we were using today unfortunately was at a very close proximity to building work which made it a bit difficult to close out the world outside.	Yoga – hard to relax as felt very inflexible. Meditation – useful as able to embrace the distracting sounds rather than feel frustrated by them. Counting very useful.
2	Much more enjoyable today. Ready to rehearse.	Yoga – first day of new yoga, so focused a lot on getting positions right. Meditation – the knocking on door was distracting, couldn't focus. Feeling stressed about work – didn't focus much.
3	The more familiar I'm becoming with the (meditation) recording the more I'm enjoying the routine. Nice.	Yoga – realised I was doing the wrong pose at one point which drew my focus. Still finding it hard to relax. Meditation – calming to free mind of stresses, found it easier than yesterday. Counting most useful.
4	The natural sunlight coming into the room today, and the knowledge that an undisturbed lay ahead added to my enjoyment of the routine.	Yoga – still not feeling benefits from yoga. Still getting used to moves. Meditation – really needed today. Feeling a lot of emotional stress, which at first nearly came out as crying when I make myself relax. After that though I calmed right down and felt ready to work.
5	Best yet. Extraneous noise reduction helped.	Yoga – still struggling to feel benefits from yoga but hoping by the end I will. Meditation – peace of mind with sign on door. Mind wandered but felt more clam about that happening.

TABLE 1   Tommy's Song Company member's daily yoga and meditation entries *(cont.)*

Day	Company member A	Company member B
6	New neighbours. Sunny outside (always helps). Nice start to the day though.	Meditation – good to have a new audio today but the noise next door made it hard to concentrate. Yoga – found it easier to focus in yoga today, perhaps from doing meditation first. First time felt focused.
7	Better without the recording.	Yoga – helped stretch out pain from running and get me in the room. Meditation – enjoyed without the voice.
8	Enjoying it without the recording.	Yoga – helped me be in the room. Meditation – silent good but drifted in and out.
9	Another nice start to the day. Head clear and hoping for a great run.	Yoga – helped stretch out my muscles from running. Find it a good way to check in with myself each day. Meditation – helps me calm down and de-stress. Still have wandering mind. Find cars comforting today.
10	"Time slows doon when yer meditating." Last day. Nice session, even with Guns & Roses'. Glad to be getting out. Not the best room for it.	Yoga – found improvements in the gym and due to sore muscles today could feel where the yoga was working. Meditation – music distracting but has always helped me focus due to stress.

TABLE 2   Tommy's Song post performance audience questionnaires

Day	Male/Female	Over/Under 50	Empathy Yes/No	Comments
W	F	O	Y	
W	F	O	Y	
W	F	O	Y	His personality and storytelling allowed us to have compassion for him.
W	F	O	Y	Great show!
W	F	O	Y	
W	F	O	Y	Engaging, involved story – 50 mins passed quickly.
W	F	O	Y	It was a complex story and character – not black and white. Some of his actions were repulsive, obviously, but a very damaged man despite his charm and optimism.
W	F	O	Y	
W	F	O	*N*	One understands why Tommy acts as he does, given the background revealed but am unable to empathize overall.
W	F	O	Y	Wondered a bit to start with, but as he got going it just got better and better – stunning – awesome memory
W	F	O	Y & N	Gallus, chancer … until … you heard about his harsh upbringing – then warmed slightly – until he beat up his father.
W	F	O	Y	Complex but quite typical story of a working-class Scottish family.
W	F	O	Y	We are all products of our environment and upbringing!!

TABLE 2   Tommy's Song post performance audience questionnaires (*cont.*)

Day	Male/ Female	Over/ Under 50	Empathy Yes/No	Comments
W	F	O	Y	Loveable rogue, victim of circumstance, but was happy where he was. Big fish in his own wee pond. Wouldn't want to step out of his world.
W	M	O	*N*	He brought it all on himself
W	M	O	*N*	
W	M	O	*N*	
W	M	O	Y	
W	M	O	Y	
T	F	U	Y	Felt very sympathetic towards Tommy. Even when you knew there were things he could've done differently, to produce a different outcome, you still were on his side and constantly rooting for him to succeed! One of the best Oran Mor's I've seen. Thoroughly engaging, charming and powerful!
T	F	U	Y	
T	F	O	Y	
T	F	O	Y	
T	F	O	Y	Real life story – well acted – very good.
T	F	U	Y	Incredible range of emotions elicited – from anger to compassion to disgust to empathy to sorrow.
T	F	O	Y	A product of his upbringing. Causing chaos but no insight into his own role in it.
T	F	O	Y	Enjoyed very much, great, great actor. Well done.

TABLE 2   Tommy's Song post performance audience questionnaires (*cont.*)

Day	Male/ Female	Over/ Under 50	Empathy Yes/No	Comments
T	F	O	Y	
T	F	O	*N*	He's a male chauvinist pig waster!
T	F	O	*N*	Sad that this could be anyone's story!! Circumstances are powerful. Great performance!
T	F	O	Y & N	Empathy? Tommy presented as a 'likable rogue' and alluded throughout to his 'wee da' as a bit of a threatening presence – if rather obliquely. I suspect we are meant to empathise, but I lost empathy as he descended into a bit of self-pity even if it was delivered humorously.
T	M	O	Y	Wonderful performance but questionable morality!
T	M	O	Y	
T	M	O	*N*	He deserved all he got! Great performance.
T	M	U	*N*	Although horrible things have happened to him, he continually resorted to destructive behaviours and expecting others to maintain a constant attitude towards him. It sucks to spend Christmas in jail, but you let emotion, drinking and apathy control you, negative things are bound to happen.
T	M	U	*N*	
T	M	O	*N*	The constant lighting changes in the first half hour did not help the actor.
T	M	U	*N*	Really enjoyable good

TABLE 2   Tommy's Song post performance audience questionnaires (*cont.*)

Day	Male/ Female	Over/ Under 50	Empathy Yes/No	Comments
T	M	O	Y	Initially, I didn't feel empathy or compassion, thinking him just a 'ned'. However, it became clear, as is usually the case, I'm sure, he was a victim himself of his upbringing and circumstance. Excellent acting – very authentic, believable – and professionalism.
T	M	O	Y	A victim of his environment or just feckless?
T	M	U	Y	I'm sure he could be played in such a way as to elicit no sympathy but in this performance, I got that he was just a prisoner of his own mess of a situation.
T	M	U	Y	He made some bad choices and deserved his consequences, but it's not his fault considering his parental abuse and upbringing. Not sure if it was just the charisma of the actor, but I did feel sorry for Tommy and in general I thought he was a good guy in a bad situation.
T	M	O	Y	at the very end(empathy)
T	M	O	Y	
T	M	O	Y	No insight, no toolkit, no parenting
T	M	O	Y	Excellent acting and quite emotional – just lets one know how life can be in 'certain quarters'. Congratulations to Tom!
T	M	U	Y	

TABLE 2   Tommy's Song post performance audience questionnaires (*cont.*)

Day	Male/ Female	Over/ Under 50	Empathy Yes/No	Comments
F	F	O	Y & N	
F	F	O	Y	Fabulous script superbly delivered, multi-faceted view of many realities.
F	F	O	Y	So, so true of a life that to a child growing up seems 'normal'. Excellent portrayal of a 'poor life' Delivery, synergy etc. Excellent.
F	F	U	*N*	
F	F	O	Y	Absolutely!!! Terrible childhoods lead to horrendous lives later. Fabulous performance!!
F	F	O	Y	Tommy basically is a good guy. Life's circumstances have coloured his life.
F	F	O	Y	The script was excellent, and Tom McGovern was nothing less than fantastic in the role. Not a word missed, and an excellent performance. Ten out of ten!
F	F	O	Y	
F	F	O	Y	Thoroughly enjoyable hour. Acting of highest quality. Would love to see more plays of his. Great storyline. But dreadful character! Thanks.
F	F	O	Y	Brilliant! When will Tommy be starring again? Will be back then.
F	F	U	Y	At the very end I did when he sang! I suppose the revelation of his childhood moved me.
F	F	O	Y	Brought a tear to a glass eye. Excellent.

TABLE 2   Tommy's Song post performance audience questionnaires (*cont.*)

Day	Male/ Female	Over/ Under 50	Empathy Yes/No	Comments
F	M	O	*N*	An unsympathetic father and mother in childhood does not excuse violence in adulthood towards parent however much provoked. A brilliant performance by Tom!
F	M	O	Y & N	Memorable quotes: I'm a guy darlin. Drinkin's what we do' 'Show's yer wee happy face' and 'She (mum) sees the bad in everything'.
F	M	O	Y	Well written and acted. Came from the heart. Great mixture of comedy and pathos. Food for thought?
F	M	O	Y & N	Been there. Tried to cope with that (fostering), jail, assault, robbery.
F	M	U	Y	Yes, even when he does terrible things, I stayed with him. I may not agree with everything he did, but I understand him – and I think that's what's important.
F	M	O	Y	Lots of men (unfortunately) lead lives like Tommy's and think it's 'normal'. Excellent.
F	M	U	Y	Powerful stuff!
F	M	O	Y	But … it's always someone else's fault!! But you can see where he's coming from. What a performance!!
F	M	O	*N*	Well written and acted (for further views see Critic's Circle).
F	?	?	Y	Tour de force!

TABLE 2   Tommy's Song post performance audience questionnaires (*cont.*)

Day	Male/ Female	Over/ Under 50	Empathy Yes/No	Comments
S	F	U	Y	Good acting, dancing and singing. Empathise with commonplace hitting children and domestic abuse, particularly in the past in poorer communities. However, as an adult we can make choices.
S	F	U	Y	Amazing performance for a one-man show.
S	F	U	Y	I thought Tommy was an extremely likeable character. Growing up in a working class town just outside Manchester he really reminded me of a lot of people I know. I also felt at times it was emotional. Also, so well acted!
S	F	U	*N*	
S	F	U	*N*	I don't. It was a different time, but everyone is responsible for their actions. He was a self-obsessed sexist.
S	F	U	*N*	Multiple opportunities to acknowledge and address his life issues. Not the responsibility of others to save 'you'!!! Fantastic performance which reflects the scenario for many, even in today's generation in society. Highlights further questions – what is the responsibility of the prison system and the individual, the abuses?
S	F	U	*N*	
S	F	U	*N*	

TABLE 2   Tommy's Song post performance audience questionnaires (*cont.*)

Day	Male/Female	Over/Under 50	Empathy Yes/No	Comments
S	F	U	*N*	Thought the actor was amazing. As was the writing for the play. I did not feel compassion for Tommy as he was self-obsessed and never took responsibility for himself, always blaming others and in need of growing up.
S	F	U	*N*	Excellent
S	F	O	*N*	There comes a time when you need to take responsibility for yourself.
S	F	U	Y	Brilliant acting. Great story.
S	F	U	Y	Very well acted and written. It's quite a talent getting slavers at the side of your mouth! Really feel like Tommy is the dude that talks your face off in the pub! Excellent play. Really enjoyed it.
S	F	O	Y	So many people suffered silently and were submitted to cruelty which society classed as 'normal'! Your background determines who you are! Wonderful play. Thank you.
S	F	O	Y	Such a complex character (and brilliantly portrayed). The backstory explains without justifying his actions and his undoubtable charm explains his being forgiven. Compassion – but with limits. A cry for better government – send the play to Westminster.
S	F	O	Y	Excellent work! Believed every word of Tommy's story.
S	F	U	Y	He's a victim of his circumstances and upbringing.

TABLE 2   Tommy's Song post performance audience questionnaires (*cont.*)

Day	Male/ Female	Over/ Under 50	Empathy Yes/No	Comments
S	F	U	Y	Amazing, very thought provoking! Empathy definitely – put yourself in his shoes, would it be different? Thoroughly enjoyable!
S	F	U	Y	
S	F	O	Y	Beautiful singing voice. Very funny and sad too.
S	F	O	Y	Fabulous play. Thank you. I jail people like that every day.
S	F	O	Y	I felt deeply affected by the trauma Tommy has had in his life. I feel total empathy.
S	F	O	Y	But in real life if someone attacked their dad, maybe not. However, as a counselor I understand the devastating long-term effects of witnessing domestic violence as a child.
S	F	U	Y	I really enjoyed the piece and the revelation of the drama. I would have liked to see the subtleties of his character explored a bit more as he was quite black and white perhaps – a bit clichéd, e.g. 'the loveable rogue'. But I thought it was a strong piece and good characterisation.
S	F	O	Y	Brilliant performance!
S	F	U	Y	Excellent!
S	F	O	Y	Very true to life in some Scottish homes in that era
S	F	U	Y	Thoroughly enjoyed the play.
S	F	O	Y	Timely reminder of perceptions.

TABLE 2   Tommy's Song post performance audience questionnaires (*cont.*)

Day	Male/ Female	Over/ Under 50	Empathy Yes/No	Comments
S	F	O	Y	Very well written play and well acted.
S	F	U	Y	
S	M	O	Y	But mixed feelings about him – can he be helped?
S	M	O	Y	Spellbinding!
S	M	O	Y	All too often this was the case for the era.
S	M	O	Y	
S	M	U	Y	
S	M	U	Y	
S	M	U	Y	
S	M	U	Y	He's a character – and loved his pal Tarik.
S	M	U	Y	
S	M	U	*N*	
S	M	U	*N*	He deserved what happened to him for what he did. Very good play.
S	M	U	*N*	
S	M	U	*N*	While I feel that Tommy's been dealt a bad hand in life, his childhood especially, he is inherently a flawed character. His lack of self-control and unwillingness to admit, both that he has a problem, and to try to change his ways is the real reason why he ended up in jail.

TABLE 2 Tommy's Song post performance audience questionnaires (*cont.*)

Day	Male/Female	Over/Under 50	Empathy Yes/No	Comments
				It is impossible to really blame him for the mistakes that he made in life, but his history of violence and irresponsible decisions really makes it hard to like him as a person. The fact that he is a womanizer, despite his protestations, only worsens the case against him. If Tommy had sought professional help from his psychological issues to deal with his abusive father and mother, he would have avoided his problems later in life and become a more happy person at the end.
S	M	U	*N*	

FIGURE 9   Tom McGovern rehearsing *Tommy's Song*
            SOURCE: PHOTOGRAPHY LESLIE BLACK, 2015

FIGURE 10   Tom McGovern rehearsing *Tommy's Song*
             SOURCE: PHOTOGRAPHY LESLIE BLACK, 2015

FIGURE 11   Tom McGovern rehearsing *Tommy's Song*
SOURCE: PHOTOGRAPHY LESLIE BLACK, 2015

FIGURE 12   Tom McGovern rehearsing *Tommy's Song*
SOURCE: PHOTOGRAPHY LESLIE BLACK, 2015

CHAPTER 8

AWKWARD: A Life in Twenty-Six Postures (2016)

Love Changes Everything: 'Compassion, Not Passion'

The third production marked the coming together of several elements of the research: autobiography and personal narrative, with yoga and meditation, and conscious collaboration *on stage*. I performed this one-off production alongside two other Bikram Yoga teachers. It took place at the Swallow Theatre in Whithorn, in the Scottish Borders. The play was self-produced, enhanced by technical support from the venue. Through Federation of Scottish Theatre (FST) membership, I attended their annual Emporium event, where performers and directors are brought together with producers, production personnel and venues. Here, tentative conversations began around the show becoming part of the Swallow Theatre's programme of summer events. As the venue is around a three-hour drive from Glasgow, I anticipated smaller audience numbers, befitting of a more intimate and immersive theatrical experience.

The rural location with delightful garden, the theatre building's previous incarnation as a cowshed, and its accolade as the smallest theatre in Scotland, outweighed the logistical challenges. The setting presented an opportunity to be in nature: to feel closer to the natural rhythms of the Universe. As yoga and meditation were to become part of the performance in this final research project, context was crucial. I organised a minibus that would ferry audience members from Glasgow to Whithorn and back again. Promoting the show involved contacting yoga groups that were local to the theatre. As on *Blood Lines*, I occupied several roles, as well as researcher, in order to make the work happen: including writer, performer, director, producer and marketing manager. I was in pursuit of a village audience that knew nothing of my work and a Glasgow audience that did; but with travelling time included would need to commit a whole day to seeing this new production. A big ask.

1 Conscious Collaborations: *Awkward*

Working with the Three 'C's model, conscious casting had first manifested during Bikram Yoga teacher training, through befriending trainees from the North and West of Ireland; one of whom had trained as a visual artist, the other an emerging theatre-maker. Through this serendipitous meeting in Thailand,

© KONINKLIJKE BRILL NV, LEIDEN, 2022 | DOI:10.1163/9789004467927_009

these fellow Celts 'felt' like the 'right' collaborators for the piece. Their 'Irishness' spoke to an interest in my Jamaican father's Irish father; a theme I had not yet explored. Their authentic relationship to the work was further mirrored in their experience of Bikram Yoga, which they would now perform on stage. This resonated with CTP's aim of enabling less experienced theatre practitioners to work with the company to enhance their skills; for the yoga teachers this meant their performance skills. For the former Assistant Director on *Tommy's Song* who returned to assist on *Awkward*, she was pushed slightly out of her comfort zone in a Production Assistant role on this third work.

There were two separate rehearsal processes on *Awkward*. Before the full rehearsal process at the Swallow Theatre, with all three performers and the Production Assistant, I worked in Ireland for five days with one of the performers. She also lived in a rural setting, with animals on site, and a Bikram yoga studio. We undertook daily meditation together and were able to practice (and teach) Bikram classes as well as working up parts of the play in the studio. Here, we developed a physical score involving the twenty-six Bikram Yoga postures. Learning through *doing* in the true spirit of PaR, we embodied new approaches and transitions from one posture into another, in the context of a theatrical performance. Simultaneously, we explored which asanas to match with the twenty-six autobiographical anecdotes contained in the script. By the end of the process, we knew how we would move in and out of the postures and the scenes. The script was fairly well developed. We had learned most of our respective speaking parts: mine being greater as the protagonist/narrator. We travelled back to Scotland to begin rehearsals at the Swallow Theatre.

2   **Ensemble**

Working and living together in the countryside was akin to being on a retreat. This setting was more conducive to working as an ensemble, to a greater degree than on the previous productions. As John Britton explains, 'ensemble training has an intention more fundamental than the acquisition of technique; it promotes the development of shared sensibility, enhanced sensitivity, common vocabulary, collective understanding' (Britton, 2013: 275). Shared understandings between company members on *Blood Lines* had perhaps been absent on *Tommy's Song*; while professional acting skills present in the *Tommy's Song* performance were absent on *Blood Lines*. On *Awkward*, the research aspired to shared understandings of yoga and meditation and the shifts in consciousness they can create; around the physicality of the practice, which shaped the structure of the performance; and of a shared artistic aesthetic coming from our respective backgrounds in the arts.

No other productions were running at the theatre over this quiet period and we spent a week 'on site' in accommodation adjacent to the venue. We ate together, meditated together and practiced yoga together every day, as well as rehearsing the play daily with the venue's production team. Some antagonisms to CTP arose here too; there was sometimes a clash with Swallow sound and light technicians who held firm beliefs about traditional theatre aesthetics. As my research is concerned with *contemporary* theatre-making practice and process, it calls for a paradigm shift away from tradition in order to contribute original knowledge to the field. To research conscious theatre practice, as opposed to traditional theatre practice, the creative team was working with the Three 'C's research model, while the technical people were not. Again, standing firm on how I wanted my work to look and sound created tension, which at the time felt necessary, nonetheless. Shared understandings between the company members did not extend to the technical team; not everyone was party to our research methodologies, and some admittedly 'last-minute' elements of producing, which caused some conflicts.

Tami Spry suggests that in performative autoethnography, connection is the most important element, including 'connection between selves, others, sociocultural context, and the language we use to articulate/represent those connections; it involves connections between personal experience and larger social issues' (Spry, 2011: 52). I suspected that venue personnel, for whom the venue was a fairly recent purchase, were somewhat wary of the work and how the local audience (that they were cultivating) might perceive it. This amounted to a lack of connection, or trust perhaps, between 'them' and 'us', although we pushed past our difficulties. CTP seeks to avoid generating negativity and I was mindful to be grateful for the more objective 'eyes and ears' of those who were less connected to our aims, which in several instances improved the work.

In terms of working with the other performers, however, there were no antagonisms at this stage in the process. It was harmonious. The work recounts a story of my life, and required the bodies and voices of my fellow performers to tell it. Spry asserts that she let go of her former argument that performative autoethnography was a "self-narrative" (2001) and came to see it 'as a narrative representation of the interrelations and negotiations between selves and others in cultural contexts' (Spry, 2011: 53). This idea resonates with the work. There was much in the script that the other performers could relate to: from our Celtic connections and yoga training to the family dynamics and relationship traumas. It was my life but also their lives and the audiences' lives; as Spry attests 'the "I" becomes a plural pronoun, a "we" narrative rather than a "me" narrative' (Spry 2011: 53). There was agency in the work, described by Spry as 'the act of empowerment in performative autoethnography,' which fused the personal narrative to wider negotiations with society (Spry 2011: 53).

3   Staging

Lee Worley contends that 'the theatrical community celebrates the profoundness of having a human life with all its blessings, responsibilities and difficulties'; mine were certainly exposed in this work (Worley, 2001:5). The use of conscious staging brought this 'human life' closer to the audience, metaphorically and literally, narrowing the gaps between us. Chairs were arranged on two sides of the playing area, very close to the action. In Royd Climenhaga's discussion of Anne Bogart's work, it is noted that one is 'not preparing a product to deliver to an audience but creating a way of being in the world in which they may share' (Climenhaga in Hodge, 2010: 303). In *Awkward*, we shared a small, intimate space arranged around a rug. Climenhaga explains that 'in Bogart's work, the stage space shifts to become an open invitation rather than a place of telling … inviting the audience in,' which was also an aspiration of *Awkward*, assisted by the staging and the play text; at one moment the audience were literally invited into the space. (*ibid.*).

The work fits with Anna Fenemore's use of the word 'haptic' in her description of a performance in which there is 'sight with the potential to touch' (Fenemore in Pitches and Popat, 2011: 45). This became increasingly true of *Awkward*, especially during scenes in the second half when performers accessed props attached to the underside of the audiences' seats, while simultaneously undertaking the yoga postures. At one moment, a performer was bending backwards, her upside-down hands reaching between audience members' legs, to retrieve an object that was hidden beneath their char. I suggest that these close encounters further eroded barriers and created humorous interstices that brought light relief to the sometimes-sad narrative.

Mimicking the structure of a Bikram Yoga class, the play was split into two parts, bridged by an interval. In a Bikram class, this interstice is a two-minute *savasana*: a resting posture designed to bring the body back to its neutral state, in this case between the Standing Series and Floor Series. Following this logic, we used the lead up to the interval to invite the audience to join us in a guided meditation. We had already engaged the audience in breathing with us during Pranayama deep breathing; the first of Bikram's twenty-six postures and the opening scene of the show, in which my first ever breath is articulated. Audience and performers breathing together in unison formed an auspicious start to the play, creating a special energy in the space from early on. For the meditation, the audience were given the option of lying on their back on the floor, or staying seated with eyes closed, meditating in the chair. Several people lay on the floor, the lights were dimmed, and a performer led everyone through a *Yoga Nidra*. Translated from *Sanskrit* as 'yogic sleep', body parts are named in a process in which participants are invited to bring attention to each part. It lasted around 10 minutes, immediately followed by the break. When the audience returned, it was the three performers that were lying on the floor.

Fenemore states that:

> Different genres of live performance already explore and exploit this embedded and visceral potential of vision and touch [...] it can be found in the work of those 'immersive' performance companies whose approach is a more total sensory approach than that of more conventional theatre.
> *ibid.*

In *Awkward* we would have liked to stimulate the senses further by bringing the meditation session outdoors into the garden. But heavy rain that day thwarted my vision of the audience spread out on the lush grass, under a cobalt blue sky, listening to the birds. Meditating in the space, however, may have created a deeper shift in the spectators' consciousness, as they became participants in these special moments of the show. Returning briefly to Meyer Dinkgräfe's analysis of Peter Brook's *Mahabharata*, he makes the point that the work was capable of affecting the 'reader's or spectator's consciousness,' which was also an aim of *Awkward*. It was not just the audience's eyes and ears that we wanted to stimulate, but also the energy between us. One of the ways in which we sought to do so, was through the use of our bodies.

4   Performance

In Govan et al.'s discussion of Physical Theatre, they point to certain practices that 'subscribe to the notion of the "experienced body", whereby the body is seen to contain a lived history' (Govan et al., 2007: 159). Coupled with the autobiographical narrative, our bodies in their black leotards; mine as an aging body, would also have been perceived as a container for lived experience. Furthermore, I suggest that the work resonates with the criteria described by Govan et al. regarding Grotowski's work, with its:

emphasis on the expressivity of the performer's body (which) places his praxis as central to the development of a more somatically based theatre [...] this emphasis of the training of the performer through psychophysical processes, and the creation of a theatre that rested on the encounter between spectator and performer, rather than scenic devices.

GOVAN ET AL., 2007:159

The Bikram Yoga postures are challenging to achieve in a room that is not heated to forty degrees. Part of the risk assessment for this research involved minimising risk of physical injury. We were concerned about performing our practice without the required heat, which softens and stretches muscles, joints and ligaments. In a Bikram studio, the sweat will also help to ease the body into where it needs to go. Here, we were working in a dark, chilly theatre space. It felt strange practicing in these conditions at first. We adapted by practicing frequently, before every rehearsal, until our bodies were used to it. There were no mishaps on stage. As performer Wendy Houston notes:

> When the emotion is connected to the action, there seems to be very little risk of physical damage. Injury seems to occur either when the ego kicks ahead of the body, when ambition moves the body ahead of its current capacity to the place where it 'wants to be', or when the mind can't find enough importance for doing it in the first place.
>
> HOUSTON in Pitches and Popat, 2011: 45

I would argue that the connection between us, through training, practicing and meditating together, kept us safe. There were times when the energy was such that it felt as though we were moving as one single organism; a feeling I had experienced once before during a Nicolás Núñez workshop, in which a long line of workshop participants closed their eyes and snaked forward by holding onto the hips of the person in front. We became one. Moving through total darkness, I experienced the sensation of being a part of a whole that was much larger than myself.

Holding our intense Bikram Yoga *asanas* on stage in such close proximity to the audience demonstrated genuine struggle, which often matched the emotion in the script. Govan et al. contend that 'as the actor tires the audience loses the sense of watching a rehearsed performance and instead sees the real characteristics of the actor themselves – their exhausted, unobliging body attempting to undergo a task' (Govan et al., 2007: 162). While it was not apparent to me at the time that we were making physical theatre, *Awkward* appears to share Dymphna Callery's five characteristics of it, defined as 'the actor as creator; collaborative working methods; the work is somatically led; an open actor-audience relationship and importance of live-ness to the work' (Govan et al., 2007: 172). We worked with a narrative script, although Govan et al. argue that even without words, the body is capable of telling its own story:

> in focusing upon the body, a number of issues are foregrounded; among these are the questions of identity, of the experiences of the body, its fusion with the mind and the manner in which bodies are transgressive. Such transgressions occur when the everyday body is pushed beyond the usual limits. It is in this space that many interesting articulations can be discovered.
>
> GOVAN ET AL., 2007: 172

As evidenced in the Immersive Contemplative Practice chapter, we performers had already pushed our bodies beyond the usual limits, as part of our yoga teaching training. Bikram Choudhury would often reiterate that we are capable of much more than we think, and that we hold our potential back because we are not self-realised. In the audio recording of his class, he posits the question:

> what's the biggest problem in human life? Personal problems. Because of lack of self-realisation, you always underestimate yourself. You always think you are too old, too sick, too fat, too skinny, too busy, too poor; that's called lack of self-realisation, you always look for excuses.
>
> CHOUDHURY, 2007

I was inspired by Choudhury's rhetoric from the beginning, when I first practiced to his commercial CD in a flat in Glasgow, before the first Bikram Yoga studio existed in the city. At that time, I could only hazard a guess at the meaning of self-realisation, but my interest was keenly piqued. Perhaps it was my own low self-esteem that Bikram spoke to as I practiced his yoga and absorbed his words. My comfort zone was in writing and making visual art. The first opportunity to perform, however, through an artist's residency with Ankur Productions was met with much self-resistance. I remember asking permission to simply stand on stage and read what I had written. This scratch performance was being directed by Shabina Aslam, a unique character, akin to Choudhury perhaps in her uncompromising ability to make people do what they think they cannot do. Before I knew it, I was performing the piece. Later, my first ever director and I attended Bikram Yoga classes together: an early embedding of the links between theatre and self-realisation at the heart of this book.

Self-consciousness on stage is an ongoing battle. The title of the work, 'Awkward', is not only the title of one of Bikram's postures, but is also a self-deprecating nod towards my own shyness and social anxiety. Lee Worley attests that 'transforming self-consciousness into consciousness of self is a noble task' and through contemplative practices my self-esteem was in a healthier place by the time I performed *Awkward* (Worley, 2001: 29). I was 50 years old, with all the insecurities around being 'too old, too poor, too fat' that Bikram lists in his CD (Choudhury, 2006). However, on-going self-realisation processes facilitated an expression of vulnerability through the work. In a discussion of her aging body, Wendy Houston captures these sentiments with humour: 'I hit 50 last year and this episode has introduced the concept of history into my life. Or has introduced the concept that my life is history' (Houston, 2011: 46). For me, *Awkward* was the creative expression that marked the history of my life, in celebration of the half-century milestone.

The work enabled a freedom to explore my own mortality, as though I was creating an artistic eulogy to my living self. This was only possible through *internal* work undertaken as Immersive Contemplative Practice over the life of this research, which finally received its *external* expression as creative output. As Lee Worley states, 'we begin by studying ourselves; before we can make art for others, we have to work toward liberating ourselves from what imprisons us' (Worley, 2001:29). Making art from one's demons expels them somehow. Worley reminds us that thinking deeply does not equate with passive work:

> We associate the word contemplative with times that are quiet and reflective, detached from the clutter of ordinary living. Theatre, on the other hand, may be designed to disturb or shock [...] contemplation should disturb us from superficial living, engage us, shock us into deeply thinking with body and mind.
>
> WORLEY, 2001: 9

I suggest this is also true of the work of David Bowie, who died two days after the release of his album Blackstar. Bowie's recording career spanned my whole life up until that moment. It was also an uncanny coincidence that he chose the same title for his final work as I had chosen for my theatre company three year previously. I was finally creating work under the Black Star moniker as Bowie's Blackstar made its entrance. This appeared to be most serendipitous. Snippets of Bowie's music through the decades became the soundtrack for *Awkward*, including Blackstar's title track. Media commentators looked for hidden clues in Bowie's work that pointed to his impending death. As suggested in an online NME blog:

FIGURE 13   Bikram Choudhury and *Awkward* performer Anna Leckey at Bikram Yoga TT

The lyrics not only foreshadow Bowie's death, but our reaction to it: "Something happened on the day he died/Spirit rose a meter and stepped aside/Somebody else took his place and bravely cried/I'm a blackstar." It's an oddly muted, matter-of-fact way to imagine your own send-off; almost as though he's asking us not to make too much of a fuss about it.

I suggest that the dark and beautiful themes of consciousness present in Bowie's final album might qualify his work as conscious music practice. His interest in yoga is exemplified in a photograph of him sitting in lotus pose. This fortuitous find completed the design of the poster for *Awkward,* in which Bowie appeared on one shoulder and Bikram on the other. I stand between these powerful artistic and yogic influences, with Buddha's head replacing mine, signifying spiritual transformation. Bikram remained with us in spirit, from Teacher Training (TT) in Thailand, to the smallest theatre in Scotland.

5   'A Space for Reflection; A Space for Sharing'

> 3. How might a research methodology applied to practice-as-research contribute to an evaluation process that questions the degree to which 'conscious theatre practice' might contribute to a shift in consciousness?

The question is the third of the three broader enquiries driving the research. Despite my best efforts, I was unable to secure the attendance of any journalists at this one-off performance so far from the city. There were two theatre-makers among the audience, however, and their respective statements, which 'speak' for themselves about the work, are presented as a further means of analysis, along with audience questionnaires. As the focus of the research regarding *Awkward* was around the possibility of a shift in consciousness among the audience, questionnaires asked specifically:

1.   Did the content of play change your perspective about anything?
2.   Would you be more likely to try Yoga or Meditation now?

> From 15 questionnaires completed by audience members directly after the *Awkward* performance, 12 answered 'yes' to question number 1; 2 people answered 'no' and 1 stated that they would have to think about it. In respect of the second question, 8 people answered 'yes'; 3 answered 'no'; 3 stated that they already do both, and one did not answer this question. As 80 percent of respondents experienced a change of perspective following the work, I evaluate that *Awkward* created a shift in consciousness among the audience. Whether the audience would be likely to take up yoga and/or meditation because of the work is less convincing, however, with just 53 percent stating that they would. As audience numbers were small, I have included all of their verbatim comments below:

Audience Feedback: *Swallow Theatre, Whithorn, 2/7/2016*
  - "Super enjoyable, revealing and insightful piece, enjoyed the structure and also the many intrigues/revelations!"
  - "The use of the space and the intimacy of the venue really helped everyone engage with the content."
  - "The play was well conceived and performed, the speech clear and I am full of admiration for the ability to hold the postures. I thoroughly enjoyed this afternoon."

- "Beautifully acted/narrated, interestingly interspersed with yoga positions."
- "It is surprising to see the humour and optimism Lou clearly radiates. I realised how judgmental I can be of people and how wrong that is!"
- "It's a really rich piece."
- "Still sitting lost for words – pure magic!"
- "You are a talented actress and a beautiful storyteller."
- "Love changes everything. Well presented. Captivating yoga postures. Thoroughly enjoyable. Don't stop."
- "It showed the ways in which our life experiences form us and the choices we have to make and how these have an effect on others – that makes me more aware of the importance of my own present."
- "You showed how yoga and meditation can help us through difficult moments, and change our outlook – thank you"
- 'A reminder to self-love and look after myself. Thank you. Your journey is inspiring."
- "I will certainly look at my own life differently now. You have inspired me to believe more deeply in my own journey."
- "It's fascinating to compare journeys through life and how we make sense of them, particularly on a spiritual level. I really enjoyed the way I could bring my own framework into conversation with yours."
- "Very interested in the meditation."
- Loved the meditation/relaxation section. Must breathe better."

Further analysis is drawn from the daily meditation journals kept by performers during the rehearsal process. One entry from a different performer each day is intended to provide a random sample:

Tired, head nodding, not falling asleep but can't pin-point the moment my head fell down. Just pick it up again. Pin-pointed sensation under my left nostril; not much but a start, relaxed, clear head, soft focus, appreciative of this opportunity. Just watch the thoughts, plenty of them but not judging or trying to understand where they came from. Breath slow and sleepy, mind content. (day 1)

This was very different. I was rested and alert when I began. This may have made it more difficult to settle. I changed position twice and was a little bit bored at moments. When thoughts like that crept in, I went back to my breathing to find my concentration again. I must have been in a deeper meditation than I thought because when I came out of it, I stretched and yawned as though I had woken from a sleep. I enjoyed hearing the dogs barking and the donkeys braying outside. It's a peaceful place. (day 2)

It was late when we meditated, and I was tired. I couldn't get comfy. I had an achy back. It was ok. I managed to find my stillness sometimes but was thinking lots. The dogs kicked off and we couldn't ignore it. This brought us out five minutes early, which I was fine with. We had worked out the whole play on paper that day, so I was still thinking about that. And was happy with our progress. (day 3)

Small moments, like miniscule moments of calm. Thoughts rushed. Breath fast. Nearly an anxious start to the practice. But once the thoughts slowed down and I stopped trying to control ... of course there were still thoughts fast and loud, but they didn't bother me and every now and again I could come back to my breath. Just the silence and the discipline made me calm and contented and after a stretch, I feel ready to work. (day 4)

Having had such a hectic Monday – and we forgot to meditate! – I found Tuesday's meditation a bit tricky. It was okay at first, but I was just desperate to get into the theatre and start work! I was finding it very difficult to be in the moment. I wanted to be in the next moment. My eyes were flickering open for the last 15 minutes. I lost my meditative state – But I did it. (day 6)

I suggest that what these entries show is the struggle to find calm and stillness in the midst of a creative process, and yet, those tranquil moments, no matter how short lived, are entirely useful. It demonstrates that the pursuit of those spaces between thoughts and actions takes effort. Lee Worley states that:

> by becoming sensitive to boring moments, we discover that if we lean into them, we can go beyond our patterns into groundless creativity. 'Boring' is a word invented by fear to avoid threats to ego-self. In sitting meditation this is known as 'cool boredom.' Practice is no longer an irritant; we allow ourselves to continue without seeking fresh entertainment.
>
> WORLEY, 2001: 60

As one collaborator noted: 'can't have a bad meditation, just a distracted one, always glad I did it,' which appears to encapsulate the practice. As I already knew from Vipassana, it is rarely easy, but always beneficial.

Statement of Support

I am writing in support of *Awkward*; Lou Prendergast's intriguing combination of yoga and theatre. This show looks back over a fascinating life and forward to new ways of being in the world.

I attended a performance of *Awkward* as a work-in-development at the Swallow Theatre in Dumfries and Galloway in July 2016. The performance took place in a small converted barn with seating on three sides of the space. Lou and her team created a space for reflection; a space for sharing; and a space for confession. The small audience were looked after and respected, and Lou's stories were beautifully written, open and honest accounts of a rich and inspiring life.

The most effective element was Lou's use of a Bikram yoga sequence as a dramatic structuring device. Yoga instruction, accompanied by demonstrated postures, was used throughout and this spoke to the subject of the piece in clever and revealing ways. At the centre of the performance was Lou's autobiographical narrative, and as she recounted episodes from her life – at turns shocking, sad, hilarious and hopeful – the audience were addressed as close acquaintances.

This style of audience address has been developed by Lou through several performances for the stage in recent years. This was particularly clear in *Blood Lines* (the Arches, 2014), her exploration of personal connections with the Scots-Caribbean experience. Even when Lou writes for other actors, as in *Tommy's Song* (*Òran Mór*, 2015), the performance feels like a personal sharing of stories and ideas. This is a vital and original theatre that uses personal experiences to speak to wider social conditions.

I would highly recommend a future production of *Awkward* as I believe Lou is an important voice in Scottish theatre with a story that needs to be heard.

David Overend

Dr. David Overend
Lecturer in Drama and Theatre

To whom it may concern,

I saw *Awkward* at the end of its development period, on the 2nd July 2016 at The Swallow Theatre in Whithorn, Dumfries and Galloway.

This was the third original production I had seen by Lou Prendergast, and I thought it was an interesting and highly appropriate development for this unique theatre-maker. Lou's work presents raw and challenging explorations of race, class, sexuality and gender, often based on her own personal experiences growing up as a mixed-race, working-class woman in Scotland.

Awkward charts her life as she presents to the audience with a series of Bikram Yoga poses, accompanied by two onstage yoga teachers. The narrative Lou creates is very compelling, and rich with the complexities of an often searingly honest and painful autobiography. Lou describes how in more recent years she found spiritual peace in the practice of Yoga. The audience are therefore not only invited to reflect on the parallels between the narrative and the carefully balanced and often awkward poses of the performers, but also, in deeper manner, the role of spirituality in allowing us to cope with and make sense of our daily lives, struggles and suffering. This sparked a great deal of rich debate between me and the other audience members on our journey back to Central Scotland, and is a conversation increasingly worth having as our society defaults unquestioningly towards secular rationality, which can yield limited answers to such questions.

Whilst the developed piece was presented to a very high standard, this was despite a very limited budget and I would be very excited to see how raised production values and working with a director would enhance the piece. The work showed great potential for touring to both rural and urban communities across Scotland, and for presentation at the Edinburgh Fringe Festival, and I would highly recommend it for further development.

Yours sincerely,

Sam Rowe

FIGURE 14   Lou Prendergast, Laura Fahey and Anna Lecky performing in *AWKWARD* * – *A Life in Twenty-Six Postures*
SOURCE: PHOTOGRAPHY THE SWALLOW THEATRE, 2016

FIGURE 15   Lou Prendergast, Laura Fahey and Anna Lecky performing in *AWKWARD* * – *A Life in Twenty-Six Postures*
SOURCE: PHOTOGRAPHY THE SWALLOW THEATRE, 2016

FIGURE 16   Lou Prendergast, Laura Fahey and Anna Lecky performing in *AWKWARD* * – *A Life in Twenty-Six Postures*
SOURCE: PHOTOGRAPHY THE SWALLOW THEATRE, 2016

FIGURE 17   Lou Prendergast, Laura Fahey and Anna Lecky performing in *AWKWARD* * – *A Life in Twenty-Six Postures*
SOURCE: PHOTOGRAPHY THE SWALLOW THEATRE, 2016

CHAPTER 9

Findings, Lessons and Learnings

He cried loud into the crowd I'm a Blackstar
BOWIE, 2016

∴

This has been an enquiry around the use of Bikram Yoga and Vipassana meditation on theatre making practice and processes. It charts the creation of the 'Three C's' research model and the consequential development of a working manifesto for a Conscious Theatre Practice (CTP). The research draws upon CTP to compare and contrast three public theatrical performances, in terms of their respective relation to conscious collaborations; conscious casting; and conscious craft. As an adjunct to the creation of CTP, this research explores the Vedic concept of Self-Realisation and the role of yoga and meditation as practices that support continual *becoming*, an ongoing process. There has been exponential growth in my personal evolution in line with practice-as-research via autobiographical writing and performance; autoethnography as a research method enabling self-discovery through immersive contemplative practice; lifelong learning and continuing professional development in yoga, all of which contributes to an ongoing self-realisation process.

Karen O'Reilly states that 'ethnography is iterative-inductive and involves constantly moving backwards from our research questions, to our data, and back, to refine questions or line of enquiry in light of what we discover' (O'Reilly, 2005: 226). Aligned with O'Reilly's theory, this research elucidated a reflexive approach. It has always been *in-process*, with anticipated endings paving the way for new beginnings, described by Kemmis and McTaggart's model of 'planning, acting, observing, reflecting and re-planning' (2008: 276).

Three broad research questions formed the basis of the enquiry:

© KONINKLIJKE BRILL NV, LEIDEN, 2022 | DOI:10.1163/9789004467927_010

1   Research Recapitulations

1.   How might 'energy practices' that create some shift in consciousness
        inform the creative processes of a 'conscious theatre practice' in which
        the work is derived from lived experience?

This question was tested in relation to all three productions exponentially,
as the research process gained momentum over the years. It began when an
intensive period of meditation inspired me to work with my family. On *Blood
Lines* my sister and I practiced Bikram Yoga on an almost daily basis at a Bikram
Yoga studio, until the demands of the production no longer allowed it. This
was beneficial in terms of our relationship and our performances. On *Tommy's
Song*, all three company members practiced yoga and meditation daily. This
was a morning ritual during rehearsals. The non-theatre space we were given
to rehearse in posed challenges for meditation; it was not conducive to a tranquil setting, which might have helped meditation novices to calm their minds.

Nonetheless, the data demonstrates positive benefits around taking this
time to practice together. All three performers on *Awkward: A Life in Twenty-
Six Postures* were Bikram Yoga teachers. We had survived the intensive Bikram
Yoga training regime together six months prior to the production and were
experienced practitioners before we became teachers. We practiced yoga
and meditated together more frequently, as these disciplines were part of
the performance. We were also far from the city surrounded by countryside.
Contemplative practices were special on this final practice-as-research production. I suggest from my relational experiences across the productions, that
the more yoga and meditation that company members share, the more harmonious the creative process.

2.   How might the creative outputs of a 'conscious theatre practice' (in which
        work is drawn from lived experience and influenced by energy practices)
        contribute to processes of socio-cultural transformation?

This book begins with a quote describing theatre as a 'spiritual practice' that can
'help heal the world' (Brask & Daniel Meyer-Dinkgräfe). If we accept increased
awareness and/or tolerance of marginalised 'others' as shifts in consciousness,
the productions did indeed change perceptions. Data gathered on *Blood Lines*
demonstrates increased awareness of Glasgow's role in the slave trade, sharing
insights from a personal narrative set within wider socio-political frameworks.
Those who had been in attendance reported that the play provoked deep conversations about Commonwealth and Empire and race.

Tommy's Song fueled lively responses, evident in the questionnaires completed by the audience. People wrote a lot. They were deeply engaged with
the performance. Data shows an overall sense of empathy for the character,

tempered with undertones around taking personal responsibility. An audience member sitting next to me, unaware of my involvement in the show, was emotional at the end. She knew I could see her crying and turned to me and said: 'that was really sad,' which made me really happy. This was not Deadly Theatre (Brook, 1968). *Awkward* also inspired shifts in consciousness among the audience, evident in their questionnaire responses; which evidence deep contemplation of the themes of the performance; as well reportedly sparking much debate among the Glasgow attendees on their minibus journey home.

3.   How might a research methodology aligned with practice-as-research
       contribute to an evaluation process that questions the degree to which
       'conscious theatre practice' might contribute to a shift in consciousness?

The 'Three C's' research model facilitated a systematic method of analysis of theatre-making practice. *Blood Lines* was analysed mostly through the Conscious Casting lens, enabling an enquiry around elements of narrative, staging and ensemble. On *Tommy's Song* the focus was around writing, directing, casting, and performance, under the broad scope of Conscious Craft. In *Awkward*, Conscious Collaborations were the main concern through analysis of ensemble, staging and performance. This bespoke research methodology achieved its aims. It was augmented by more traditional evaluation methods including data generated from questionnaires, discourse analysis around digital and print media reviews, a physical focus group discussion with invited theatre-making peers; and written statements from others, contributing further insight to how the work was perceived. From these findings I conclude that the creative outputs; my plays, were the highlight of the research.

2   Outcomes for Theatre Practice

The research findings have informed the Black Star Projects manifesto (presented below). I suggest this seventeen-point blueprint for a conscious theatre practice is a further highlight of the research. It is a set of statements concerning how we train, how we treat each other, how we create work. The 'Three 'C's' research model, which guided the productions and facilitated the trying and testing of various approaches and/or questions, was an early incarnation of the manifesto. Yogic restraints, the *Yamas* and *Niyamas*, were a further influence, along with insights from Vipassana. It was through the creative processes that the manifesto was honed and modified, however.

This working document can continue to develop, guided by the realities of practice. The manifesto contains a Hindi couplet I encountered on a Vipassana retreat. This concept of burning away dross speaks to a number of the strands I have been working with. In PaR, we do not create theatre by intellectualising; we learn through doing. We physically make the play, dropping the parts that do not work and refining the parts that do. Through this process, we eventually find 'gold'. This chimes with *Tapas* in yoga, and purification in Vipassana, where the fiery heat of discipline eradicates impurities. The Hindi couplet is also appropriate to Bikram Yoga, which utilises heat to heal the body. Choudhury compares the healing and rejuvenation of the human body through his method as akin to putting a piece of junk metal into a furnace, melting it down, and remolding it to something shiny and new.

This remodeling does not come easily, however. As the couplet attests, we must 'strive ardently [...] and burn'. We must be passionate, intense, fierce and fiery to get to where we want to be, in the hot room of the yoga studio, in the rehearsal space, and on the stage. Striving ardently is a way of working that demands concentration and effort. This is the energy the manifesto attempts to convey. Just as Grotowski shared his twelve principles with collaborators, the manifesto attempts to serve as guidance for how we interact with each other. It was not a prerequisite for theatre-making collaborators to declare any desire to engage with a self-realisation process, or conduct themselves according to the yogic *Yamas*, relationship with self (internal); and *Niyamas*, relationship with others (external to self). Perhaps it will be in future, as I endeavour to work with it professionally; and get better at living it personally.

3   Black Star Projects Manifesto

Strive ardently, oh man, and burn! Purity comes from burning away the dross. Gold must pass through a crucible in order to be refined.[1]

1.   Undertake daily yoga and meditation/mindfulness to shift our consciousness through increased awareness, focus and energy

2.   Apply a strong and determined 'embodied' work ethic, as we learn to do in yoga and meditation, working through our difficulties by *doing*

3.   Push our potential for self-realisation through taking risks and embracing new challenges that expose our fears and vulnerabilities

4.   Aim to be flexible and open, in body, mind and attitude

---

1   A Hindi couplet (doha) chanted by Sri S.N. Goenka in his 10-day Vipassana courses.

5.   Present 'true' narratives from marginalised sections of society
6.   Keep audience close, utilising 'nowhere to hide' staging where possible
7.   Be mindful of generating attachment or aversion to ideas
8.   Remain experimental
9.   Work with actors with some authentic relation to the work
10. Actively seek diversity in casting – across gender, race, class, sexuality
11. Select company members intuitively, because they 'feel' right
12. Practice kindness, empathy and compassion towards each other
13. Seek the truth/Speak the truth (with kindness in our communication)
14. Avoid generating negativity
15. Enable less advantaged/experienced practitioners to work with the company to enhance their skills
16. Adopt ethical guidelines for treating company members fairly
17. Encourage company members to contribute creatively

4   CTP Antagonisms and Limitations

The presentation of the works at their respective venues; the Arches (2014), Oran Mor (2015) and the Swallow Theatre (2016) were each preceded by very different but equally intensive short rehearsal processes. Theatre-making collaborators were not the 'subject(s)' of this study. Hammersley and Atkinson assert that 'ethnography forces one into relationships with the people being studied' and in this autoethnographic account, the person being studied is myself (Hammersley and Atkinson, 2007: 229). The relationship with my myself is a potentially challenging one, in all the ways Katie O'Reilly suggests in 'the irreducibility of human experience, and acknowledging the complex, messy nature of human lives and understandings' (O'Reilly, 2005: 226). Add the pressure of deadlines across shorter than required rehearsal periods due to budget limitations, and emotions will occasionally escalate. Given that learning from one's mistakes is congruous with 'realising the Self' in all its glorious weaknesses and shortcomings, my one spectacular emotional eruption, which shook the walls (and the cast), was limited to the first production only.

In my respective roles as Researcher, Producer, Director, Writer, Performer and Marketing Manager, *Blood Lines* was particularly challenging. Managing the dynamics of family members that had been estranged for several years; and managing their first forays into theatre, and managing my first full-length, funded production, amounted to too much pressure on one small human. The notion of self-care was unknown to me at that time. A sense of responsibility around caring for everyone else felt more pertinent. I wanted everyone to know and feel their importance to the work; to enable a sense of democracy, especially given the themes of racial oppression pertinent to its themes. In *Staging Social Justice* (2013), devised theatre makers Ainsworth and Pippen recount challenges they encountered working with non-actors:

> The transition from devising to producing a show in such a short time becomes the most challenging aspect of the process [...] the compressed time frame, the high-pressure concerns [...] of numerous family, employment, and other personal frustrations, a pressure cooker of emotion is created that needs to be negotiated.
>
> AINSWORTH AND PIPPEN, 2011: 201

Across my three productions there were singular instances of collaborators: being late back from lunch; publishing photos of the set and performers in costume on social media after being specifically asked not to do so ahead of the show opening; expressing resistance to turning up at all, after a request for a full day off during a short rehearsal period was necessarily denied; repeating a key element of my play in their work, uncomfortably soon after, potentially jeopardising funding applications describing my work as pioneering and original. However, O'Reilly cautions that 'what is needed is to be able to locate yourself in your study honesty and openly, in an admission that observations are filtered through your own experience, rather than you being the detached voice of authority' (O'Reilly, 2005: 223). Thus, I hold my hands up and note that others may perceive these situations somewhat differently.

Nonetheless, negotiations and challenges such as these had to be carefully threaded through all three productions; working with professional actors posed different challenges to non-actors, perhaps because of the self-expectation that comes with professional experience. An actor must put their faith, and to some extent their fate, in the director's hands. Non-actors appeared to be more willing to take risks, perhaps because they had less to lose. Ainsworth and Pippen state that 'the director needs to be given permission to create something that sits well with the company's production standards and those afforded (or not) within the project budget' (Ainsworth and Pippen, 2013: 200). The experiences they describe on a devised, community production on which they faced resistance, resonate with my own:

> the director finds that one actor wants to resist all of his suggestions, another struggles intensely with learning lines, and others express

frustration with the power differential by arriving late, disrupting the ensemble, and falling in and out of focus.

AINSWORTH AND PIPPEN, 2013: 200

However, given the way that the performance described above moved the audience and broke down barriers between different factions of the community, it appears that the challenges were worth every moment. I would make the same claim for *Blood Lines*. As Tammy Spry asserts 'it is not that she now "gets along" with others better because of performative autoethnography, but that she may perhaps be a bit more ready to engage the complexities of being and doing with others' (Spry, 2011: 2010). I am unconditionally grateful for these sometimes-challenging creative processes that involved 'being and doing with others'. We created valuable artworks. The rawness of the performances lent an authenticity to the work. I include my own performance in this analysis.

In the months leading up to rehearsals I had already performed in two of director Alan McKendrick's productions (*Cain's Book* (Untitled Projects/The Arches) and *Emancipation Acts* (ACCG/Culture 2014). My confidence as a performer should therefore have been optimal. The pressure that I was under in my respective roles however, left little time and/or mental space to work on my own performance. Directing the cast presented many of the challenges and took my focus away from my own preparations. A few sessions with a dramaturge and project consultant provided an invaluable outside eye, assisting with overall structure and flow, but I was largely directing my own performance. One cannot see oneself from the outside. In this situation one can only *feel* one's way through. It was not until the fourth and final performance that I had truly embodied my spoken and physical parts and had relaxed sufficiently to shine on stage. People rose to their feet to applaud.

Multiple roles on the productions also required the balancing of relations and tensions with those outside of the immediate 'family' of company members, which might normally be handled by producers. Any private challenges inherent to CTP among collaborators were multiplied when it came to the public sphere of venues and their respective protocols around collaborations, casting, craft and commerce; processes that were not necessarily 'conscious' in my sense of CTP, and sometimes clashed with it. As Hammersley and Atkinson point out:

It is the responsibility of the ethnographer to try to act in ways that are ethically appropriate, taking due account of his or her goals and values, the situation in which the research is being carried out, and the values and interests of the people involved.

HAMMERSLEY AND ATKINSON, 2007: 228

All venues had their own agendas and audiences to consider. One is always a guest when presenting at venues and should act accordingly, or risk not being welcomed back. This can create inequitable power dynamics; especially for the emerging artist that is attempting to gain some foothold in a professional the-atre arena in which older, female, working class, mixed-race artists are margin-alised. My research interests were not pertinent for anyone else. Hammersley and Atkinson remind us that 'the ethnographer is very much part of the social world he or she is studying, and is therefore subject to specific purposes, con-straints, limitations, and weaknesses; like everyone else' (Hammersley and Atkinson, 2007: 229).

Across all three productions there were singular instances of venue person-nel: undermining/overriding my creative decisions; attempting to disrupt cast-ing processes that did not fit their own 'ways of doing'; 'assisting' with a budget and then refusing to accept accountability when it later emerged that an error in a formula was going to create financial hardship for me personally. I felt it necessary to call in the funding body for a resolution to this crisis, as I was also accountable to them. This again did not bode well with venue staff. As Tami Spry states of performative ethnography 'it becomes a practice of vulnerably engaging the collisions and communions with others as we seek to find ways of living that allow for a diversity of being, a multiplicity of stories'; multiple roles; myriad challenges (Spry, 2011: 209). I am unconditionally grateful to the venues and personnel that facilitated the presentations of the work(s).

5   Implications

Ultimately, my research processes and the elements of self-realisation, self-discovery and self-cultivation embedded within them had to be balanced with artistic collaborations, negotiations with others inside the work, and the power dynamics, established protocols and culture of theatre venues that were outside of the work(s), but integral to its presentation(s). The theatri-cal productions involved laying bare my heart and soul for the entertainment and/or heightened awareness of distinct public(s), including theatre-making peers, journalists, and essentially audiences. Feminism's mantra, the personal is political, shifted my autobiographical narratives into public arenas where wider socio-political implications came into play; 'speaking' to people in direct ways, inspiring them to create change, or at the very least to think a little more deeply about society, if only for a brief, utopian moment.

The research is multidisciplinary and multi-layered. The other aspects, 'Self Realisation' and 'Conscious Theatre Practice' are separated and deconstructed, enhancing understandings of each. Practice-as-research and autoethnography are justified as the most appropriate research methodologies. Furthermore, Daniel Meyer-Dinkgräfe's wisdom around 'the model of consciousness proposed through the Vedic Science developed by Maharishi Mahesh Yogi' is drawn upon to explore the efficacy of Bikram Yoga and Vipassana meditation upon an emerging autobiographical theatre practice. The concept of *Dharma* as 'all that is helpful for evolution – from Self to society is essential as a guiding premise for this work. Jill Dolan's *Utopian Performatives* and Peter Brook's *Holy Theatre* informed the research. The legacies of Grotowski and Stanislavski have been essential to this study; the latter arguably the first theatre director to bring *asana* and *pranayama* into theatre-making processes in the West.

In terms of the project's implications for embodied knowledge, it owes much to contemporary energy practitioners Phillip Zarrilli, who has since sadly passed away – I am truly grateful to have experienced his teaching – and Nicolás Núñez, both of whom guided me through intensive trainings/workshops. Psychophysical Performance Research led by Deborah Middleton at Huddersfield University has been pivotal to deeper understandings; as well as personal introductions to theatre-making peers with shared interests and/or creative outputs. This research endeavours to add new, original knowledge to existing studies, contributing to the academic canon of work in this field of contemplative performance praxis; and may also be of interest to yogis.

Intersectionality as a critical methodology befits my feminist position of enunciation and self-identification as marginalised 'other': mixed-race, older, lone parent, grandmother, coping with neurodiversity (dyspraxia) and *dis*-ease (autoimmune conditions). The analysis of Self is pertinent to my 'bodymind', including altered states of consciousness and the pursuit of holistic health and conscious medicine: alternative healing methods with a focus on childhood trauma as root cause; as well as more traditional allopathic methods concerned with treating symptoms. Laterally, my research has led to the discovery of the work of Canadian physician and author, Gabor Mate. I attended his engaging talk at the 'Aces to Assets – Fostering Resilience in Stressed Culture' conference in Glasgow (June 2019). His work provides illuminating insights into autoimmune conditions, including two of those I suffer from:

> A disturbed immune system reacts against the body's own tissues, particularly against connective tissues like cartilage, tendon sheaths, the lining of joints and the walls of blood vessels. These illnesses are characterised by various patterns of inflammation that strikes the joints of the limbs or the spine; or surface tissues like skin or the lining of the eyes; or

> internal organs such as the heart or the lungs or in the case of SLE (sys-
> temic lupus erythematosus) – even the brain.
>
> MATE, 2019: 170

There are no surprises here; who *feels* it knows it, and I described how I *felt it* in the hips, the knees and the spine throughout immersive contemplative practice; and in the heart and lungs via a blood clot on my lung caused by kidney damage, outlined in the Sick Self section in this book's first chapter. Mate's insights around the bodymind connection are true revelations. He cites a medical-psychiatric study, which concluded that 'despite the diversity in the group (of people with the same or similar diseases to mine) the patients' psychological characteristics, vulnerabilities and life conflicts were remarkably similar' (Mate, 2019:170). The study points to the common characteristic of 'pseudo-independence' described by the authors of the study as 'compensating hyperindependance', common in those whose parents separated in their early life, causing feelings of loss and abandonment.

Mate explains that the angry child got into trouble and experienced rejection. The anger and the rejection had to be deflected inside, against the self, in order to preserve the attachment relationship with the parent ... leading to 'strong feelings of inadequacy', a 'poor self-concept' (Mate, 2019: 173). Mate describes how the child's repressed anger turns inward. Consequently, in autoimmune disease, the body's defenses turn against the self (*ibid*). The understanding that one's biography becomes one's biology (Nakazawa) augments the notion of Know Thyself; this research has contributed striking self-wisdom. It has opened new lines of enquiry that warrant further investigations around Heal Thyself; or at least implications around engagement with work that might help others to heal; to 'help heal the world' in new ways, in and beyond theatre.

6   Applications

The application of this research is tangible in the establishment of two legal entities and one physical space. Theatre company, Black Star Projects, was incorporated at Companies House in 2013. The concept of Conscious Theatre Practice will guide Black Star Projects. Immersive Contemplative Practice undertaken during this study, including Bikram Yoga Teacher Training, has been applied directly in the setting up of the BodyMind Studio, a yoga facility established in late 2016. The name of the studio honours this research. In January 2018 the legal status of the company was changed to Community Interest Company (The BodyMind Studio C.I.C.), resonating more appropriately with its vision and aims. The studio is now located in the Glasgow burgh of Partick. Working with other self-employed instructors and offering several styles of traditional as well as hot yoga, and other fitness disciplines, the studio has become a space for movement; and will potentially become a space for making theatre, for rehearsing productions and even as a performance space.

Following numerous rejections from theatre organisations around presenting *Awkward*, it could be staged here; befitting of my creative mantra that if you want something done, do it yourself. It is a thrilling prospect to move the work beyond research and apply it to future work with new collaborators, informing new creative processes. The manifesto is ready to be assimilated by mine, or any other theatre organisation who might tailor it to their specific working practices. It has potentially far-reaching implications for contemplative theatre. Lee Worley extols the merits of a theatre in which one might be 'inspired to create an approach to mainstream theatre that encourages people toward kindness, dignity and love' (Worley, 2001: 5). How inspiring it would be to delve into those deep questions posed by Worley, such as 'what is your connection to the universe? why do you live? what do you value? what can you contribute? what is real?' with the manifesto as a blueprint for making the work (*ibid*).

My desire to form an ensemble is tempered with the self-awareness that I might stand in my own way. Having a long way to go yet on the self-realisation path, I anticipate potential complications with this approach, as John Britton states:

> Most ensembles grow through the initiative of a charismatic individual. It is generally individuals who have the inspiration to assemble a team, the vision and drive necessary to sustain and develop it and, sometimes, the intrinsic personal flaws that will prove to be its ultimate undoing.
>
> BRITTON, 2013: 208

One learns more from doing than from not doing, however, and potentially even more from 'undoing'. CTP is a learning process. The focus on self-cultivation in Somaesthetics, purification in Vipassana meditation and the calming of the ego through psychophysical practices, all amount to knowing ones bodymind better, aiding one in ironing out 'intrinsic personal flaws' (*ibid.*). CTP is potentially transformative, although leadership can be complex. It was my energy, vision, focus and drive that made the productions happen; and not necessarily through shared power dynamics. Britton asks, 'are the 'democratic,' 'non-hierarchical' working practices so valued by some who work in ensemble compatible with 'structure' and 'leadership'? (Britton, 2013: 208). Similar questions were raised during the *Blood Lines* focus group, around a clash between CTP and professional theatre: are there rules, and if so, laid down by whom? The manifesto was in its early stages at that time. Now completed, its seventeen statements form the rules; laid down via Conscious Theatre Practice.

John Collins of the Elevator Repair Service (ERS) suggests that ERS might appear from the outside to be non-hierarchical and entirely democratic, but this appearance may belie a more complex dynamic. Britton quotes him thus:

> Far from utopian, the underlying narrative of this ensemble suggests that maintaining exclusive, club-like membership may not be the only (or even the most effective) path to a theatre company's longevity. Instead, longevity may be best achieved through embracing a paradox: the most enduring ensembles are always falling apart.
>
> BRITTON, 2013: 2010

Perhaps this paradox alluded to by Collins embraces change; change viewed in a positive light. Ensemble, in CTP terms, aligns with notions of conscious collaborations that are both harmonious on a personal level and creatively productive on a professional level. The optimum scenario for Black Star Projects would involve making theatre with artists who emanate wonderful, inspiring energy, who practice yoga and meditation to enhance their own evolution as human beings, who care about the plight of other human beings. These artists are generous with their talents and seek to share their merits. Respecting the practices and ideologies of CTP, we set about making theatre that moves, touches and inspires people in extraordinary ways; challenging, fearless theatre that is not afraid to prod and poke at the real issues facing real people.

The wider sociopolitical implications of this study include Black Star Projects within my new term, socially conscious theatre practice (SCTP); a not-for-profit theatre company, and the BodyMind Studio, a venue in which to explore/deliver socially engaged narratives to/with minority audiences that might not normally attend theatre. My vision for the studio is that it becomes a space for arts practice as well as yoga, meditation and movement. Its services are currently utilised by yoga students who pay for classes; and beneficiaries for whom services are free, including individuals in recovery from substance addiction and female survivors of domestic and sexual abuse. The studio has become an essential space for recovery, providing crucial connection to others. There are no hierarchies. The studio is a level playing field that breaks down barriers and connects vulnerable people in unique and supportive ways, in a safe space where individuals can talk and laugh together; motivate and inspire each other.

Two yoga courses expanded my knowledge around yoga as a tool for healing from addiction and/or trauma. In 2018, I attended leadership training in Y12SR – the Yoga of 12-Step Recovery. Based on the 12 spiritual principles first introduced by Alcoholics Anonymous, Y12SR blends the more cognitive elements of the 12-Steps, with the somatic approach of yoga. It takes the form of a two-hour session that involves discussion or a 'share', an important aspect of 12-Step style meetings, immediately followed by yoga. The share takes place on the mat. The emotional shift in energy that arises with the issues and feelings that are 'shared' with the group, are then worked through, and out of, the body through yoga *asanas*. This pioneering approach was created by Nikki Myers. The official Y12SR programme description document sates that:

> Y12SR offers a mind and body approach using both the mind and the body for relapse prevention. Using the cognitive tools of the 12-steps and the somatic experience of yoga, Y12SR assists people to develop body awareness, to learn to feel what's going on in their bodies, and to self-regulate.
> Y12SR marketing information, n.d.

This programme is offered in the US by addiction treatment centres. Y12SR addresses any/all addiction issues, not only substance abuse. It may attract those with gambling, sex, or over-working addictions, or obsessive, compulsive disorders. Anyone affected by addiction may also attend, including the families of addicts, and/or their health care professionals. It is entirely inclusive. Y12SR sessions are growing globally. The BodyMind Studio is the first facility in Scotland to host these sessions, funded formerly through the Big Lottery Community Fund, and laterally through the Scottish Government's Childhood Abuse Support (SOCAS) fund. This funding acknowledges the links between childhood abuse and addiction. Y12SR is highly appropriate to the concept of bodymind and conscious practice, recognising yoga as part of a holistic recovery route:

> Addictive behaviors separate and disconnect us from our loved ones, our environment, so much more and ourselves. Conversely, yoga itself means union, integration and balance. Yoga and its practices teach the fine art of balancing our multidimensional lives while living in a complex world [Y12SR] creates a model that truly addresses addiction as the physical, mental and spiritual disease that it is.
> *ibid.*

The launch of Y12SR sessions in Scotland is further evidence of the wider implications of this research in its potential to move into new holistic health and/
or social-care contexts. I have undertaken further training that supports this
aspiration, via the Trauma Centre Trauma Sensitive Yoga (TCTSY) certification
programme, described on its website thus:

> TCTSY is a program of, and has foundations in, both Trauma Theory
> and Hatha Yoga practice with an emphasis on body-based yoga forms.
> Complex or Developmental Trauma have such a deep impact on the
> entire organism that there is a strong consensus among professionals
> that treatment approaches need to reach beyond talk-based or cognitive
> therapies.

Addiction is *dis*-ease that is linked to childhood trauma. It has become apparent through this research, as Havi Carel pointed out, that illness can prompt
a new awareness of oneself, leading to personal growth. The 'know thyself'
adage can apply to addicts too; I suggest that self-discovery is an important
part of their recovery. In the first chapter of this book, ideas around knowing
our true self through Vipassana meditation were introduced, along with the
belief that it is necessary to solve our own problems before we can resolve the
wider problems of the world, a notion articulated through Y12SR as putting
your own oxygen mask on first. Bikram Choudhury also advised that through
yoga we could help to heal the sickness all around us. Zarrilli spoke of the quiet
ego and calm emotions achieved through psychophysical processes, allowing
one to perform more positively in life and on stage. Meyer-Dinkgräfe explains
how self-realisation and *dharma* are helpful for evolution. I aspire to apply my
research to new realms, both in and beyond theatre, in health and wellbeing
contexts.

7   Back to My Future

As an artist, the need to express myself creatively will always surface. There
are tentative ideas around creating theatre with individuals recovering from
trauma. This is already happening to great effect by Glasgow theatre company,
Incahootz. On their website, they describe their approach of using the arts to:

> produce theatre shows for local communities, using the arts to engage
> people in positive and inspiring activities that will enhance and improve

their wellbeing, confidence and skills [...] we believe these will, in turn, impact positively on all our lives and be of benefit to the wider society.
incahootz.co.uk

I experienced their work when invited by one of my yoga students who was performing in their play, *Pigeon*. It moved me to tears. Skillful writing by Martin Travers and Lee Hollinshead was brought to life by director Katie Black. The most compelling part of the work, however, were the unpolished performances of the community actors; all of whom were in recovery from addiction or still in active addiction. This struggle was etched on faces, in scars and pallid complexions. The production's pared down set, of not much more than a few rows of chairs creating the setting of a housing office, powerfully delivered the work's stark themes. This was 'poor' theatre, in the sense of Grotowski's work and beyond, encapsulating notions around class and inequality in clever ways. Humour was also used to subtle effect. The production ran at the Scottish Youth Theatre. My tickets cost £2.

This work contrasted sharply with *Dark Carnival*, a production by Vanishing Point that ran at Tramway. My tickets cost £24. As the name implied, I anticipated something dark, but in that sense the show did not deliver. The house band were impressive. However, the rhyming couplets delivered by the professional actors caused my attention to wander; whereas in *Pigeon* I remained present, alert and carried along by the Glasgow vernacular being delivered by non-actors. In *Pigeon*, the intersectional marginalities of the performers were palpable. Their speech-acts drew me in; unlike the alienating middle-class enunciations of *Dark Carnival* performers, with their trained 'drama' voices. I assume that the set of *Dark Carnival* cost a small fortune; I nonetheless felt unmoved by it. There was a separate area (the living world) created above the main playing area (the afterlife), where actors were sometimes in silhouette: a grave digger, an angel. It was not until these two performers joined the rest of the cast for curtain call that I realised they were black. How ironic that Vanishing Point cast black actors and literally kept them in the dark; their race and ethnicity becoming a further vanishing point.

I suggest that the work(s) I created are positioned somewhere in between the two productions discussed above: while working with non-actors, we did strive for beautiful sets and high production values. If the opportunity is afforded to develop and produce work in collaboration with trauma survivors at the BodyMind Studio, the established protocols of other venues will not be contentious to CTP.

Autoethnography as a research method; autobiographical playwriting as creative output; and yoga and meditation as contemplative, complementary research methods all worked in unison to create shifts in Self. I had some prior embodied knowledge of the benefits of Bikram Yoga upon performance through acting roles in Alan McKendrick's *Cain's Book* (2013), and its second incarnation when a further hour was added to the production (2014). In this almost durational theatre work, I was able to find poise through my breath and moments of stillness and flexibility in my body when required, through yoga training. There were further aspects of yoga and meditation that I wanted to explore, however. It appeared most expeditious to work with the concept of self-realisation across the research journey.

Reflecting upon my own trajectory since 2013 when I first began my research, two of my plays had already been produced: *Fifty Shades of Black* (Ankur/ Citizens, 2013) and *Whatever Happened to Harry* (Arches, 2012). The latter, which won the Arches Blackbox Visual Artist Graduate Award, was reviewed by Eric Karoulla in the 'the Skinny' magazine, as 'an intelligent piece (that) pushes theatre performance into a unique place, quite outside the proverbial box' (Karoulla, 2012); and Mary Brennan in 'Herald Scotland' who stated that it 'made the pulses race and the nerves tingle – wow!' (Brennan, 2012). These early works and their positive reception augmented a trajectory that had resulted in artistic academic achievements.

My theatre research facilitated the incisive inclusion of Bikram Yoga and Vipassana meditation as analogous methods in arts making processes. This union was congruous with the overall research strategy because both PaR and CTP pursue embodied knowledge. According to Swami Sivananda, self-realisation *is* knowledge. He states that 'self-realisation or direct intuitive perception of the Supreme Self is necessary for attaining freedom and perfection' (Sivananda, 1971: 3). In this yogic philosophy, the Supreme Self, is 'pure, all-pervading consciousness' (Sivananda, 1971: 1). I wanted to shift my consciousness; the research assisted that ongoing aim.

Black Star Projects and the BodyMind Studio are the new vehicles through which I will endeavour to create art; and remain alive. Systemic lupus is a ferocious disease. To know the probable cause of one's death requires ongoing reconciliation with the self. Writing and presenting autobiographical theatre helps me realise this aspiration for myself; and facilitate it for others. I have struggled all my life with the learning difficulty, dyspraxia, only diagnosed at Glasgow School of Art (GSA) when I was in my forties. Dyspraxia has an overlap with autism; both falling under the umbrella of 'neurodiversity'. This is defined as leading to 'difficulties with organisation, concentration, time, direction, perception, sequencing, poor listening skills – leading to low self-esteem, anxiety and depression'. The positive flipside is that individuals affected by neurodiversity are 'creative, original and determined', which I recognise in myself. The above traits have simultaneously posed challenges to, and creatively enriched, the arduous completion of this book (theblogwithonepost.wordpress.com).

I suggest that my (mis)understandings, unstable beginnings, poverty, *dis-ease*, neurodiversity, racial diversity, social conscience, feminist perspective and ongoing pursuit of self-acceptance, are factors in my theatre-making diversity, contributing original knowledge to the contemporary theatre-making field. A funding contribution towards self-development on this project, provided by Playwrights' Studio Scotland has been conducive to positive changes in my life, both within and out with the research. I am eternally grateful. Furthermore, it has sparked the potential to help improve the lives of some of the most disadvantaged individuals and resilient souls in society: the black stars. Under the auspices of Black Star Projects and the BodyMind Studio, we performers epitomise the 'anomalous performers', the 'black sheep' on the margins of society that I defined at the beginning of this book. For I am a black sheep too.

Afterword

I write as we emerge from the ravages of Coronavirus. The vaccines are rolling out. My research, my plays, were completed long before Covid-19 reared its deathly head. I was lucky to have performed in director Stewart Laing and writer Pamela Carter's *Them!* in the summer of 2019, before the world changed. I had been Associate Director on *Slope* in 2015 and it was thrilling to be making work with this award-winning writing/directing duo again.

The *Them!* cast was truly diverse, consisting of a bunch of performers of literally all shapes and sizes, colours and creeds. It was fun. I was part of a group of 'dancers', jumping about to big loud beats in a Nike tracksuit in a 'smoky' club that had been installed for the production at Tramway. This role demanded energy! I also performed in the film element of the work that was screened as part of the show. My 'big screen' debut of a few short seconds.

This is one of the wonders of being involved in theatrical performance; to be contacted out of the blue and find oneself quite suddenly plunged into something so alive; so vital. I miss live performance. This week marks one whole year of theatres being closed. I personally did not take my performance practice online. Neither could I bring myself to watch theatre on Zoom. I went online with yoga facilitation in order to keep our special community together.

It has been a poor compromise, but served its purpose in terms of human connection, albeit through a screen. My yoga studio is still standing. I am fortunate. It will reopen next month. Recently I have been permitted into Phoenix Futures Rehabilitation service to do yoga with people in recovery. I can only describe my emotions after working in proximity to people again, and sharing their energy in physical space, as jubilant; buoyant. I floated home.

The Covid interstice afforded the opportunity to complete TCTSY training, to help people recover from trauma and connect with their body. This role feels more important than any performance role at the moment. As theatres open, and the irrepressible urge to create art resurfaces, I will no doubt make work.

It felt, after *AWKWARD – A Life in Twenty-Six Postures*, that narratives around older, mixed race, working class women had been surpassed by other essential female stories in theatre, especially around those who had transitioned. Perhaps as we come out the other side, space opens for an inclusivity of tales.

© KONINKLIJKE BRILL NV, LEIDEN, 2022 | DOI:10.1163/9789004467927_011

As we approach the anniversary of George Floyd's murder; as the British Monarchy's racism towards the mixed-race woman who joined 'the firm' is revealed, as poverty rises, and the pervasive abuse of women and children is painfully apparent through trauma work; there is much to explore and express.

These themes may sound sombre, but where there is darkness, there is always the possibility of a little streak of light, for hope, for healing, for humour. And while we can laugh, we can also find love for our lives. We are the survivors.

Blood Lines

Lou Prendergast

The audience enter the space to a recording of Enoch Powell's 'Rivers of Blood' speech. A Commonwealth definition is projected onto a black screen, which is situated above the musicians' instruments. Five performers are inside a classic blue Mercedes Benz. They exit the car and stand in a rough circle, facing outwards, inside the outline a map of Jamaica drawn on the floor ...

⁘

on screen

The Commonwealth is a voluntary association of 53 independent countries, almost all of which were formerly under British rule. The origins of the Commonwealth come from Britain's former Empire. Many of the members of the Commonwealth were territories, which had historically come under British rule at various times by settlement, conquest or cession.

   (*extract from the official website of the British Monarchy*)

humanity-equality-destiny: the motto of the Commonwealth Games

MICHAEL

   Nothing is more misleading than comparison between the Commonwealth immigrant in Britain and the American Negro. The Negro population of the United States started literally as slaves and were later given the franchise and other rights of citizenship, to the exercise of which they have only gradually and still incompletely come.

NEIL

   The Commonwealth immigrant came to Britain as a full citizen, to a country which knew no discrimination between one citizen and another, and he entered instantly into the possession of the rights of every citizen, from the vote to free treatment under the National Health Service.

GRAHAM

   As I look ahead, I am filled with foreboding; like the Roman, I seem to see "the River Tiber foaming with much blood." In numerical terms it will be of American proportions long before the end of the century.

SOPHIE

But while, to the Commonwealth immigrant, entry to this country was admission to privileges and opportunities eagerly sought, the existing population found themselves made strangers in their own country.

LOU

They found their wives unable to obtain hospital beds in childbirth, their children unable to obtain school places, their homes and neighbourhoods changed beyond recognition, their plans and prospects for the future defeated; they began to hear, as time went by, more and more voices which told them that they were now the unwanted.

GRAHAM

My name is Graham Campbell. I came to the UK as a Commonwealth immigrant from Jamaica in 1969. We've all been reading from Enoch Powell's 'Rivers of Blood' speech, which was delivered at a Conservative Party meeting in April 1968.

walks over to his guitar

MICHAEL

My name is Michael Abubakar. My father Ali Abubakar came to this country as an immigrant in 1958. From Zanzibar.

walks over to his keyboard

NEIL

My name is Neil Stewart. My sister was Roby Stewart, who had two children, my nieces, with Harry Prendergast. I was born in Glasgow in 1955.

walks over to his drums

SOPHIE

My name is Sophie Prendergast. I'm the first-born child of Neil's sister Roby Stewart and Harry Prendergast, who was a Jamaican immigrant.

walks over to the car

LOU *as she is walking over to the car*

My name is Lou Prendergast. I am the sister of Sophie and the niece of Neil. I came to Scotland from London in 1968 when our parents, Harry and Roby, moved their young family to Glasgow ... the same month and year that Enoch Powell made his speech in response to the American race riots sparked by the assassination of Dr. Martin Luther King.

SFX musicians strike up a quiet ska rhythm to underline narration

Harry Prendergast began life as a country boy

Born in Spanish Town, Jamaica

In 1938, perhaps,

Black mum, white dad, an Irish soldier I've been told.

I imagine him
Playing in the yard with your brothers and sisters
Cooking yams on the fire
A move to Kingston toughened him
And he stowed away to England!
Britain has a shortage of workers
Tens of thousands of West Indian immigrants come here, by invitation
With British passports, as British citizens as they were then
To rebuild the 'mother country' after the war.
To fill the jobs that couldn't be filled.
So Harry comes too ...
But he doesn't want those jobs either
Refusing to conform, as he did,
To any submissive role or lowly position ...
He was charming ...
and devious!

SFX *Ska beat comes in*

But who could resist you dad?
As London's early Ska music scene burst into life
Your brethren bringing forth the black music from your island
You meet my mother in the Roaring Twenties nightclub, on Carnaby Street
So handsome with your straw hat and cane
And she, with fringes round the hem of her dress, caught your eye.
"He made some comment and I was hooked ..."
I hear you were creative, could draw; and sing
A sign writer my birth certificate tells me.
But another kind of creativity surfaced in your life below the law
No public transport work for this immigrant bwoy!
Flash Harry had bigger fish to fry ...
And he ends up here (*music stops*) in Glasgow
Not a bus driver nor a hospital auxiliary
But providing commodities that this city demanded
Hashish. And women ...

SFX *Ska rhythm morphs into Marin Gaye's 'Let's Get It On' sung by Michael
after song Michael walks forward to frame, in character now*

MICHAEL

I knew your dad. I grew up in Glasgow in the early 60s, in Cowcaddens, which
was an Italian district at that time. An' the part of Sauchiehall Street where
the prostitutes worked, we called the drag. The American Navy wis based at

Holy Loch, Dunoon. The sailors would come to Glasgow at the weekend. Me an' ma mates, aged 10, would walk up to them and say 'any gum chum? gies thrupence!' And they'd say 'what's that?' and pull out a handful of change and we'd point to a two-bob bit (*laughs, shaking head at own mischief*).

When we were teenagers we'd offer to take them where they could get a burd and a drink. We'd take them to Billy Bodkins'. Billy was an African that had a shebeen, an illegal drinking den. 99 Grant Street in Woodlands. We'd get a drink aff Billy fur bringin' him business. I was listening to Prince Buster, Desmond Decker.

In the late 60s, early 70s, a big squad of Jamaicans came up wi' their prostitutes. The laws were different in England than in Scotland. In Scotland, for the 'living off immoral earnings' law to work, they woman had to say 'he's the boss' for her man to get charged. But the girls would get charged and they'd have to go to the Central Court, just down from Glasgow Cross. 'Working Ladies' came under Central Police command and would go before Judge McLaughlin.

When I was 12-years-old there was a craze for coffee bars in London and Jimmy Fusco opened 'Fuscos' here, in Cambridge Street. That place attracted a lot of vice. Homosexuality was illegal at the time and all the gays and the prostitutes would hang out at Fuscos. Prostitutes would work Buchanan Street Rail Station.

We used to call a prostitute a gas cooker, hooker, so you'd say, 'yeah, she's a gas.' ... I married a gas cooker! I met her when she was on weekend leave from borstal. We had three kids but it didn't last too long. Prostitution was woven into the fabric of society. Your mate's maw would be a gas cooker – you never thought nothing about it.

So I'd see Harry in the boozers. His pals were Sugar, Freeman and Dudley – who looked like Sonny Liston – and Smiddy – he was another dead good pal. They'd all be in the Carse Kegg, passing time with Jimmy Fusco. West Indians were crazy mad fur watches and chains. I had an Omega C Master watch an' your auld man tried tae buy it aff me. I says it was a gift fae ma auld man – it wisnae fur sale!

Your dad had women working for him at Billy Bodkins. He wouldn't be called a pimp though – that was American – here, you father ... he was a stick man.

Michael moves back to band. Neil comes forward to frame opposite Lou, who stands in front of car bonnet

LOU

My father was a stick man.
But I didn't know at that time, in the formative family years,
With him, my mother and sister Sophie

That his dodgy dealings
His ill-gotten gains, extended to prostitution

NEIL

I spent a bit of time with them, my sister Roby, and Harry.
I had a great time.
I mean, it was Glasgow, late 60s and they had the best parties
They were the king and queen of their scene
Harry was a happy guy ... a young Jamaican living in Glasgow!

LOU

These sparring partners that were my parents
The hippie and the gangster
Split when I was seven
And she became tight-lipped on the subject of him

NEIL

He used to get all his pals round and they'd be listening to reggae music.
I used to play his records – he had the only quadraphonic system I know of,
with big round speakers. It was brilliant.

SFX *Michael brings in 'Shaft' melody on keyboard*

LOU

Dad was in cahoots with a corrupt police officer from Strathclyde CID
John Brown was his name – bent as a two-bob bit
He paced around my home as though he owned the joint

NEIL

Isaac Hayes ... the album cover, had a big gold cross on it ...
Harry's record collection educated me, not only to black music, but to what
black people were saying.

LOU *singing 'Shaft' lyrics*

Who's the cat that won't cop out
When there's danger all about? (*Graham* 'right on')

NEIL

There was a lot of racism around ... not everyone wanted to see a black man
doing well in business. He had something to do with a club in Sauchiehall
Street, the Revolution. Him and his pals would hang out there.

LOU

Who is the man
That would risk his life for his brother man? (*Graham* 'can you dig it?')

NEIL

He had various guys working for him. They didn't always get paid on time
but they still wanted to be around him
Ronny was Harry's driver. He drove Harry's motor.

He came in for me one morning and off we went.

Big Silver Buick, electric windows and everything.

LOU

He's a complicated man.

But no one understands him like his woman

NEIL

We drove to Maryhill to collect some money. No problem.

On the way out we turned a corner and a team of guys stopped us in the street, thumping on the car and that.

LOU

But other people told

The terrible tales

Of Flash Harry Prendergast

NEIL

You tell your boss if I don't get my money he's getting fuckin' stabbed.

Michael shouts in unison with Neil "he's getting fuckin' stabbed"

SFX 'shaft' fade out before 'stabbed'

We gave Harry the news and warned him it was serious.

He seemed disinterested, "It'll be alright man," he said.

I didn't see Ronny much after that.

But things did get violent at times.

LOU

Acquaintance of the Gorbal's own Jimmy Boyle

And Maryhill's Arthur Thompson

NEIL

I mean there was a time I remember his face got slashed.

I don't think he knew he'd been cut at first. It happened so fast.

GRAHAM

I know the guy that slashed your dad. It was Willie Mad Patch McGill, fae the Cowcaddens TOI. He was a nutcase. Willie was a chib man. You'd have chib men in those days and that's what they did – they chibbed people. He grew up in the nick. He got 10 years in the 80s. That night, at Billy Bodkins, he was hanging about in the doorway. Harry told him to 'beat it' and Mad Patch pulled out a razor, slashed Harry and ran. Harry chased him. Your Da made an effort but Willie got away – being a bit quick.

NEIL

He had this second-hand furniture shop on Maryhill Road

But that was just a front really –

There was a bit through the back, up the stair

And he had women up there – prostitutes, you know?

LOU

> A gold-toothed Jamaican pimp operating right here in the dear green place
> Selling women from the upstairs of a second-hand furniture shop.

NEIL

> There was this Jamaican woman that came down to the flat
> And she says: *Graham* "Me nah gwan sell me pussy fe Harry no more"
> Until he paid her back the money he owed her – the money he owed her!

LOU

> Hustler, Liar, charmer! Father?

NEIL

> Harry was a gambling man and he loved to take risks.

LOU

> My powerful pimp daddy!

Sophie enters stage, looking into Lou's eyes

SOPHIE

> Powerful? Really?
> It's a funny thing power.
> It shifts and changes.
> What sort of power could a black man really have had in the late 60s?
> Powerful in the criminal underworld, perhaps
> But not within the establishment ...
> Power over his prostitutes at least?
> Well not necessarily.
> Because there's prostitutes
> and there's prostitutes.
> From the vulnerable streetwalker
> drug addicted and pregnant
> To the high-class escort
> She don't need no pimp!
> She's powerful enough
> In her own right.
> Consider that story
> My uncle Neil just told
> Of the Jamaican whore
> Who worked here, for Harry
> She came and went like anyone else
> Complaining bitterly
> That Harry owed her money
> All services were postponed

Until she got her cash.
She had some power.
The power to say NO.
She was not forced.
At least not by him.
But by circumstance?
Forced by her class?
By her colour?
By colonialism?

Graham enters stage and stands on frame, Sophie leans on car
Neil plays militant style colonial drumming during Graham's speech

GRAHAM

In the colonial period, from the 16th century to the mid-20th century, European powers established colonies in Asia, Africa, and the Americas. Kings and queens throughout English history have had connections to slavery. In 1562 Queen Elizabeth I sent the first English slave ship to Africa. In 1624 the English colonised Barbados and St. Kitts. Around 23 years later, the first sugar from Barbados was sent to England. In 1655 England captured Jamaica from the Spanish and the slave trade had yet another place in which to thrive.

In 1672 England set up Royal African Company to control the slave trade. King Charles II was a shareholder. The company shipped 5000 slaves per year, aided by grants from Parliament totaling £90,000.

The Grand Old Duke of Duke of York, he had 3000 slaves.
He sent them off to the plantation,
And they never went home again.

SOPHIE

What ... *the* Grand of Duke of York?

GRAHAM

Yup. That one. He branded his slaves on the left breast or the left buttock with 'DY' before shipping them from Africa to the Caribbean.

Graham goes back to join band

SOPHIE

On Caribbean plantations, sexual exploitation of black women by white men was systematic. For the enslaved black woman, the problem of getting the slave master off her back in the daytime and off her belly in the nighttime, was very real. The black woman's hell would begin on the slaving voyages, where she was stripped naked, and ever vulnerable to sexual abuse and torture. On the plantation, the female slave was at risk of rape, not only from the white masters, but also from the black slaves. There were no laws to protect her. Even now, in the global, social hierarchy, the black woman has the least power. Slavery is defined as the buying and selling of people as commodities. And the origin of the word 'prostitute' from the Latin, in the 16th century, means 'offered for sale.' So, for the prostitutes who worked for Harry, he too was a master of sorts.

Graham, Neil and Lou come forward and stand in a rough circle facing outwards again, recounting short 'reflective' accounts from characters before freezing, statue-like until their time to speak again

NEIL

I knew your dad. They called him the King. He was feared.

LOU

I knew your dad. Ach he was lovely! Harry? Oh aye!

GRAHAM

I knew your dad. Harry and all of them guys came up here because of prostitution.

NEIL

He always had a big posh car and he always had a lot of money. He would buy all the drinks for everyone.

LOU

He used to let us play with his hair, 'cause it was different, you know? You wanted to touch it.

GRAHAM

I had heard about how bad your dad was, but when I met him he was a nice guy – if he liked you.

NEIL

He had a Pale Green Nash Rambler at the time, a four-door saloon.

LOU

I was young and I'd never seen anyone like him. So he used to let me comb his hair and his beard.

GRAHAM

He was just looking after himself and his family. Them guys don't go out looking for trouble. They just do things their way. I don't blame them. Jamaican's got a bad reputation because they looked after each other

NEIL

He was a magnificent actor. He would pretend to be angry and shout a lot and do a thing with his eyes that terrified people.

LOU

And we'd go: 'Mon show us your dancing Harry, teach me how to dance.' As if you can teach somebody to dance!

GRAHAM

All the Jamaicans would hear about Billy Bodkins and go there. Rube boys they were called at the time. They had a scam going with cheque cards.

NEIL

here was a big tall guy called Nick the Fisherman. He had no place to stay. He had an amazing vibe about him. He was a musician. He came to the door and I gave him something to eat and washed his feet.

LOU

But he was always dancing. He was great mover. And a natty dresser. He was always dressed nice. Sometimes with a hat.

GRAHAM

They would hit different cities writing cheques. In those days there was no way of telling if the cheque was good or not until it bounced.

NEIL

Harry took him out and bought him shoes and let him stay in the flat he owned for nothing. Then Harry had an idea that he could pro-mote him.

LOU

He was very cool. He was so charming, you know? A real people person. But he didn't like some of her friends. She had all sorts of weirdos hanging around and he didn't like that. No. He didn't like that.

GRAHAM

One night I was in there with Bobby Green. All the boys were playing dice. Bobby Green had a sixth sense and pushed me to the floor.

NEIL

He hired a church hall to have a gig. He got a license to sell booze. But it got raided and there was a big fight.

LOU

And they disagreed on style. Uh-huh. Because she loved old things, like vin-tage furniture – all the old things. And he wanted all the new 60/70s furni-ture – the flash stuff.

GRAHAM

Next second someone started shooting at the place from outside. Bullets were flying. They were looking for your daddy. *Goes back to band area*

NEIL

All the drink got left behind and Harry lost all his money. You win some you lose some. *Goes back to band area*

LOU

They'd go to a shop and he'd say 'what do you think of that?' And she'd say 'no way' and he'd buy it anyway! That's what she had to put up with.

sfx band play Toots and the Maytals' 46 -54 that's My Number
Lou and Sophie get into the car, and speak in unison

LOU & SOPHIE

Glasgow, late 60's.
Gliding round town in a black Mercedes Benz
Looking out at the night, from the safety of the car
I was thrilled to be up so late.
Mercedes by night,
Ford Mustang by day
A long, low, fast thing
Electric blue, shiny and sleek.
You parked it on Renfield Street one Saturday afternoon.
People were staring
At the big black man with the big blue car.
Who the hell was he?
Some super soul star?
At your birthday party
You wore a purple velvet suit
With a white ruffled shirt
My sister and I (*look at each other*)
were dressed the same, in bell-bottoms and capes
Women, were dancing inside cages.

SOPH

Oh, I've heard all about
Your eye for the ladies

LOU

And insatiable appetite ...
Which I didn't really need to know

SOPH and LOU

But we sensed it for ourselves
Kids have sharp little instincts
We watched your interactions
With a white woman
We once went to see
With a platinum, pink-tinged afro
And a platinum pink-tinged poodle
Black false eyelashes – first time round
We watched her eyes widen
When you sent us out to play ...

LOU

Not much to play with right enough

SOPH

In an overgrown back court

LOU

Waiting

SOPH

waiting.

SOPH

Or outside the bookies

LOU

Waiting

SOPH

Waiting

LOU

Outside Billy Bodkins

SOPH

Waiting

LOU

Waiting

SOPH

Outside the Carse Kegg

LOU

Waiting

SOPH

Waiting

SOPH and LOU

Outside the Halt Bar ... "I'm waiting for my daddy."

*SFX musicians play 'Forget About You' written and performed by Graham
Sophie and Lou sit stand in front of car and do a simple dance (like band backing
singers, clicking fingers to the right and the left)*

LOU *takes centre stage*

By the age of four or five, I was delivering dope to your friends

Aware it was our family secret

I saw a policeman and stashed it in my shoe.

I reported this to you, on my return.

Seeking and receiving approval

How proud you were!

You lifted me up, told your friends,

laughed heartily, gave me money.
Shhh, you'd say, finger on your lips
Pulling slabs of hashish from the family oven.
(*Sophie shouts from the car*) It was never dinner that was cooking!
Your loyal workers
Bagging up grass from a mound in the room
A circular production line Running to the rhythm of reggae.
They were blacker than you –
Some with gold teeth.
They pinched our cheeks, my sister and I.
Rough Jamaican love.
And conversations in thick patois
That back then, we understood.
I liked the sound it made
When you sucked your teeth
Or whistled for a black hackney – Cabbie!
The wave of a camel-coated arm
The flick of a gold braceleted wrist
They always stopped
Spinning on the spot
What presence, I thought
What power
What about the advice you gave
When you told your wee girl
That if anybody ever did me wrong
I should wait until their back was turned ...
Graham And throw a rock at the back of their head!

Graham, Sophie and Michael form the circle for the next round of reflective accounts from unnamed character

GRAHAM

Your Dad's friend Smiddy, his woman Anne was a prostitute. He used to put her on the street. Smiddy was a different kind of guy to Harry. They lived in Arlington Street. A sectarian organization was trying to exhort money from him and the other dealers and stick men. Smiddy got shot in his bathroom in 1973. It was a Saturday night. Me and my younger brother Oakland arrived at the house because we were going out with Smiddy that night. Police were there. Sergeant John Brown was there. Oakland identified Smiddy's body.

exits stage, back to musician's area

MICHAEL

Harry had this aquarium, a tank full of pirahna fish. The hash was stashed underneath the tank in a metal plate between the tank and the counter. Sergeant John Brown and Brenda, a big mad dyke, were working under for Inspector Beattie at the time. John Brown's title would change from Sergeant to Constable Brown to Sergeant Brown again, depending on whether he'd been demoted or promoted. Anyway, Brown goes over to see the fish and wiggled his finger in the water and Harry shouts GRAHAM: 'Nah man – dem fish bite off you han!' It was a genius way to protect the dope, man.

exits stage, goes inside car

SOPHIE

What do I remember about Harry Prendergast?

What do *you* know about Harry Prendergast?

He was a fucking ponce!

We were all into stuff – a bit of this, a bit of that, but him!

He was right in the cops' pockets, that fucker.

He was thick as thieves with that bent copper fae the CID –

Sergeant John Brown

The two of them were working together.

Maybe it's just rumours – I don't know – but I heard that anyone who bought more than 2kilos got grassed in …

And that John Brown got promoted on the back of the arrests …

Police corruption?

You couldn't make it up!

Sophie joins Lou at car

LOU *taking centre stage*

The day we left, from a tenement flat, on a Glasgow Street

In a furious flurry – a red-hued rage

You were chopping up our furniture.

You worked methodically

in a clockwise direction

I wonder what it was

That led you that day

To take out a sword

From the display cabinet on the wall

Housing beautiful blades

It was 70s style
To match the bar ...
Brass studs in black vinyl
And the sofa!
My seven-year-old eyes had never seen
Such an extravaganza of coloured foam cubes
Spewing forth, with every blow you struck
Wow. I thought.
So that's what's inside a couch?
We had these painted tree trunk stumps
They almost stopped you in your tracks
The dense wood gripped your blade
It was a power struggle.
You yanked it free with superman strength
And worked on: hacking, slashing, chopping
The adults were pinned to the wall
Like the wall of death at the fairground.
We edged slowly towards the door
And out the door and up the hall and into the bedroom.
She calmly put our clothes into suitcases.
That was the end of patriarchal family life.
Lou walks to Sophie and takes her hand as they cross the stage to the frame
SFX Neil begins a drum beat evocative of a train

I glimpsed you as we left though, laying back
As burst as the couch, being comforted
by our landlady who lived two doors along *as an aside, to* SOPHIE:
we liked Bessie. She always had corn on the cob for us.
Holding a wet cloth on your troubled brow –
"Harry's had a brainstorm," she mouthed to my mother.
Aww, poor you, daddy.
Sophie repeats sarcastically Aww, poor you, daddy
Sophie sits on frame, Lou stands at front of it, gesturing back to Sophie..
LOU *as Roby*

A pair of purple bed sheets and a brass Buddha.
A ten-year relationship and that's what I left with – and you girls of course.
That was the way it went with your dad.
One day you'd open the wardrobe and it would be full of luxurious fur coats.
You'd open it two days later and they'd be gone.
He wasn't like that at the beginning when he first come from Jamaica.
But he just got more and more corrupt.

Flash Harry they called him.

Flash cars, fancy suits, gold jewellery ... he always looked the part.

No carpets in the bedroom though – in the places people didn't see.

Bloody Mercedes Benz but no prams for the babies!

He could be tight with his money an' all.

He'd turn his back and peel a few notes off a wad he didn't want me to see. Tight bastard.

He came home with a mate one time and the pal came in first saying: "Harry's had an accident," and Harry followed him in, holding his face like this ...'cause it was hanging open!

But he got this great surgeon, em – Swiss! Swiss I think this guy was You could hardly see the scar.

Sometimes I'd take you girls and leave, go to Brighton.

But he'd always find us ... I mean,

Jamaican culture, it's not good for your woman to leave you

He'd come and get me and – we'd go back.

I knew how to get him mad.

I was scared of him but I still did it.

I even went though a phase of refusing to do any housework

He had to get a cleaner in: Margaret, she came a few times a week.

He admired certain qualities in me and wanted me to be more part of the business

But I acted like a spoilt child around him sometimes

I'd make a fuss or sulk if I didn't get my own way.

Would me getting involved have changed what happened though?

I don't know ...

Lou joins Sophie on frame, Michael pops out through the sunroof of the car

MICHAEL

In the Late 1600's, Scotland was experiencing poor international trade, as in- they weren't very good at colonising other nations for their own gain. But they tried, they tried really hard. It's the classic Scottish attitude; pull all your resources for one big mad scheme that might just boost the nation's wealth.

A rich young Scot named William Patterson heard of a place called Darien on the east side of the Panamanian Isthmus. From here, you could see both the Atlantic Ocean and the Pacific Ocean, and Patterson thought that if you established ports on both sides of this Isthmus you could control much of Global trade. He decided to set up a colony there.

The Scottish parliament were like 'ya beauty!' and in June 1695 they backed the creation of 'The Company of Scotland trading to Africa and the Indies'.

England did not offer any funding due to their displeasure at a possible rival for global trade.

Six months later, the people of Scotland had raised £400,000 – this was half of the Country's capital (and worth about 35 million pounds today). Being the wise businessmen that we are, and having heard that the natives had particularly long hair, we took a fuck load of combs to trade with them upon arrival ... not just combs – mirrors, shortbread and tweed – just the essentials.

On July 12 1698, 1200 colonists set sail on five ships. 43 died on route, which was acceptable at the time for a voyage of such length. However many more died upon arrival, which was mildly perturbing.

They landed at a place they named Caledonia bay in November 1698. Patterson had been to the Caribbean but never Panama. He had heard of the Darien region being full of low valleys, easy to build a road through. Wrong!

It was dead sunny when we got there, taps aff an' that. But then the rain started, not like our rain, proper rain, rain that would drown you, rain which did drown you. It was a swamp, a giant bog, a marsh the size of the highlands.

By March 1699 200 colonists were dead, which was alarming. And eventually this rose to 10 per day, which was a fucking disaster.

Much to our surprise, it turned out the locals had no use for combs and mirrors, and when food supplies began to rot as a result of the weather, we starved.

There was no real leadership. Fights and disagreements became commonplace.

Oh, and we also overlooked the fact that the Spain had previously laid claim to Panama. So they came back and gave us a warning to leave or be destroyed.

Those who had survived until now bolted, stopping off at Jamaica, which was owned by England at the time – a wee home away from home.

But before word could get back to Scotland that the task had been abandoned, the company had sent more people out. It was a total fiasco.

Survivors were despised on their return Scotland, for losing their country-men's life savings. We were so broke that we were forced to strike a deal with England.

England paid Scotland's debts of £398,000 and the 1707 Union was forged. That was the end of Scottish independence. But not to worry, the Union allowed Scotland to get in on the slavery act ... and Glasgow flourished.

Sophie and Lou from the frame

LOU

It's weird to think of being ... the ancestors of slaves, like, from a slavery blood line, eh?

SOPH

Mmm ... s'pose so

LOU

Don't you find that interesting?

SOPH

Well, I don't go about thinking of myself as coming from slave stock. I'm not even sure if I'm black ... Are we black now?

LOU

Hmm. It depends on the context.

When I was in Jamaica a couple of years ago people were shouting 'come 'ere white girl!' in the street and it took me a minute to realise it was me.

But we would have been considered black in Jamaica in the slavery days. We would have been termed 'quadroon' meaning one quarter black. But there wasn't always breeding among slaves. Jamaica was regarded as the graveyard of the slaves at one time you know.

SOPHIE

How come?

LOU

In places like Brazil, the slaves were encouraged to breed. But in Jamaica, slaves were worked to death. They didn't want new slaves from the plantation population, they wanted 'salt water blacks'.

SOPH

Salt water blacks?

LOU

Yeah, the slaves that came over the sea from Africa.

SOPH

Salt water blues more like.

LOU

Ain't that the truth.

SFX Graham plays blues riff on the guitar over the following recording as Sophie and Lou attach themselves by rope and perform repetitive 'slave dance' movement

At the opening of the eighteenth century Glasgow was an insignificant town on the banks of the Clyde; by the start of the next it had become a major Atlantic port, a trading powerhouse, the Second City of the Empire!

Scottish society had been transformed.

But where did these riches come from?

Well, history books would have us believe that it was down to the native genius of Glasgow's traders, tobacco lords and sugar barons; striding around the Merchant City where the streets still bear their names: Glassford St, Buchanan St, Ingram St.

But what's often left out of history lessons is the shameful plight of the Scottish owned slaves who sweated and bled in the plantations of the New World, to grow those most lucrative crops: tobacco and sugar.

Only 27 slaving ships left directly from Scottish ports, yet Scots were instrumental at every level of Atlantic slavery.

Thousands of ships with Scottish owners, captains and sailors winged towards West Africa to purchase slaves; some stopping off at Bance Island in Africa, for a round of golf, where slave caddies would be decked out in tartan.

11 million Africans were transported across the Atlantic, packed on their sides on ships, like any other cargo.

Up to 20,000 Scots travelled to the Caribbean in the 18th century, where they made up one third of the white population of Jamaica.

The slaves they owned sometimes danced the Scotch reel and spoke a Scots patois – and sometimes, even Gaelic.

In Jamaican patois, Scottish phrases continue to exist – as even Bob Marley sings about feeling 'crabbit' in the morning.

On maps of Jamaica we see the town names: Edinburgh, Stirling, Dundee, Penicuik, Bannockburn, Hampden. And in the archives we find the slaves had names like Perth and Paisley and Glasgow.

Lou removes Sophie's collar before recording finishes and goes to car, Neil, Sophie and Michael perform 'reflective character' scene again

MICHAEL *jumping out of car*

Glasgow, 1973. I knew your dad. Two black guys with Liverpool accents came into my family's shop and asked me to take them to Harry. They were delivering a car for him – a Coup De Ville two-door convertible, 22 feet long.

SOPHIE

Well. He was a bit devious ... But he got on well with everyone. He went to my family home Hamilton Drive once. He was actually invited in by my mother because he was so charming. He told her he knew me from the Art School. He'd never been near the Art School. It was just one of his stories. But it worked! My mother let him in and that was – that was quite something.

NEIL

He was the first person to show me a gun. I was about sixteen.

MICHAEL

I wanted to buy it but my father said no, you don't know if it's got the right papers.

SOPHIE

Yes, there were a lot of West Indians coming up from London at that time
Their girlfriends would come up too, but the CID would send the girls back.
The guys stayed though and were welcomed by the students in Glasgow
With their drugs. Yes, they were more than welcome.

NEIL

I went up to the house to score a bit of dope. And he brought out this gun.
I nearly shit myself.

MICHAEL

Anther time Harry came into the shop, with a canteen of cutlery made of pure gold. He wanted £1000. I refused it. A guy bought it for £3000 and sold it to an auction house. A dealer paid for £30,000 for it.

SOPHIE

And there was a jazz club, off Berkeley Street somewhere, called The Cell.
Musicians from the Locarno club at Charing Cross would go there afterwards.

NEIL

There was this big nervous Great Dane jumping aboot that got fed steak pie suppers.

MICHAEL

Your dad loved a punt on the horses. He wanted to put this accumulator bet on. He sent wee Joe round to the bookies. But Joe never put the bet on. In fact, he spent the money. All they horses won and Harry was due half a million. He was looking for Joe, but Joe had disappeared.

SOPHIE

And we'd all be there, Harry and everyone. But the cops were never far away. The club was in the basement and this policewoman, Brenda, you'd just see her big black shoes coming down the stairs, and you'd know it was a bust.

NEIL

And a tropical fish tank in an alcove in the lounge. He sold those fish ten times over. I heard that, days later, there was a string of guys turning up at the flat wanting their tropical fish. There wasn't so much as a goldfish bowl left in the house by then. And Harry? Harry had done a Houdini.

recorded speech is played into space. Graham pulls up stool and sits at frame, writing with quill on parchment

The plantations of the Caribbean relied on an enslaved labour force transported from Africa, supervised by a layer of poor, white indentured servants, of whom our own Robert Burns was nearly one.

In 1786, Burns accepted a position on a sugar plantation at Ayr Mount, Port Antonio in the North East of Jamaica. During this dramatic year he bade farewell to friends, family and Scotland in many letters, poems and songs.

This planned emigration was abandoned and Burns found fame instead as the national bard.

Michael stands up on frame

We'll never know what would he have made of Caribbean slavery had he gone, as there is a surprising lack of comment on the subject in his later writings.

GRAHAM

In the 1960s, the boxer Cassius Clay, who later changed his name to Mohammed Ali, visited Ayrshire. He stood in the cottage where Burns was born and recited the Slaves Lament by heart and cried.

MICHAEL *singing a cappella*

It was in sweet Senegal that my foes did me enthrall
For the lands of Virginia-ginia O;
Torn from that lovely shore, and must never see it more,
And alas! I am weary, weary O!
Torn from that lovely shore, and must never see it more;
And alas! I am weary, weary O!
All on that charming coast is no bitter snow and frost,
Like the lands of Virginia-ginia O:
There streams for ever flow, and there flowers for ever blow,
And alas! I am weary, weary O!
There streams for ever flow, and there flowers for ever blow,
And alas! I am weary, weary O!
The burden I must bear, while the cruel scourge I fear,
In the lands of Virginia-ginia O;
And I think on friends most dear, with the bitter, bitter tear,
And alas! I am weary, weary O!
And I think on friends most dear, with the bitter, bitter tear,
And alas! I am weary, weary O!

Sophie and Lou join Michael for the slave movement section, moving forward on the second "And Alas ..."

recording continues

But what sort of slave masters were the Scots?

Among the worst, as the following three eyewitness accounts testify:

"The poor negroes in the West-Indies, have suffered enough by such religion as the philosophers of the North produce; Protestants, as they are called, are the most barbarous slave-holders; none can equal the Scotch floggers."

the three drop down to one knee

When the bodies of the Negroes are covered with blood, their flesh torn to pieces with the driver's whip, beaten pepper and salt are frequently thrown on the wounds, and a large stick of sealing-wax dropped down, in flames, leisurely upon them."

drop down to Japanese style sitting, hands outstretched, heads bowed

On the estate of 'Paisley' in the parish of St James, overseer, the 'Dionysis of Dundee' instructs gunpowder to be rubbed into the festering wounds of an old woman who had been whipped. Calling for a match he lights a 'segar' and uses it to set the gunpowder alight, engulfing the live body in flames.

slowly bend forward, bringing forehead to floor and hands on floor to front
SFX Neil (after a pause) begins a drum beat
Sophie, Lou and Michael lift heads and rise slowly. Michael returns to musicians,
Sophie and Lou go to car, Sophie takes centre stage

SOPHIE

I missed you later Dad
And Glasgow
And all its different peoples
When we were whisked off to a mining village
Below the Ochil Hills
It was grim up north
In a deprived estate
Where packs of dogs
And packs of kids
Trotted the streets looking for mischief
It was raining that first day
When mum sent us outside
Children gathered round us
And the sun came out
And we pulled down our hoods and revealed our hair
And someone shouted:
band joins in "They're darkies!"
What did I expect?
I wasn't one of them.
I wasn't quite white enough.

And the only thing worse than having a black dad
Was having an absent dad
And a single, white mum
Who cooked rice and peas
Played Bob Marley too loud
And put a poster of Jimi Hendrix just inside the front door -
"Is that your dad?"
The kids would ask.
Why couldn't she just like Sydney Divine like everybody else?

Sophie comes to car, Lou takes centre stage

LOU

Fourteen years later, I've come home to Glasgow
And I'm on the phone telling my mum I've earned a bonus
At my wee job at British Airways in telephone sales:
Two long haul tickets to anywhere
D'you wanna to go to Jamaica?
I had heard that you were back there
And off we went, my mum and I
Me, heavily pregnant with your second grandchild
Who, somewhat unsettled by the journey
Might also have been born in Jamaica -
and not up the road in Yorkhill maternity
It was an all-inclusive deal
We ate and lounged by the pool
And ate and lounged by the pool
But we could have been anywhere
I wanted to experience the 'real' Jamaica
To know your land, to know my roots
But the hotel weren't keen
On guests straying beyond the security boundaries
They insisted we went with a guide
And I said no thank you,
And they said yes
And I said no,
And they said yes
And when we got there –
I was bloody glad we had him!
It was rough.
Rough, and poor, and edgy

And one woman's scorn towards us rich, white tourists was palpable:

"What are you looking at miss?!"

What did I expect?

I wasn't one of them.

Not quite black enough.

But Dad tell them!

Tell them that I am yours and you are theirs

And doesn't that make me theirs too?

I searched the phone book for you.

There were thirteen households in Jamaica in 1994

With our Irish surname!

I called a couple of them up ...

But nobody understood my Scottish accent

So I put a request out on Irie FM Radio

SFX band play the Irie FM radio jingle

GRAHAM

We have a young lady ere, she from England or Scotland – I don't know which ... anyway, she looking for her daddy ... if anyone know a 'Arry Prendergast, get in touch so we can 'elp the girl find er daddy ... keep it tuned to Irie FM ... your Jamaican station

LOU

And it blasted out all over the island, causing great excitement

"You looking for you daddy?!"

The staff would ask me.

We'll find him.

And I waited for you to get in touch

I was twenty-eight years old

And still waiting for my daddy.

Leaving day arrived.

And not a word.

Ach well.

It was one for Poirot

The mystery of you, was as yet unsolved.

Lou joins Sophie at the car, Michael comes forward to frame, echoing his first speech at start of play

SFX musician's perform Jah Light, written and sung by Neil

MICHAEL

I knew your daddy. From when I was ten-to-thirteen years old. I loved the man. He was a better father to me than my own father.

I met Harry in Gordon Robertson's garage in Maryhill, where my mother worked. Harry had an open top red mustang and I jumped in it.

My ma told me to get out, but Harry says 'just leave 'im, he alright' From then on he would take me out and about in the car with him. I was a cheeky wee boy and Harry liked that, but I was never cheeky to Harry. I respected him.

He never had a cross word for me though. Don't get me wrong, I've seen him angry – he never suffered fools lightly. There was a wee Canadian called Scottie. He was a jagger (*makes injecting motion*) Harry told him straight 'don't be taking that shit in my house'. He was direct – he would just tell you.

I would get bad beatings from my father and Harry would take me in. He would let me stay for a few days but he'd always say 'you need to go home.'

He wanted to go and sort things out with my dad, but I said please don't, my mother will get hurt. He understood me. He told me how to go about things. He would say 'you got a brain – use it.' (*points to temple*)

Your house was packed every night. But for me, it was peace, and safety. I'd babysit for you two. We would have our own party in the room, with sweets and ginger. Your dad says ' keep an eye on mi girls – 'dem precious to me.'

I was a street-wise wee guy. One day I came out the house and spotted loads of cars in the street with guys sitting in them. I knew something was up and went back in and warned Harry. Everybody started running about and getting rid of stuff. The cops came in seconds later, it was supposed to be a big bust but they didn't get a thing.

Harry owned a few antique shops. And he had a house in Napiershall Street. There was a woman, a blonde, he liked his blondes and he says 'jus watch what she doin'.

He was out his depth in Glasgow but he managed to turn it around. Last time I saw him he was going to London, Golders Green, for a major score. I hitch-hiked down to find him, with a mate when I was 15.

We went to the Jamaican community but nobody had heard of him ... unless he was using an alias.

When I couldn't find him, I cried.

But he had itchy feet, Harry. He would never hang around anywhere. He could be impatient. If he had a meeting with someone and they were late, Harry would just leave ...' mi see 'im later man.'

He used to get up and dance, he loved to dance. He said, 'never ever be scared to dance. It's a way for people to express their self.'

If we found out he was still alive I'd give that guy the biggest hug.

He was like an apostle – a teacher. An apostle preachin' the reefer.

Michael goes back to musicians

GRAHAM *from the mic*

Your father set the ground for you. That anybody who knew him would take care of you. Your father had the reputation but as far as I'm concerned, he was just looking after himself. He was one of them guys he don't take crap from nobody. Don't get in his way. Your father had his good side. He had his bad side but he was just doing what he does best. You might say he was an unaccomplished gangster. He wasn't a violent man. He wanted to be big time but he was just too nice a guy.

Sophie and Lou get into car

SFX musician's play cover of Toots & the Maytal's Pressure Drop

Sophie and Lou in quiet moment again – chatting then looking down, heads bowed towards a piece of paper they take from glove compartment

SOPH

So, you know that story about dad's friend Smiddy's woman being a prostitute ... he put her on the street?

LOU

Yeah?

SOPH

Well, did that never make you wonder whether mum ...

LOU *sort of laughing*

Ahh ... I know what your thinking. No, mum wasn't a 'working lady'. I wondered about that too. But after the Daily Record article, when all those people who knew dad came forward and gave me their stories, I asked a couple of them about that. And they were quite upset by the question. They defended mum's honour.

SOPH

Ah okay. Just checking. It's so nice to finally know people who knew them.

LOU

I know. People who them as a couple when they were together.

I've actually got another bit of information to share ...

SOPHIE

Oh? What's that?

LOU

You know that signed photo that Dad sent us in the 70s? I sent it away to a handwriting analyst. I didn't tell her anything about him, but I got this report back. Quite amazing what she could tell from four words and three kisses ...

SOPHIE

Let's see it then ...

LOU

You want me to read it to you?

SOPHIE
Yeah!

Lou reads the report

Your father wanted to be seen as a smart and respectable person, in control of himself and moving towards fulfilment of his ambitions. He put a lot of effort into looking his best and behaving with decorum and probably despised unkempt or slovenly people.

I can imagine him spending time in front of a mirror, checking that his appearance achieved exactly the image he wanted to convey.

He did his upmost to be as good and worthy a person as he could, both out of a desire for self-fulfilment and to avoid attracting personal criticism, as it made him feel deeply uncomfortable.

Probably shy deep down, he nevertheless gave the appearance of being quite self-assured. He felt at ease in elegant surroundings that made him feel valuable and proud.

Charm he had in plenty. He could be passionate, friendly, sensitive and generous, with the ability to make someone feel really special. He must have been popular with women! Relationships though, had to be on his terms: he would decide what to give and when and how, rather than lending a listening ear and adapting to his partner.

In romantic relationships, he would be sweet and fun, but also maddening; in time he would become restless, both emotionally and sexually.

It is likely that, as a boy, he was fussed over a lot and, in some ways, in adulthood he still behaved rather like a child. He was sensitive, with intense emotions that he struggled to contain. Sometimes he must have felt he was burning inside and may have had outbursts of tears or anger.

He was a logical thinker of great intelligence, with an ability to concentrate well when his interest was aroused. However, once he became bored, he lacked realism and perseverance, which meant many of his ideas were not brought to fruition. He was reluctant to look back and learn from past mistakes, preferring to envisage new opportunities yet to come.

At the time of this writing, he remained optimistic that he would realize his ambitions and continued to hope for a bright future. It would be interesting to know what happened as he got older: did he develop more perseverance or did he remain somewhat naïve and increasingly disillusioned?

The way he has written the word Dad shows that it was a special and loaded word – and role – for him. It conveys a mixture of contradicting emotions: pride and trepidation, novelty and hesitation, affection and detachment. The impressions coming through when looking at his splendid portrait are I think, confirmed in the handwriting. Your father comes over as a special person.

Sophie and Lou get out of car, wearing the same collars, this time evocative of noble ladies, and do a version of the 'slave dance' as recording is played into space, as with other previous historical material

In 1833, thanks to the abolitionists, many of whom were Scots, many of whom were women, Britain abolished slavery. But the slave owners wanted compensation.

In the chattel system, slaves were property, just like cattle, or furnishings, or land. Parliament, therefore, could not deprive these noble traders of their livelihood without remunerating them. Scotland made up just 9% of the UK population at this time. Yet 16% of the 16.5 billion pounds of compensation was distributed to Scotland. And the hotspot, was Glasgow.

By that time the large Scottish presence in the Caribbean had already channelled wealth back to the Mother Country swelling the coffers of the Scottish merchants and landowners, who funded the institutions of the Enlightenment.

By the mid 1800 almost half of Scotland's males were employed in industrialization. This industrial revolution also marked the beginning of capitalism. And then, Scotland forgot. Through the centuries, a collective amnesia clouded the nation, which conveniently blamed Liverpool, London and Bristol for the practice of slavery. But the evidence of Scotland's gains from slavery was in its tobacco trade; which elevated the nation to economic excellence. By the 1960s Scots saw themselves as victims "It's the Scots who have been colonized!"

Well, tell that to Jamaica.

Thanks to plantation owners and tobacco lords such as Mr Cochrane, Mr Oswald, Mr Glassford, and Mr Buchanan, those same ships that carried the human stock between Africa and the Caribbean returned to Scotland with a new cargo of sugar, cotton and tobacco to sell ... which is why we have Virginia Street and Jamaica Street ... and Glasgow flourished!

as recording ends Lou and Sophie are back at car. Lou takes centre stage

LOU

My father told my mother
stories of how, back in Jamaica
when women tried to flee their men
they would catch them
and lame them
so they couldn't run again.
Like that's not a hangover from slavery.

Tough love.
Rough land.
In colonized countries
men became more patriarchal
more domineering of their women.
Excluded from the public sphere
they became tyrants at home.
Wielding their power
In the domestic space.
My father bore all the features
Of that post-colonial male.
King of his own castle
And a black king
Can be every bit as wicked
As a white one.
No longer colonised by Britain
But still marginalized by her ...
But the Commonwealth
enabled this diversity (*gestures to band and audience*)
Humanity. Equality. Destiny
And blame ... is just negative energy
We move forward.
We evolve.
And we forgive.

Tommy's Song

Lou Prendergast

Scene One

Tommy approaches the stage from the aisle between the audience's seats
SFX racing commentary
LFX warm wash

Me an ma da's in a bettin syndicate. At the bookies. Tenner each, we started wi, but I won thirty quid oan ma tod, an I split it wi him. He was dead chuffed. He says, 'aye, that's the winnings goin up, up up!'

Ach. Ma wee da's got lung cancer. I'm back at ma ma's the noo, helping them oot wi the hoose an that. I hung that wallpaper fur ma ma that goes up horizontal. I'm in her good books fur a change. I've never been ma ma's favourite person, you know? But she's ... luvin me the noo, so she is.

pause

They gied ma da wan o they motorized scooters. It gets him oot an aboot, but he disnae like people tae see him oan it. It's a sin. I nip roon the bookies an stick bets oan fur him. Me an' ma mate were gonny take um fishing, but he's no eatin.

LFX change as Tommy stands and performs on thrust

So I wiz up seein ma ex-burd. I wiz tellin her aboot the bookies. I says, see 'if that horse I backed that came third, had came second the day, we'd have won a coupla hunner quid. No bad, eh? Two hundred poun darlin!' She says, 'it didn't come second though.' I says, 'it could've though! She says, 'it didn't though, so what's the point in talking about it!' I says 'ach, see you, you're a bloody killjoy sometimes.'

I wiz up her hoose doin a bit o DIY fur her. I've laid ply on the flairs an noo we're startin the bathroom.

Between her an ma ma, everybody wants a piece o me the noo.

pats his chest with both palms

Yup. Tommy Boy's in big demand. Ach, it keeps me busy while I'm no workin. Otherwise I jist end up oan the computer all day.

I like tae spend quality time wi my ex. An she gets the stuff done that she canny afford tae pay fur. I wouldnae take money aff an auld pal – an ex burd? No way. Favour fur a favour but, she says she'll come tae ma ma's fur Christmas dinner. I'm pittin oan a big spread fur ma da. I'll need tae get cash fae somewhere. I telt ma da Christmas Day's oan me. He says,

© KONINKLIJKE BRILL NV, LEIDEN, 2022 | DOI:10.1163/9789004467927_013

'pigs might fly'. I says, 'I'll get a bit o work before then Da. An there's a boy that owes me money. He's been warned. It's time tae pay up.' I'm makin the dinner an aw – I'm some cook by the way. Trained as a chef. Loves ma cookin, ma ex-burd. She's a bit o a grubber though. I love watchin her eat, mmm ...

laughing, making a 'stuffing it in' motion

'Are you saying I'm fat Tommy?' I'll go, 'Whit? Not at all! ... yer jist ... cuddly!' See if I'd have said that tae ma wife, I'd have goat a boot in baws. But this burd, she's sensitive. Always take the bait.

I'm jist glad she talks tae me noo. Blanked me fur years, so she did.

LFX change to 'memory state' as Tommy sits on stage again

Aye, we were madly in love once. There's nae kissy-kissy stuff noo, but we're pals. I help her oot n that. She's good company, so she is. Ye can huv a conversation wi her. She's one in a million. An intelligent burd?

Ma da likes her an aw. She'll blether away wi ma da. It'll make his day if she's roon fur Christmas. I want ma da tae see me wi a wummin – always windin me up, so he is, about no huvin a burd. He's done it fae I wiz a wean.

pause

LFX change to a warmer state again on the next line

Anyway, she's stonin at the cooker makin square sausage. I says, 'whit d'ye fancy fur Christmas dinner then? I wiz gonny dae a turkey, an a ham an aw the trimmins? Roast totties, mashed totties, sprouts, carrots, gravy, cranberry sauce, Christmas pud fur efters? What you think?' 'Whatever,' she says. I says, 'don't sound so enthusiastic.' She says, 'I'm not getting myself excited Tommy, it might not happen.' I says 'whit? it's tae cheer up ma wee da!' She goes, 'do you forgive your stepdad then?' I said nothing. I forget she knows stuff aboot me. She says, 'you should try talking to him, give him the chance to apologise, make amends, before ... well, before that's not an option anymore.' She thinks she's ma therapist. I says, 'that wiz a long time ago! Me an ma wee da's good the noo.' She says, 'but you were just a little boy.' 'Different days darlin,' I says. 'An men don't talk like that. I jist want a nice family Christmas, wi nae hassels. Like the Christmas adverts, when the whole family are aw at the table the gither, eatin and chattin and an everybody's goat their Christmas hat oan? Ma da'll love a Christmas day like that.'

I says, 'it's goat tae be a good wan. It's gonny be his last, darlin.'

'that's a shame, she says. D'you want tea?' 'You nothin stronger?' I says. 'Did I no leave some bevvy in your fridge the last time?' 'It's half past ten in the morning,' she says. 'I'm a guy darlin. Drinkin's whit we dae.' She thuds a can o Strongbow doon beside ma roll an sausage. 'Alkie'.

pause

She says 'Is that how it's going to be on Christmas day, drinking from the morning? That'll be a recipe for disaster.' I says, 'obviously I'll be huvin a drink oan Chritsmas day! Anyway, you like your drink an aw lady. She says, 'I never had much choice when I was seeing you!' I says, 'naw, naw. Whit aboot oor whisky day?' I spots a wee smile creeping at the corner of her lips. 'Oh yeah,' she says, 'I made spag bol, steaming drunk.' I says, 'Aye. Tomato sauce up the wall, onion skins all over the floor.' We laughed. I says, 'dancing to Elvis ...

LFX change as Tommy sings

blue Spanish eyes, teardrops are falling from your Spanish eyes ...

LFX change back to previous state

She smiled. 'Your song ...' she says. 'I've not heard that for a while.' She's nice like that. When she isnae bustin ma baws. Like when I first met her. She loved me tae bits (looks Spanish, so she does – dark hair, blue eyes). I says, 'you used tae go, 'sing me your song, Tommy', when you were pished. I'd grab you roon the waist and twirl you aboot the living room ...

LFX change as Tommy sings

this is just adios, and not goodbye ... please, say si! si!, say you and your Spanish eyes will wait for me ...

LFX change back to previous state

'Oh shoosh! I sobered up,' she says. I says, 'aw, you blushing lady?' She started laughin. I says, 'that's better. Show's yer wee happy face.' She drew me a dirty look. I says, 'you're getting jowls. Ye better stoap making faces like that – everything's going south.' 'Oh yeah,' she says. 'you like them young now don't you?' I says 'aw don't be bringing her up again. She's dumped.'

pause

'you still goat that Elvis CD? Bring it tae ma da's and we'll get a wee dance on Christmas day. 'I wont be dancing in front of your dad,' she says. 'I'd be too shy!' 'Shy?' I says. 'You wurny shy at your fortieth ... you niver sat doon!' She says, 'until you got barred.' I says, 'ach, how do you only remember the bad bits? Did I no make it up tae ye back at the hoose?' She smiled. 'You really did,' she says. 'I got out the taxi with my pals and saw that

LFX a light flashing on and off on Tommy's face

big star flashing on and off in the window.'

LFX change back to previous state

I'd been doin ma secret squirrel while she wiz oot. Hung fairy lights aw ow'er her hoose. 'An don't forget the live entertainment,' I says. 'As if,' she says, 'that scene's etched into my memory forever. You and your two daft mates wearing nothing but the thongs you'd found in my underwear drawer,

standing in a row singing Elvis.' 'Good times.' I says. 'We'll have a laugh at
Christmas an aw.' 'Hmm,' she says. 'The good times didn't last long after *that*
party though, did they? I spent the summer visiting you in Barlinnie.' She
hud tae spoil the moment.

LFX change to 'memory state'

She's still bearing a grudge cause it wiz the day before we were movin in the
gither. We hud a tiff cause I widnae leave the pub tae come an see the new
flat wi her. She wiz jist signin the lease. It wiz aw in her name – I widnae o
passed the credit check – she didnae need me there! She says that wisnae
the point. She wanted me tae show commitment. Be supportive. I said, 'fuck
this darlin. If aw yer gonny dae is nag me, I'm gawn back tae the pub. I lifted
the keys fur the work's van. She shouts, 'you're not drivin that van drunk
Tommy!' Tries tae wrestle the keys aff me. 'Get Tae fuck'. I speeds away, hits
traffic at Great Western Road and skids intae a black hack. Guess who wiz in
it? Four plain-clothes cops. That wiz it. Four months in the pokey. She says
ah sabotaged my ain happiness. Lot o pish.

pause

LFX change back to previous state

I says, 'your face – that you in a bad mood noo?' She says, 'I'm sick of living
in a building site.' 'It'll no take me long, darlin,' I says. 'Uh-huh, once you're
actually here,' she says. 'It's the days you don't turn up.' I says, 'Your personality's changed a lot darlin.' 'Oh?' 'No bloody wonder', she says. I says, 'you
used to be fun.' 'Don't start,' she says. 'You drained me when we were going
out.' I says, 'how did I drain you?' She says, 'you drained me physically, emotionally, psychologically and financially. That's how.' I love windin her up, so
I dae. 'Something amusing you?' she says. I says 'No.' She says 'Gimme that
tea-towel. I'll finish drying these and we'll go to B&Q.'

LFX change with the character's location change to outdoors

In the motor I telt her she'd be cheaper up the Barras. So, we're in Bill's Tool
Store an she lifts a tube o Pollyfilla. I says, 'don't get Polyfilla darlin – it's crap.
I picked up a packet o stuff you mix yersel. I says, 'here, get this. We use this
in the trade.' An she's arguing wi me, in front o the wee wummin behind
the counter. I says to the wummin, 'I'm a painter and decorator darlin, and
she still think she knows best!' The wummin smiled an gied me the change.
Nice wee wummin. Reminds me of a prostitute I hud a thing wi in Spain.
Ootside she goes, 'my change, please!' wi the paw held oot. I laughed and
handed it ow'er. 'No flies on you today,' I said. 'No,' she says, 'I learned the
hard way. Get in the car.' 'Gies the keys then,' I says. 'Don't even go there,' she
says. I've goat a lifetime ban, it's a fair shout. She says 'we'll get stuck into this
bathroom as soon as we get in, right? You've been fed and watered. No more

interruptions.' Then she goes: 'Seriously Tommy. I need the bathroom put back before Christmas. I've got family coming.' I says, 'Relax, darlin.

points to himself with both thumbs

Big Tam's on the case. An Christmas is still a month away.' I like tae spin the work oot. Gies me an excuse tae go back.

We're nearly hame when ma mobile goes. Wee Tariq. He's been at a burd's hoose fur three nights. I wiz winding him up. I says, 'you hud the same knickers oan fur three days ya dirty wee bastard?' 'Aye,' he says, 'It's awrite but, I turned them inside oot.' Pissin masel laughin. Turns oot he's in the Partick Tavern. 'See you in five minutes, buddy,' I says. She spins her heid roon like a scene fae the Exorcist. 'In case you've forgotten,' she says, 'we're on our way back to finish a job!' I says, 'I've no seen ma wee pal fur ages darlin. I'm huvin a pint wi um.' She forgets I'm the gaffer. Next minute she's pulled ow'er. Starts shoutin and cursin. I says, 'don't swear darlin.' I hate tae hear a burd swearin. 'You never could refuse a bloody pint,' she says. 'Get out my car!' Leans across me, opens ma door, and paps me oot at Charin fuckin Cross! (2049)

LFX change to transition between scenes in time with music
SFX Elvis – Spanish Eyes

Scene Two

LFX back to original warm wash

Ma wife's efter money. We separated years ago, but we're still in touch. I says, 'I'm tryin tae get money masel darlin, fur the Christmas dinner. I've aw the booze tae buy. I'm treatin everybody.' 'Lucky them!' she says, 'whit aboot me? You still owe me £300.' I says, 'you're no still gawn oan aboot that hoaliday, are ye? That wiz years ago!' She booked us a 'make or break' trip tae Goa but I never goat my passport sorted. I niver gied her the money fur the flight, an it wiz too late tae refund ma ticket. She says, 'I made you a same-day passport appointment and you never fukin showed up.' I says, 'don't swear darling.' She's a nippy sweety ma missus. Widnae be the first time she's lamped me wan. I said, 'I'd been up aw night neckin eccies! I could hardly see straight, niver mind walk or talk. 'Aye well,' she says. 'It wiz you that fucked up. An I've waited long enough.' I says, 'I'm owed money an aw darlin. Fae that arsehole. An I'm no aboot tae hand ow'er cash fur a holiday I never went.' 'Aye!' she shouts 'I hud tae go ma self!' I says, 'ye made pals, fur fucksake! What's wrong with you?' Kicked me oot the minute she goat back, so she did. She's a pain in the arse (Sexy but. Big tits. Nae hips). I sent her a text last night when I wiz drunk. She sent me back a pound sign. I didnae appreciate it. Pound sign. Cheeky cow.

laughs

There's cash comin but. Thank fuck. Price o turkey these days! Aye. Tariq goat us an interview wi Amazon. They want mair staff fur Christmas. Big warehoose oot in Fife. They pit a bus oan. We've done aw the assessment tests. Long as they don't Disclosure check, or we're fucked. I met Tariq in the jail. Six year I done. Tariq wiz ma wingman in there. He hud ma back. Be a laugh workin' wi um. An a need the dosh. It's Christmas in three weeks. Time's marchin oan.

I've no heard a word fae 'Miss I want ma bathroom done before Christmas' since she papped me oot the motor. She's no gonny get her bathroom done before Christmas if she disnae come oot her huff before Christmas. She's blankin ma calls. I've been tryin her every day. Just the wan text message I goat aff her, sayin the stuff I made her buy tae plaster the cracks in the bathroom walls wiz fur outdoor, no indoor use. When she sanded it doon the bathroom wiz thick wi black cement dust. Noo the plughole's blocked. An the toilet's leakin. I didnae pit it back right, blah, blah. She forgets. I wiz doin her a *favour*.

Ma da wiz askin efter her the other day. I says, 'aye da, ye'll get a wee festive tipple wi her on Christmas day.' 'I thought ye hud a new burd?' he says, 'that young lassie that wiz in the hoose?' 'Naw,' I says. 'That's finished.' And gonny no mention her at Christmas.' He says. 'Your wife wiz oan the phone tae your ma the other day an aw. I canny keep up.' 'Aye well,' I says. 'The missus and the young burd are history. They hud their chance!' Ma da shakes his heid. 'Player,' he says.

I need tae get the Christmas kerry-oot sorted. Miss Bathroom likes her Advocat, wi a splash o lemonade in it. Whit d'ye call that again? – a Snowball. Aye. A Christmas snowball fur ma Spanish senorita. Talk aboot the good times. Stick the king oan – here! I wonder whit Elvis had fur his Christmas dinner. I bet big Gladys heaped his plate. That wiz Elvis' ma, Gladys. Ma ma canny cook. But Elvis' mammy? She fucking loved um. Even slept in the same bed, him an Gladys. Aye. Christmas day. Happy families. Like the M&S advert. Canny wait. Show ma da we can be normal. I can be normal. Wi a lassie there ... a nice lassie tae, wi manners an –

LFX change to more dramatic state

fuck!

pause

We were getting oan so well tae! – she said she wanted the bathroom done before Christmas, then she blanks ma calls! Just because I wanted a pint?

quieter

Wummin, eh?

Fickle as fuck.

Between the Missus and Miss Bathroom – psychos, the lot o them.

pause

LFX *change to 'memory state'*

Ma ma. She's beginning tae faw apart at the seems. It must be forty years she's been wi my da – I was jist wee when they goat the gither. I wiz in the garden the other day and I spots ma ma an da through the windae. She wiz fixin his hair. They're no affectionate in front o people, but I spied them. She wiz lookin up at him, sortin him oot. The look o love between them said it aw. Brought a tear tae ma eye.

LFX *change back to original state*

She niver looked at *me* like that.

She's worried she willnae get tae spend Christmas wi um. I says, 'ma, ma da's hingin oan. Look at that fucker Megrahi. He hung oan fur years!' She goes

makes tutting noise

He's still no eatin, but. Ma ma's trying tae get um oan they wee drinks. Eleven hundred calories in they wee bottles. Aw ye need fur the day. But he disnae like them. Shame he missed the fishin tae, he wouldv've goat a laugh.

I wiz tellin um, we wur on the boat aboot 100 metres oot, and there wiz a bunch o rowdy boys fishin oan the bank, drinkin Bucky and huvin a laugh. We gied them a wave an that, an we're aw shoutin funny shite back an forward. But when we started up the engine, I noticed we were towing somebody's fishing rod ... so we pulled it in and here's this fifteen-and-a-half pound pike on the end of it – big fucker! It must've been one of they boys had caught it, then oor boat caught their rod! It wiz aboot a hunner's poun worth o fishing tackle, so we sped up and fucked off before they noticed! I ran in tae tell ma da when we goat back, tell um aboot the size o that fish! Know what he said? 'I don't believe you.'

I says, 'Da. I'm tellin ye whit happened.'

But naw.

'I don't believe you.'

See, when I wiz a wean I woulda goat a crack fur that.

Fur tellin lies.

pause

So the mair ma ma worries aboot ma da, the mair she nags me. She says, 'you're oan that computer aw day long Thomas. Whit ye lookin at fur oors oan end?' I'm Googled oot ma nut, tryin' tae stay oot your road! She says, 'how ye no oot doin that lassies hoose?' 'Ach,' I says. 'We fell oot.' 'Again?!'

says ma ma. 'Whit did ye dae this time?' Everything's ma fault wi ma ma. 'I'll
sort it,' I says. 'She'll be here on Christmas Day, don't you worry.' 'You better
finish painting that woodwork then,' says ma ma, 'the lassie'll be talkin aboot
us.' I said 'I need tae sand it doon first mum. I'll dae it efter I've signed oan.'
I jumped into the bettin shoap on the way roon tae Jobcentre Plus. I stuck
my last fiver oan. Trying tae get another result fur ma wee da. Cheer um up
again. Fuckin thing came last. Last! Anyhoo, I'm at the front o the queue an
as I'm walkin up to the burd behind the desk, I clock this fat security guard
parkin his sel beside her. She starts telling me I've not to sign on. I won't be
getting any benefit. I didn't fill in the form properly. The bit that asks whit
you've done tae find a joab – I only pit seven things doon. An that wisnae
enough. I says, 'I'll write doon mair things the noo – gies the pen darlin.'
Nope. She wisnae huvin it (Pakistani. Beautiful tae). She says ma money's
been stopped. I says, 'I've a Christmas dinner tae buy darlin. Ma da's no well.
I need ma benefit.' She says, 'you can appeal, but it takes weeks, especially
with the holidays coming up. 'Magic,' I says. 'That'll be Austerity then, thank
you very fuckin much.' Now, fat boy must've known whit the burd wiz gonny
say. He's came up in case I kicked aff. Dunno what use they think Fatty
Boombatty would've been. He wouldnae have stopped me before I jumped
the desk and strangled her – I see him in the bookies aw the time, serious
gamblin habit, that boy – not that I would. Strangle her, I mean. I don't hit
burds. That young burd I wiz hingin aboot wi, she's been telling people
I tried tae kill her. She wiz batterin me ow'er the heid wi a big pan!
I only put ma foot across her neck fur fucksake.

demeanor changes

tone becomes quieter, menancing

LFX *change back to previous more 'dramatic' state*

Right. This is serious. Canny be skint fur Christmas. I'm gonny need tae track
doon that aresehole that owes me money. He's done a bunk again. I spotted
um in the toon the other week, walking right towards me. I says tae masel,
'thank you god. Somethin's finally goin

claps his hands into prayer position

right fur me'. He sold ... well, 'stuff' I gied him, then fucked off wi ma money!
I wiz kicking doors in, lookin for the arsehole. Vanished fur months, so he
did. An there he is, like a mirage! He sees me comin and stops dead. Frozen
to the spot in the middle o St. Enoch Square. People everywhere – I could-
nae even punch um. I grabs um by the collar. The face goes grey. I yanks him
doon onto the bench. Captured! 'You. You bastard. Where's ma money?' He's
agreed to pay me fifty quid a week. I says, 'You better pay up, or I'll be passing

on the debt.' 'What does that mean?' he says. I telt him a coupla boys wid take him away in a motor an! ... well. Anyway. Treatin me like a prick.

An Miss Bathroom? Still no answerin her phone! I swung by her hoose last night. Tryin tae carch her in. Nae joy, but. Place wiz in darkness apart fae the Christmas tree in the windae.

LFX a light flashing on and off on Tommy's face again

She's annoying me noo. It's two-weeks tae the big day and she canny return a call. Where's the respect?

LFX change to transition between scenes in time with music

SFX Elvis – She's Not You

Scene Three

LFX back to original warm wash

swaggers on singing Elvis' 'She's Not You'

And when we're dancing
It almost feels the same
I've got to stop myself from
Whisp'ring your name

Fuckin result! God bless the bookies. Ma da gied us a coupla quid tae stick oan. It wiz jist wee bits tae get started, but I picked a winner in every line. The winnins built up, an I ended up pittin £100 oan a three-tae-wan shot – an goat £400 back! That wid get anybody's juices gaun. So while I'm waiting fur that tae get paid oot, I stuck a tenner oan a twelve-tae-wan shot, an it came in an aw! I wiz hardly in the door an the wummin gied me £530!

sings and dances again

Her hair is soft and her eyes are oh so blue
She's all the things a girl should be,
but she's not you ...

I glanced ow-er and spots that fat security guard sitting wi his eyes glued tae a race. I says, 'here, James Cordon,' see when you're back in the Joabcentre the morra, mind tell that burd she can stick her benefit where the sun don't shine. Tommy Boy no longer requires your services!

I phones Tariq. I says, 'get your wee toosh intae Oran Mor buddy, there's a pint sittin wi your name oan it! 'Whit we celebratin?' he says, 'did you hear fae Amazon?' I says 'Fuck Amazon!' We're celebrating Christmas. Santa's came a week early!'

Next call. Ma wee Da. Best call I've made in along time, so it wiz. Tellin um we were quids in. 'Ya beauty,' he says. 'Well done you!' It's no often you

get a 'well-done' fae ma Da. Aye. He wiz ow-er the moon. I says, 'so that's
Christmas day paid fur. I think five hunner poun should cover it don't you? –
fuckin ... Christmas A La Carte!' Pissin masel laughin. So wiz ma da. He says,
'an are we still expectin company of the female variety?' I says, 'da, I've telt
ye a hunner times she's comin.' I says, 'I'll see you when I'm hame. I'm gaun
fur a pint then I'm gaun food shoppin. Tell ma ma the good news!'

Third call. Miss Bathroom. It rings once then cuts aff. I tries it again. Rings
once, cuts aff. Whit the fuck? So I phones Three Mobile. I says, 'is that a technical fault?' 'Actually no sir,' the guy says (Polite boy. Indian). 'The number
you are trying to reach has blocked your number.'

pause

LFX *change to 'memory state'*

Fuckin hell. Changed days. See when I wiz in the jail, oan remand, she used
tae visit me every day. Every single day. Then efter I wiz sentenced, she'd
come tae aw the visitin sessions. Used tae write tae me aw the time tae. An
pay in money fur ma canteen. Cheered me up so she did. Ma Senorita. Kept
me gawn. Noo she's blocked ma number?

She is a moody burd, but. Fell oot wi me the night I goat oot the jail. In bed.
Roarin and greetin. I says, 'Whit's up wi ye? Is it cause I'm no makin mad,
passionate love tae ye? I says, 'gies a break darling – I'm jist oot the fuckin
jail.' Wummin, man. They think yer a machine. Switch ye oan an aff when-
ever it suits them.

pause

LFX *change back to previous state*

Wan burd I canny get a haudae; another wan I canny get riddae. My mis-
sus. I'm sittin oan the computer last night an she phones. I says, 'you're up
late.' 'I know,' she says. 'I hud a coupla hot Buckies an I canny sleep.' I says,
'Buckfast in the hoose, ya rebel?' She says, 'naw, at the theatre.' I says, 'ootae
somebody's hawf bottle?!' She says, 'naw! they sell it at the bar.' I laughed.
Bucky at the theatre. 'Of the mulled variety I'm supposin?' 'Aye,' she says.
'Hot Buckie. It wiz rank.' I says, 'mulled wine, whit weirdo thought that up?
She says, 'probably some German.' I says, 'I'm gonny Google it.' She says,
'anyway, I didnae phone you tae talk aboot mulled wine.' 'Aye awrite,' I says.
'Whit ye wantin?' She says, 'whit d'ye think I want?' I says, 'don't start digging
me up aboot money. I'm desperate masel darlin.' She says, 'not ma problem.'
I says 'listen cheeky chops, you know ma da's no well. First money I get's
gaun tae the Christmas party at ma ma's.' She says, 'an does your ma and da
know you still owe me money?' I says 'whit? whit's it goat tae dae wi them?'
She says, 'your ma's paid debts fur you before, maybe *she'll* gie me the money
you owe me.'

I hung up.

So I'm in the boozers wi Tariq an we're getting torn intae the hawfs. Havin a laugh aboot the jail. I says, 'whit aboot that time we wur in at Easter?' 'Aye,' he says. 'Did they no gie us a cream egg?' I says, 'they gied me a cream egg. I wouldnae a thought they gied you a cream egg. 'How no?' he says. 'I says, 'you fuckin requested the Halal menu. You canny huv it aw ways. You're either a Christian or Muslim.' Funny as fuck. 'Here! he says, 'did you hear aboot that boy that owes you money?' I says, 'do you know where that arsehole is?!' 'Aye!' he says. 'Where?!' I says. Don't get too excited,' says Tariq, handin me ow'er ma double whisky. 'He's in fuckin Thailand.' 'Bastard!' I says. 'Escaped again!' 'Aye,' says Tariq, pissin his sel laughin, 'but that's no the best o it ...' I says, 'how whit?' He says, 'he's fucked off wi that young burd you were seein!' 'Ach,' I says, 'that pair o pricks are perfect fur each other.' 'Get it up them!' says Tariq, clinkin ma glass. 'Get it up them,' I says. We laughed.

SFX Elvis – Peace 1

LFX change with the character's location change to outdoors

It wiz snowin when we stoated oot the pub. Tariq's jumped oan a bus, an I'm drunk drivin a trolley roon Iceland. 'Where's your turkeys darlin?' I says tae the wummin. 'The biggest bird you've goat.' I'm chuckin aw sorts o fancy stuff in that trolley – fozen peas, dream toppin, packets o sage n onion stuffin – bought aw the bevvy tae. I even remembered the Advocat fur you-know-who. I came oot there laden like a donkey and flagged a black hack. Tae hur hoose. Nae time like the present tae crack oot the snowbaws! She'll no be sayin 'it might not happen' noo – when sees aw this grub! She of little faith!

SFX Elvis – Peace 2

LFX change soft, sparkly, romantic state

As we draw up I can see her lights are oan. The front door opens and there she is ... an she's walkin doon the path towards me, smiling. Like an angel.

I wiz jist getting ready tae pay an she opens ma door. 'Hello,' she says. I coulda kissed her. 'Eh. Hello at last?' I says, 'it took you a while! Blocked ma number – whit's that aw aboot? She says, 'you're steaming Tommy.' I says, 'so will you be in a minute – look! fur the party next week. We're gonny huv a wonderful day, so we are.' I starts getting oot the taxi.

She says, 'Tommy. Stop. You're not coming in.'

I laughed. 'Aye, very good,' I says. 'Grab a coupla bags.'

'Tommy!' she says. 'You're not coming in. And I'm not coming to your dad's. She leans her heid in, and says, 'take him home, driver.'

I says, 'woah! Wait a minute here ...'

pause

I says tae hur, 'ma wee da's dyin darlin.'

She says, 'I'm sorry Tommy. I'm seeing somebody.'

An she shuts the taxi door.

SFX Elvis – peace 3

LFX change back to previous state

Ma ma's hoverin aboot the kitchen while I'm emptying the bags. I could tell she hud a bug up her arse. 'You're drunk Thomas.' Ma ma disnae drink. 'Aye mum,' I says. It's Christmas. That's allowed. 'your wife phoned.' 'And?' I says. She says, 'you've owed that lassie money aw that time? Fae that holiday she went?' I says, 'exactly. The holiday *she* went. I owe her nothin.' 'Shockin Thomas,' says ma ma. I says, 'Ma, gonny no start. I'm really no in the mood. No the night.'

I pour mysel a large wan and go up the stair tae the computer.

An jist this wan time – wan time an aw! – I'm lookin at a bit o internet porn. Next minute, the door gets flung open and there's ma da stonin. I tried tae shut it doon, but he could see! I wiz like, oh fuck, fuck! An I clicked the rang hing an made the screen bigger ... Aw man.

There it is.

pause

Two guys.

Cocks an arses everywhere.

pause

'Oh ho!' shouts ma da, 'I fuckin' knew it!'

I says, 'it's no whit ye think, da. I wiz jist lookin!'

'You,' he says, 'you're a fuckin' bender.'

I says, 'naw da – it's no whit ye think. Are ye no allowed tae look? I've no goat ma cock oot!.'

He says, 'is that how you've no settled doon? Is it wan o your bum chums fae the jail you're waitin fur!

I says, 'Dad. You know me. I'm no gay fur fucksake. I'm a man's man. I like burds.'

'Aye right,' he says. 'Now we know how ye canny keep wan – yer no man enough! Can ye no satisfy a wummin! Canny get it up?!

He says, 'nae wunner that lassie's fell oot wi ye.

She wiz scrapin the bottom o the barrel wi you anyway.

I flipped.

LFX change to 'dramatic' state of aggression

SFX Elvis – If I Can Dream

starts attacking the Christmas tree

I pulled ma fist back and smashed him in the mouth. His false teeth split. Blood spurted onto ma ma's good carpet. He staggered fae the blow and grabbed the back o a chair. I hit him again. And again. He bashed his heid aff the table and ended up on the flair. I goat this rush. This flashback tae him crackin me ow'er the heid wi a chair leg. I wiz aboot fourteen. He widnae stoap. I remember the pain wiz so bad a wid o jumped oot the windae to get away fae the cun. It wiz like we wur back there. Only this time it wiz me that widnae stoap. Sinkin the boot in. I wiz like a wild beast. Kickin an stampin. And kickin! And stampin! And kickin! And stampin!

SFX music out after applause on track
has violently pulled down a curtain and moves into the reveal space
LFX change to a cold wash we haven't seen before

Scene Four

LFX Gobo of prison bars on flat (back of cell) and shadow on floor

I spoke tae her oan the phone. Miss Bathroom. I'm waitin fur a letter fae her. There's mail sitting oan that screw's desk, but he canny be arsed. I asked him fur it, know white he says? 'The backshift can give it out.' Bastard. That's aw there is tae look forward tae in here, your mail. That fucker's sittin wi he's feet up oan the desk playing cards on the computer and there's guys gawn aff their heid waitin tae here fae their missus. Then the screw takes his time, opening the mail in front o the prisoner, to check there's nothing in it – some guys just lose the rag. The screw ends up getting pulled up and doon the landin by the hair, shoutin 'help!'. *laughs* Aye, mail's a serious business in here. Mine's due the day.

pause

The judge deferred sentence till they get the psychiatric reports. You should've seen the psychiatrist – he wiz aboot 12-year-auld! Big daft boy asking dafter questions. Draggin up stuff that's aw in the past. He even hud ma Primary School records aboot ma burst eye.

LFX change to previous 'memory' state

That wiz when ma da flung the saucer at me for running oan the carpet wi wet socks. Caught me right under that eye. Like a frizbee.

presses under his eye with his fingers

You can still feel it aw ragged there, where the bone chipped. It puffed up like a golf baw, so it did. I telt the school I fell. But mibbes they knew. I dunno. This young psychiatrist fella, he seemed to know, anyway. I telt um I didnae want tae talk aboot it. He says 'I'm trying to help you Thomas. Get your sentence reduced. The more the court knows about your background, the better.' I says 'my background? it wiz the same as everybody else's who grew up skint. There wiz two aulder, two younger than me. An ma da ran a tight ship. He was oot at the club drinkin every night. Ma ma never complained. He wiz the boss. We'd aw get lined up, the boys anyway, or pit ow'er ma da's knee and hit wi the slipper. Or the Jesus sandal. The guy doonstairs but, he was a Green Beret – we used tae hear they weans getting it worse! I telt the psychiatrist, 'we wur lucky!' He says, 'what about your mother?' Have you ever had a heart-to-heart with her about your childhood?' I says, 'whit?' I says, 'ma mum's no got a bloody heart. Sees the bad in everything. She'll go 'how come I've worked hard all my life and they're on the social and driving about in fancy cars?' That's her mentality.

She gets embarrassed cause I've been in the jail.

pause

She fuckin tried tae throttle me once!

pause

When I wiz a wean – a toddler. I canny remember it. She done a bit o time in the loony bin fur it. The psychiatrist says 'did you ever seek counseling for that?' I says 'counseling?' I says 'don't talk bloody stupit. It's no as if it's affected my life!'

Ma ma's finished wi me noo anyway. Santa disnae come tae bad boys. He didnae when I wiz a wean. And he's no gonny noo.

LFX change back to previous cold state
pause becomes introspective

That's me locked in fur the night. Time slows doon when yer locked up.

LFX fade to dark briefly and come up as character changes position
pause sighs through nostrils

Jist in, an I'm moanin like a lassie.

LFX fade to dark briefly and come up again as character changes position
pause bites thumb nail begins to sing under breath

... please don't cry ... this is just adios, and not goodbye ...

LFX fade to dark briefly and come up as character changes position
missing out a few lines

... say you and your Spanish eyes will wait for me

LFX change back to original cold wash

I've pit ma name doon fur a joab in the kitchen. I learned the chefin workin in hoaliday camps, when I first left hame. Blackpool, I went tae. Then off-season I'd work in hotels. I've worked in the kitchen here tae. I know the ropes. The best joab in the jail but, is a pass-man, but. Cushy wee number. I hud that joab the last time I wiz in when I wiz banged up fur drink drivin.

The powers that be leave the pass-man tae deal with the new comers. So they don't need tae dae it. You get them their stuff, their beddin and toiletries an that. Show them the lay o the land. Make sure they're awrite. Some o the young boys canny handle it. You've goat menial duties in the hall. You get the keys tae the store cupboard. You even clean the screw's office. Aye. They only gie that joab tae prisoners they trust. I hud the run o the place, so I did. But the kitchen's a laugh tae. That'll dae me. If I get through the interview.

I've goat ma gym pass noo. I went this mornin. Did ma induction. I reckon I'll get workin oot four, five days a week. It'll no take me long tae get in shape. I've goat good, eh ... whit d'ye call it again? muscle memory! I've goat good muscle memory. I've pit ma name doon fur the Bar L barbers an aw – there's a twelve-week waitin list, but. Twelve weeks! I'll be like a yeti by then ... fuckin ... Chewiebacca.

raises both arms and makes a Chewbacca noise

Naebody'll regognise me. Nah. Somebody wid always regocnise me in here. Everybody knows me. I've been in and oot Barlinnie like other people come and go fae Benidorm. The screws aw know me. I'm a *pats chest with both palms* bit o a legend. The wan the teacher ran away wi. My wife. I met her in here. She wiz teaching me a marketing module. Ended up shaggin in the cell. Wouldnae get away wi it noo. When I got oot, she came wi me. Chucked the joab. We got married up Park Circus. Ach. We were young. She says I wiz a nightmare. She's probably right. Says she didn't realise I wiz institutionalised when she fell in love wi me. Institutionalised. Talks some shite, so she does.

I said tae her tae pit her name doon fur a visit. We could get a cup o coffee. Fur auld times. She says, 'I don't think so.' I says, 'Calm doon darlin. It wiz only a cup o coffee.' I mean, the visitin area's awrite in here. Done like a cafeteria. Roon blue tables an benches. Wee weans don't even know they're in a jail. You can get tea, coffee, juice. Polystyrene cups right enough. An you've tae keep the lid oan or the screws will be over like a shot. There's nae sharin food or drink wi yer visitors. In case somebody spits drugs in it. Or a razor blade. Ye can buy sandwiches. Cheese savoury ... ham an tomato. Quite cheap an aw. Anyway. The missus knows aw that. This is her auld work, int'it? She coulda popped in. She's lucky I'm talkin tae her efter that shite she pulled phonin ma ma about money. Cheeky cow.

Funny as fuck, but. Turns oot she's been working as a dominatrix. Wee Tariq spotted her oan the Internet. Wi a whip, standin in a pair o spiky thigh high boots. I thought she might deny it, but naw. 'Aye,' she says, 'I done it fur years. Made a right good livin aff it.' She's just sold her dungeon. Made a packet.

Hud customers fae aw ow'er, flyin into Glesga fur a session wi her. Says it
wiz therapy. Every blow she struck was meant fur me. Fifty Shades o Black
n Blue.

laughs

gets his mail

Oh ho. I think I know who's writing this is ... Miss Bathroom -

'Soon, I'll return, bringing you all the love you're heart can ho ...'

aw she's sent me a Christmas card ...

smiling, opens the card, unfolds the letter inside it and reads it out:

LFX change to more 'dramatic' state

Stop phoning me Tommy.

Oh here we go. Nice way tae start a letter.

You let me down badly with the decorating. I had to finish that bathroom
myself. I should have known. You've never been reliable ...

But what you did to your dad! How could you?'

How could you? She fuckin knows he's pit me doon aw ma life.

That Culpable Homicide charge, you always said it was self-defense: 'him or
me.' But a defenseless old man Tommy? I won't be visitin this time. Won't be
driving to Riddrie in rush hour. Or sitting waiting with the junkie wives. Or
opening my mouth for the prison officers to search – as if I was guity!

Oh exclamation marks! She's oan wan noo ...

I don't want anything to do with you. Stay out of my life'

Stay oot my life?

LFX change back to original cold wash

Happy fuckin Christmas to you too lady.

She wiz the cause o it tae.

I mean, it wiz when he brought her in tae it ... I jist fucking – I jist loast it.

pause

The judge says it wiz a sickening attack. He says given the victim's age and
medical condition, this assault posed a serious threat to the victim's life.

pause

He disnae know ma da.

I hear the auld yin wiz back oan his scooter the day efter he goat oot the
hospital. Away roon the bookies.

pause

It's been good the last coupla years tae.

Father and son stuff. The bookies. A pint. Fishin. ...

... castin aspersions on a heterosexual guy but – a womanizer – that wiz the
last straw that broke the camel's back.

I wiz only lookin.

I'm a man fur fucksake!

Guys'll look at anythin –

Disnae mean yer gonny dae it.

Ach I'm stuck in this shithole fur Christmas noo.

An ma ma's oot there murdering the turkey.

Gobble fuckin gobble.

Here! if I get ma auld joab back in the kitchen, it'll be me that's makin the Bar L Christmas dinner. Yip. Tommy boy serving up the turkey. An aw the trimmins – roast totties, mashed totties, sprouts, carrots, gravy, cranberry sauce, Christmas pudding for dessert. We pit it oot oan big servin trays an wheel them oot wi the plates and cutlery. The men come oot an wait in a queue, get their dinner and go back tae their cell. You even get a selection boax aff the guvnor, so ye dae. An you know whit the Christmas Kerry-oot's gonny be? ... Hooch! Aye. That'll be planked and fermentin away somewhere the noo. You jist get broon breed and a bit o yeast. An huners o sugar an fresh fruit – oranges, apples, raisins, whatever you can find an let it soak fur a few weeks. Wance it turns tae alcohol you drink it there an then. Blows yer heid aff. Back tae the cell pished. A very merry Xmas!

Ach Aye.

Christmas dinner in the cell.

Nae hassles.

Stick the King oan the CD player.

LFX change to original 'singing' state

Decorations of red on a green Christmas tree

Won't be the same dear, if you're not here with me'

And when those blue snowflakes start falling

That's when those blue memories start calling

You'll be doin' all right, with your Christmas of white

But I'll have a blue, blue blue blue Christmas

You'll be doin' all right, with your Christmas of white,

But I'll have a blue, blue, blue blue Christmas

lights up. Curtain call. After first bow, departs up aisle between seats before the audience leaves

SFX Elvis – Blue Christmas (song takes over from the actor)

AWKWARD: A Life in Twenty-Six Postures

Lou Prendergast

Characters

ONE, female or male
TWO, female or male
SHE, female
Character One and Two are of any age and race.
Character She is mixed-race, middle aged.

Cast

ONE
    Anna Leckey
TWO
    Laura Fahey
SHE
    Lou Prendergast

Scene One

ONE
    please listen carefully
TWO
    This is the unwrapping of a story.
TWO is removing the fabric shrouding that SHE is wrapped in, slowly revealing her human form
SHE
    This is love story. This story, 'a life in twenty-six postures' is the story of a search for love. I could have called it 'love in 26 Postures'
ONE
    but you might have thought you were getting the *Kama Sutra*.
SHE
    Maybe next show.

© KONINKLIJKE BRILL NV, LEIDEN, 2022 | DOI:10.1163/9789004467927_014

ONE

first is the breathing exercise, Pranayama Deep Breathing Good for your lungs and respiratory system

SHE

The first love of my life was my mother – whereupon exit from her womb, I took my first breath. Life begins – and ends, with a breath.

ONE

inhale, head down, arms up, start please Full lungs, Exhale, head up
ONE & TWO continue Pranayama for five breath. SHE stops after first two

SHE

My mother was a one-off. An artist. Ahead of her time.

My mum was doing yoga when other people still thought yoghurt was a bit weird. She had brass Buddhas, wooden elephants, albums by Ravi Shankar – never been to India right enough! But these Eastern influences must have crept into my consciousness too.

ONE

half Moon – Ardha-Chandrasana with Pada-Hastasana

TWO

arms over your head sideways, palms together
interlock the fingers
release the index fingers
thumbs crossed

SHE

My father was born and bred in Jamaica. White dad/black mum – same as Bob Marley. My grandfather was an Irishman. Now what he was doing in Jamaica in the ... 1920s? maybe? I don't know ... but I heard he was a soldier. An Irish soldier I've been told.

TWO

was he Catholic?/

ONE

was he Protestant?

SHE

Who knows! I never met my father's family. My parents separated when I was a child and although I saw him occasionally – I was fifteen the last time – I feel there are bits of me missing. Irish-Caribbean parts yet to be discovered. These two nations get along celestially, allegedly, with a love of music and liquor/and

TWO/ONE

the craic!

SHE

Now, I wouldn't want to fuel the stereotype of Jamaican men as drug dealers and pimps. So lets just call my dad ... em, what can I call my dad? an
entrepreneur! He and my mother matched each other's intelligence. But a
certain dysfunction, already in my mother's bones by dint of her alcoholic
parent – my other Grandfather, a Scot from Campbeltown – when mixed
with the patriarchal culture of the Caribbean, created a cocktail of conflict.
Sparks flew between them.

ONE

awkward pose – Utkatasana
right foot step to the right
six inches gap between toes and heels
don't change your feet throughout the entire posture
arms up parallel to the floor

SHE

It was the mid-sixties when my sister came along. I'm sure my poor mother
believed that the arrival of the first-born would mark the settling down of
my father. It didn't. And before anyone could quite get their head round
what was happening, I arrived. Precisely one year and one day after my sister. This play is my gift to her. Things between us are a little bit/

ONE/TWO/Awkward?

SHE

Awkward.
My love for her is unrequited perhaps – but this she would deny.
We were sibling soul mates once.

TWO

stand up on your toes like a ballerina

SHE

It wasn't neglect in the sense of nobody caring, no mistreatment, not cruelty.
Our parents were non-conformists: art, music, parties, psychedelic drugs.
It was the swinging sixties and sometimes someone ... would forget
to feed
us. Salivating at Danish Bacon adverts on black & white
TV. Alert to the rustling of wrappers like a little
dog, caught in a cupboard eating jam from the
jar, under the bed eating crusts. My
sister trying to boil eggs for us in the
kettle at 3/4 years old. She knew
the eggs went into the water. But

the kettle had boiled and the
eggs were still raw!

ONE

come up a little bit on the toes
bring your knees together
Turn your back while I take my medicine, one babysitter would say, sweet
and loving was she.
It was later in life,
that we realised
that the medicine
was heroin.
And then there was the grooming:
One of the gang.
Friend of mum and dad.
Paedophile.
Nobody knew.
Inappropriate conversations with him/

ONE/TWO

as giggling little girls
do you lie bare-naked with your girlfriend?/

SHE

knowing it was wrong, yet being encouraged. It went further with my sister. It was later in life, before she told. Of the awkwardness for her, at five-
years-old, when she had to see him again after their alone time; the sheer
embarrassment.

ONE

feet together, don't move

TWO

eagle pose – Garurasana!

SHE

My father's criminality was catching up.
His best friend was shot dead and he had to flee the city.
It was time to get out.
We would never live together as a family again.
My mother took us to her mothers'. From the streets of Glasgow to the pretty
countryside on the outskirts of Dunblane – a tied cottage, Grandma worked
for the farmer: glorious flower garden, bees and butterflies, milk from the
urn. A dog called Prince and a cat called Tabby.
Playing in the burn with my cousins.

Grandma's love was much more hands on. The fridge was always full. I never felt scared there.

Except for one time when my mum was going away somewhere and I asked her when she was coming back and she told me she might not come back at all! This thought haunted me.

Until the day she returned. And a life-long craving for my absent father's love ensued.

I really missed him!

Why didn't he miss me back?

TWO

standing Head to Knee – Dandayamana-Janushirasana
shift your weight to your left Leg
interlock your 10 Fingers and grab the right Foot
your left leg should be solid, concrete, one piece, lamppost, unbroken

ONE

continuously repeat quietly: solid, concrete, one piece, lamppost, unbroken

SHE

Granddad, and my older uncle drank to excess.

Quick-witted and amiable as the drink flowed.

An aunt and younger uncle lived there too –

this uncle didn't drink whisky and smoke Woodbine though. He played the drums and smoked those funny cigarettes like my dad. Everyone was musical! Guitar, banjo, ukulele: singing the blues.

Except Grandma.

she was a Londoner –

sings 'my old man, said follow the van!'.

continues to sing/hum the tune, moving round in close proximity audience

TWO

over the humming
inhale breathing: slowly, gently, right leg lift up and
stretch forward towards with all five toes turning in
if the standing leg is bending the posture has not started yet
kick your heel out, turn your toes in, try to get both legs locked
if both knees are locked, and still you can balance there comfortably
then only, you can bend your elbows down towards the floor
until your elbows are touching the calf muscle
eventually elbows should go down below the calf muscle

SHE

But there was conflict here too. The parties would sour. Someone would turn. I learned that family could be kind one day and verbally abusive the next/

ONE

don't dare talk when the football's on!

SHE

But they didn't terrify the house, the men, like
my dad had – they didn't brandish swords or chop
up
the furniture, didn't beat the dog ...
neither did they laugh like my daddy had.
My Grandma never shouted or swore at me in her life.
But others were changeable.
Falling out ... falling in, falling out.

TWO

standing Bow Pulling Pose – Dandayamana-Dhanurasana

SHE

In 1973, Blue Peter presenter, Valerie Singleton
- did she and Peter Purvis have a fling? -
came to Dunblane Primary School for the 'Plant a Tree in '73' Campaign.
A new love was developing here, a love of art. And that feeling you get when
others are 'loving your work.'
I'd painted a portrait of Valerie – 'is that me?' she asked me!
Twenty-three years later, Thomas Hamilton opened fire on that little
school.
My cousin's daughter was there that day.
In Primary one.
Her class ... was
not in the gym at the time of the massacre.
It would be several hours
before that was known for sure.

TWO

balancing stick – Tuladandasana

SHE

We couldn't live at Grandma's forever.

ONE

Your mum got her own house?

SHE

Yup. In Clackmannanshire. The 'wee county', as it's known.
Comedians make jokes about being poor:
'we were so poor, we lived in a shoe box,'
Well we were so poor we lived in a tin.
Prefabricated metal housing thrown up after the war.

ONE

Was it a bit chavvy then?

SHE

It was, an area of deprivation, yes.

And we were so different, on so many levels

ONE

What, you mean your mum?

your dad wasn't there?

Your dark skin?

SHE

Our hair!

And so the balancing act began, of trying to reconcile one's home life with one's environment, in order to fit in.

To be loved.

A little boy from the other school punched me in the face.

Have you ever been punched in the face?

ONE/TWO

No!

SHE

It's a shock to the system.

But we loved school. And school loved us back.

We were little black stars: 'half-castes' as people called us then.

So bright yet so poor.

The headmaster asked why we hadn't put our names down for the school trip, and we explained our dilemma: pocket money or school trip; and there was a comic I wanted to buy. He let us go for free. I liked him a lot. Until primary 7 when he belted thirteen of us for playing an innocent game of 'kiss, cuddle or torture'.

The love I thought I had from Primary School was now sullied.

I felt betrayed.

Maybe I'd find love at the big school.

lights go down, 30-second clip of 'Blackstar' by David Bowie fades u

Scene Two

TWO

standing separate leg stretching –
Dandayamana-Bibhaktapad- Paschimotthanasana

SHE

Taking seven O' Grades.

My mother got into college.

She wouldn't always come to parents nights – 'what's the point,' she'd say, 'they're just going to say A for this, A for that.'

Sorry to disappoint you mum.

And there were ruffians that I was attracted to

– an affliction that has stayed with me –

I wanted acceptance, to part of the crowd.

To be loved.

But the 'friendships' were not to be trusted.

The gang turned. I was bullied.

I began to drop subjects.

Or not go in at all.

My mother was accepted to Glasgow School of art. It was along commute, so she took a flat in Glasgow Monday to Friday.

My sister was sixteen, my legal guardian.

But we fought bitterly over dinners and housework, with no parental support. Mum would come home and complain.

About everything.

I sat my English O Grade, but didn't go in for the Art exam.

Until my art teacher turned up at my door and

practically dragged me up to school.

How wonderful of him, to

care.

TWO

Triangle – Trikanasana

SHE

It was an exciting time musically. When I was thirteen, my Punk Rock passion that I'd copied from my cousins gave way to Two-Tone. In monkey boots and a Crombie coat, I strutted through the Thistle Centre in Stirling, and caught the eye of a boy. The first date was sweet, holding hands in the cold. On the second date we were in a flat with his 15-year-old friends.

And they were drinking.

And he said casually that they'd been 'shagging'.

And I was mortified.

He was trying it on with me.

I fought and I fought!

His strong arm reaching down, fingers hooking under, I

used both hands to try and pull it away. He
was biting my neck, over and over.
I was wearing a leotard as a tee shirt;
he was trying to pull it up!
But that didn't work, and
he tried to pull it down!
And that didn't work and eventually he gave up
Jumped up.
And threw me out.
I was chucked.
Alone at the bus stop
mascara tears and *love?* bites
on my innocent neck, my
first crush ended
with virginity intact.
Saved by a leotard.

TWO

standing separate leg head to knee
Dandayamana-Bibhaktapada-Janushirasana

SHE

Sweet sixteen

ONE

Is this a cheery one?

SHE

Sort of cheery.
Summer holidays from school.
But I was going back to do my Highers, like my sister.
I was fairly committed to that, until I met Mr. M.
He was nineteen and ever so worldly.
He'd been up and down to London for a couple of years.
He said he could get work on a building site to keep us.
And did I want to go?
I went home and packed a bag.
Luckily my mum wasn't home, so
I left her a note/

ONE

What!

SHE

I heard she cried.

We didn't have a penny between us.
Hitchhiked down to Carlisle the first night
pitched a tent in the public park.

SHE

In London, he parked me in Centre-point, a homeless unit, until
he got us accommodation. He was too old to stay there.
But I wasn't like the others.
They frightened me.
I hadn't run away
I had just left home.
We got jobs and a lovely bedsit in South Ken with French doors.
I worked in the ice cream parlour in Harrods.
This was love.
But a controlling love.
There was no going out.
He was insanely jealous
and slapped me once.
Once was enough to
keep me in my place.

ONE

Cheery!

SHE

All I have left from that time in my life
is this David Bowie book from Kensington Library, which ...
 I appeared to have, ahem! forgotten to return

ONE

I guess that fine might be too large now.

TWO

tree pose – Tadasana

SHE

I stayed for a year but tired of his behaviour. I came home and got a job
in Pizzaland. My training was in Edinburgh and while there, a met a guy
I knew from Stirling that I'd always liked. Mr. T. was a much gentler person,
never aggressive to me. And we'd go out, to the Hoochie Coochie club on
Lothian Rd.
I was seventeen and clueless.
By the time we went home
I was pregnant.
Mr. T didn't really want to know,

or ... didn't really know what to do, maybe?

He never left completely. He would show up at my mum's, or I'd see him in town. No mobile phones then, no landline either. No running out to get me a tuna and banana pizza.

I had to make all the preparations myself.

He didn't come to see his son in hospital until he was two days old.

Didn't support us.

But he loved his son – still does – and we tried to make things work.

I got a house and put down roots.

ONE

Toe Stand – padangustasana

SHE

With my boy in nursery I got a part-time job,

selling sunbeds.

As soon as the boss saw my dark skin I was hired.

I was back in the world of work. I had choices.

I got a full-time job in telephone sales.

I was ambitious.

I wanted more.

I was bored of small-town mentality.

I found a job in Glasgow.

I was going home to the city!

I commuted for three months, dropping my son off at nursery before travelling to Glasgow, picking him up from his Nanas in the evening. I was making a transition.

This is always hard work.

But after three months,

I got a mortgage,

At 21-years-old a home, for my son and I.

No more disappearing partner-dysfunctional-love.

I wanted a functional love –

A love

Where we worked as a team.

One rainy day, I was stressed and rushing for an interview. I got caught in the middle of Hope Street

as the traffic lights changed. I lurched forward but

a car coming up the inside lane

caught my left hip. I was catapulted

into the air and landed

on the pavement. As I lay

there stunned and bruised, the driver stood over me and uttered the proverb

ONE/TWO

'more haste, less speed' dear'.

SHE

And I said, 'sorry'.

It taught me that I am merely flesh and bone.

It taught me that I needed to slow down and relax more.

We *all* need to relax more. ...

We're going to help you do that right now.

ONE

Dead Body pose – Savasana

To take us to the interval, I'm going to lead you through a relaxation technique. You are welcomed to come and lie down on the floor in the pose of savasana – lying on your back with your palms facing up. Alternatively you can stay seated, and take part in the relaxation from your chair. This meditation is called Yoga Nidra, or Yogic Sleep. It involves leading the bodymind into a state of consciousness between waking and sleeping –

a state of complete relaxation.

INTERVAL

Scene Three

As audience enter, David Bowie's 'Fashion' begins to fade down.

The performers are lying in the posture.

ONE

Wind Removing Pose – Pavanamuktasana

SHE

With no Higher education, I'd sold sunbeds and seafood, I sold wine and spirits and cigarettes. I got into recruitment and sold human resources. Finally, I moved to a contract cleaning company and was hired to develop their telemarketing operation. But it wasn't very sexy. Too much sales talk – hot air being blown. I needed a wind removing position. I found a way for people like me, without the require qualifications, to get into University, and signed up for an Access to Communications college course.

One teacher there showed great faith in me. She nurtured my creative talent and I discovered I could still write. Twenty-one years later, I wrote

and directed a play in which I cast a real-life lecturer from Strathclyde
University. We didn't know it then, but it turned out he is *that* teacher's son.
The Universe works in mysterious ways. Now he's written an academic tome
about Scotland and the Caribbean, in which my work is featured.

ONE

Yeah right.

So where can this book be found?

SHE

Right under there, as it happens (*points*)

TWO *reaches under the seat of an audience member, retrieves the book and reads
from a page in a lofty tone*

"Through a trilogy of plays, she has brought questions around race, gender and Caribbean slavery to the centre of the Caribbean stage for the first
time. She has written, directed and starred in plays related to her difficulties
locating her 'lost' father. The final installment represents and evocative *lieu
de memoire* that explores her ambivalent feelings about his 'dodgy dealings' and the shifting nature of power relations that characterise Scottish-
Caribbean relatio/

SHE *takes the book away from* TWO

SHE

Right. That's enough of that.

ONE

The hot air of Academia.

SHE

In 1993 I started Uni. I met a man I was attracted to. Mr. R dealt in toxic con-
sumables, and appeared to exude power. He was my friend to begin with. He
had a 'her indoors' that nobody had ever met. We rode around in his friend's
Mercedes Benz, as I had done as a child in my father's Merc, feeling same
sense of security.

We would go from nightclub to nightclub, not having to pay. I was with the
big boys now. One cocaine-fuelled night, we

crossed a line.

We had, a moment.

It was just before New Year.

It was a one-off.

I didn't see him afterwards – our association appeared to have ended.

I felt like I might be in love with him.

Weeks passed.

I missed him.

I also missed a period.

Or two.

all three do the Sit Up

SHE/ONE/TWO

Pregnant?!

SHE

I talked to my mother

ONE

But you're just in your first year of Uni – how will you cope?

SHE

It would be due in the holidays mum,

and there's a crèche on campus.

And I talked to my to my sister

TWO

If you go ahead with this, you'll need some support. I'll move in!

And I talked to my nine-year-old son

ONE

But what about the Dad?

SHE

It will still just be me and you – and the baby

ONE makes a happy, child-like gesture

And I spoke to the Dad

TWO

You know I'm involved in something else. I can't just walk away.

SHE

I know. I'm thinking of doing this on my own.

TWO

Well if you do it on your own, you're really on your own. You'll be setting yourself up for a lot of hurt.

SHE

And that's exactly what I did.

If it had hurt me that daddy number one took two days to see his son, daddy number two took two years to meet his daughter.

But when he did, we began a two-year relationship.

To enable our daughter to have that biological bond I craved so much, I left a relationship to pursue this connection.

That was a mistake.

He was a nightmare.

More controlling than my first love, his rage

was fierce and tumultuous.

He didn't need to hit me.

My fear was palpable.

ONE/TWO

Be careful what you wish for

SHE

As my mother used to say

SHE/ONE/TWO

For it will surely be yours.

TWO

Cobra pose – Bhujangasana

ONE

hands-palms flat on the floor

SHE

Mum had had a sore ankle that wouldn't go away.

ONE

you have one leg like a cobra, don't open it.

SHE

Mum woke up yellow with jaundice one morning.

ONE

inhale breathing, come up!

SHE

Mum was getting tests.

ONE

trapezius muscles visible

SHE

Mum had a tumor the size of a grapefruit in her pancreas.

ONE

chest up, chest up

SHE

Mum was given a year to live.

ONE

hold it there, freeze

SHE

Mum died on April 10th 1998 at the age of 53.

ONE

and gently come down

SHE

I got to say goodbye. (*quietly, with ear on floor*)

I got to say goodbye. (*coming up onto elbows, more happily*)

TWO

Locust pose- Salabhasana!
A birth often follows a death. My new baby
was my own Arts PR and events company called Firehorse –
that's my birth sign in the Chinese zodiac.
Firehorses are fabulous!

ONE (*dryly*)

Who told you that?

SHE

It's in the Chinese Horoscope book!
It's *so* accurate.

ONE

Where is it? (*sighing*)

SHE

Under there (*points*)

TWO reaches for the Chinese Horoscope book and reads the definition

TWO

"This is the leader of the herd, the alpha female or the magnificent stallion, well able to take on all potential opponents and quite willing to cross sword, intellectually of course/

SHE

of course/

TWO

"with almost any other Chinese animal type. There is passion, energy and adventure here in such quantities here to make less progressive types shudder just to observe. Although a good friend, anxious to please and very giving, the very essence of the Firehorse nature would *not* be ..."
oh!
"inclined to infer *loyalty*"/

SHE snatches the book away

SHE

You really can't take these things too seriously.
I threw myself into this new business venture, in an attempt to bury my grief. It was a time of socialising and of glamorous clients: theatre directors, artists and DJs: 'we're out and about and we know what's happening' my tag line read.
A journalist wrote a feature on this up and coming mover and shaker, who as a child, had shared a house in Glasgow's west end – 'a hippy commune' they called it – with Hollywood A Lister, Robert Carlisle. He'll always be Bobby to me. We loved him, my sister and I. He was always kind to us. I gave a mutual

friend a photograph to give to Bobby, of him and us. In 2012, my childhood pal emailed/

ONE

No he didn't.

ONE

Where is it? (*wearily*)

HE (*just points*)

TWO reaches for the printed out email and reads it

TWO

"I should explain that any image of me from the past is l gold dust. Reason being … all me and Dad's stuff, photos etc. were lost a long time ago. Abandoned in a left luggage department in some train station in the mid 70s. p until a few years ago I had absolutely no photos of me as a child at all. With the ones you have given me. … I've now got 4!! So, you can imagine the buzz w one turns up! I'm back at the beginning April and so look forward to meeting you then. So much to talk/

SHE plucks the paper from TWO's hands

SHE

Yeah.

He never called.

ONE

full locust – Poorna Salabhasana arms out to the side like airplane wings.

SHE

My son was 17. He'd left school and I was taking him to Jobcentre Plus. It was raining. My boyfriend, Mr. E, was waiting in the car. Before we got to the entrance, my son stopped me and said

TWO

Mum I've got something to tell you/

ONE

palms down and fingers together/

SHE

What is it?/

ONE

Chin on the floor/

TWO

I've got a boyfriend/

ONE

legs and feet together/

SHE

That'll be why there hasn't been any hint of a girlfriend for the last three years/

ONE

hip and leg muscles tight, solid, concrete, one piece/

SHE

Is this because I brought you up myself, as a single parent?/

ONE

knees locked, pointed toes/

TWO

No mum!

Don't YOU try and take the credit for MY sexuality/

ONE

make sure you only have one leg/

SHE

Did somebody interfere with you son?/

ONE

look up to the ceiling, take a deep breath/

TWO

No mum! Don't be daft/

ONE

arms body, head, legs, everything lift off – 747 taking off!/

SHE

Why didn't you tell me before?/

ONE

go up, everybody look up, chest up, arms up, arms back/

TWO

Mum you knew! You bought me a Robbie Williams video/

ONE

chest, up, chest up, chest up/

SHE

I thought it was his *music* you liked!/

ONE

exhale breathing come up one more time!

SHE

But he was able to tell me.

What a weight must've been lifted off him.

TWO

Bow pose – Dhanurasana

Love, from my mid-twenties until my late thirties, involved several two-year relationships – with Mr. K/Mr. G/Mr. R/Mr. E and Mr. S respectively.

Not at the same time.

Well … apart from a little bit of crossover between Mr. G and Mr. R. I'm not sure what Mr. K is doing now. We loved each other, but we threw it away. Mr. G is married with a couple of kids. That was love; but I threw it away. Mr. R., father of my daughter, I put *all* my love and energy into, but I *had* to throw that away. Mr. E has a baby now. He really loved me, but I also threw that one away. Mr. S has a couple of kids. We had loved each other too, but there was a big age gap and … well, true to form,

I threw it all away.

light's fade down. 30-second clip of 'Can You Hear Me' by David Bowie fades up

Scene Four

ONE

Fixed Firm pose – Supt-Vajrasana!

SHE

I got a bit burned out with Firehorse. Having to be out in the evenings. My son was looking after my daughter a lot and it wasn't fair. I needed a day job. I'd enjoyed the writing side of PR and I applied for a Postgraduate Diploma in journalism. Upon completion I got myself some casual shifts at the Evening Times. This was hard news: murders, fires and 'death knocks'.

That's the term we use when a reporter is sent to just turn up where someone has died, knock, and get their foot in the door. I was sent to a family whose little girl had died of leukemia on a trip to Lourdes. I was warned by the editor, not to come back without a photograph of the deceased child and some emotional quotes from the mother. I did my job. The next day the story made the front-page story – the Splash – as we called it. But it raised moral dilemmas for me.

Wasn't this just Capitalist exploitation of grief?

TWO

Half Tortoise – Ardha-Kurmasana

ONE

But didn't you go to the Daily Record after that?

SHE

I Did. But my role there was reviewing show homes. It was fun at first. But there was no love there. The show homes had no real substance. It was soulless.

ONE

Yeah. How many different ways can you describe beige?

SHE

Exactly. I had a new mortgage and a Mercedes of my own by then -
but happiness doesn't come through material possessions.

There were office flirtations, but sex without love is also superficial.

SHE

Mr. R, father of my daughter got in touch. After seven years he wanted to see
her. He was in India and sent the airfares.

It didn't go well. He was playing the disciplinarian Dad, as his dad had, and
my little girl didn't need that from him.

I was the worm that had turned.

No fear now.

We fell out.

But I'd seen a part of the world that I liked. Goa was a place I could go on my
own, but not be alone. And so began another enduring love affair – with my
beloved India; and with it, a new perspective.

TWO

Camel pose – Ustrasana!

SHE

I left the Record with hopes of working freelance, but my confidence soon
plummeted.

My self-esteem was on the floor and just then,

I met Mr. C.

I knew it wasn't a good idea, but like the proverbial moth to the fire, I had
a killer attraction to this wild, riotous risk-taking charmer who took my
breath away.

TWO

listen very carefully, word by word
stand up on your knees

SHE

Generous to a fault and inconsistent as hell

he was kind to my daughter/

ONE

always fighting my corner when I got into trouble!

SHE

We decided he'd move into mine. But the night before, we had a fight.
I couldn't get him out the pub. He came home drunk and we rowed. He
grabbed the keys to the works van, jumped in and sped away.

TWO

take a deep breath

SHE

The following morning I received a call from the police station.

ONE

Caught drunk driving.

And not for the first time.

He won't be coming home.

SHE

I slid down the kitchen wall and cried.

Four months I spent, visiting my love in Barlinne prison, taking to his lawyer, sending him cash for the canteen, accommodating his dad and other family members. I bent over backwards.

We spoke on the phoned he'd write me letters ...

TWO

drop your head back and grab your heels

TWO reaches under backwards and grabs a letter from beneath an audience member's chair

TWO

Is this one of them I spy under here?

TWO comes out of posture to read the letter. SHE and ONE stay in the pose

"Hello beautiful. I loved speaking with you today. You make me feel great and wanted and loved, when you've got your positive head on. I don't want you to be feeling insecure anymore. There's absolutely no need for it my wee darlin'. I just love you to bits – and for a million reasons. You'll see for yourself once I'm outa here. You will f like one of the most loved women alive. I've been in this wee trance most of the day, thinking about some of the things that I like – and love – about you: I like it because you are smart and we have good conversation. I love your honesty and your thoughtfulness. I love your smile. I love it when we dance slowly when we're alone together. I love you when you say my name when we/

SHE

Okay! That's enough of that thank you!

SHE comes out of the pose and grabs the letter (ONE remains in the pose)

I arranged a holiday for when he got out/

TWO

continuously keep pushing, don't stop pushing/

SHE

but he didn't get his passport sorted/

TWO

everybody push, push more, everybody push harder/

SHE

It was the final insult/

TWO

360 backward bending for gravitation/

SHE

It was over.

beat

ONE

Rabbit pose – Sasangasana!

SHE

2006 was a new beginning.

I was soul searching, to see what I might be. I thought back to what I'd been good at naturally.

I would study art!

Back to college and into Glasgow School of Art

– as my mother had done –

with a portfolio of work about my incarcerated lover.

ONE/TWO

Saved by art!

SHE

Training in sculpture meant working with materials that seemed to be having an adverse affect on my joints. strange symptoms ensued.

Undiagnosed for a couple years, I finally find out I had an autoimmune disease.

A few diseases actually, including Lupus, which affects the skin and the joints and the organs.

Own body attacking own cells, as if they were invaders.

What's that all about?

Alternative health theories suggest that being overly s

self-critical is key.

I started meditating.

I started doing Bikram Yoga.

The heat really helped me/

ONE/TWO

Saved by yoga!

ONE

head to knee with Stretching – Janushirashana with Paschimotthanansa

SHE

If you keep bending backwards, you can't move forward. I started to focus on my forward bends. I needed to get to know myself a little better. I did a Masters course, then went straight into a PhD in playwriting.

I was becoming a luvvie.

ONE/TWO

Saved by theatre!

SHE

Meditation brings self-realisation.

I wasn't cut out for call centres and death knocks.

I was attracting the wrong people because

I felt wrong about myself.

The lure of sex and drugs and rock 'n' roll was waning.

If I couldn't be loved and respected, I wouldn't be giving my body away.

Meditation teaches *com*passion, not passion.

And since 2012,

I chose celibacy.

TWO

spine Twisting – Ardha Matsyendrasana

SHE

I started doing Vipassana

10-day silent meditation courses, to help me get onto my true path.

Now, everyone's on their own path,

you can't control anybody else's.

And while my sexual activity was taking a break,

my 18-year-old daughter's was just getting going/

ONE

turn around and sit facing the left side of the room
bend your left knee on the floor, left knee facing the left side mirror
put your right foot exactly over the left knee corner
h-E-E-L, your heel should touch the knee. Foot flat on the floor
both hips should touch the floor comfortably
to keep your spine perfectly straight, perpendicular, 90% angle
hips touching the left heel. Point your left toes/

SHE

the boyfriend she'd had since 14, no.1, she had finally split up with, and started dating no. 2. Both boys were raised with the usual inner-city issues around exposure to drugs and violence and a lack of self-confidence and education. My daughter, like her mum and grandma before her, has a penchant for a bad boy/

ONE

bring your left arm over the right knee, elbow exactly against the knee
push your knee back, with the help of your left elbow
turn your wrist, and grab the left knee, with your left hand
now, look down. Make sure your knee, hand, and the heel
all three things touching each other, at the sane spot, on the floor/

SHE

No. 2 got involved in an assault and ended up in a young offender's institution. And during this time, my daughter, it turns out, was pregnant. After the shock I asked her if she'd told no.2, which she hadn't, because the baby was a result of a one-night stand with no.1 while 2 was inside! The repetition of family patterns!/

ONE

stretch your spine up towards the ceiling
right arm on your back, palsm facing out
try to grab the thigh behind you with your right hand fingertips
chest up, spine straight, rib cage open
inhale lift up, exhale twist
lift up, twist,
twist, twist, twist/

SHE

No.2 was devastated as you can imagine.
But then something beautiful happened.
These two young people talked openly and honesty to each other, and no.2 pledged to raise no.1's child, as his own. And now they are raising their THREE children together. I have three grandkids. The boys are still babies, but the bond with my granddaughter?
Now that really is *love.*
And just like my Grandma, I'll never shout or swear at those kids.

TWO

we started with the Pranayama Breathing Exercise, good for the lungs
we end with another Breathing Exercise, Blowing in Firm Pose

SHE

In 2014 I travelled to France to see my sister, I had an awkward altercation with her controlling partner at the train station, and didn't see *her* at all. This hurt me deeply. It caused a rift with my son, who then stayed with her,

and said partner, even though I wasn't welcome. Well. It is his auntie. She
had been with me just six weeks previous and we performed a play together.
When the physical demands of the work met the emotional pain of the conflict, my bodymind attacked itself with relish/

ONE

Breath. Pain-Breath/

SHE

My breath so shallow/

ONE

Breath. Pain-Breath/

SHE

a clot of red blood

ONE

Breath. Pain-Breath/

SHE

blocking the oxygen

ONE

Breath. Pain-Breath/

SHE

to my right lung/

ONE

Breath. Pain-Breath/

SHE

Every inhale/

ONE

Breath. Pain-Breath/

SHE

Puffing out/

ONE

SHE

Breath. Pain-Breath/Stopping.

beat

SHE

No.

TWO

blow out by your lips very strong, pull your stomach in and out
no inhale, only exhale. Inhale happens automatically

SHE

I got out just before Christmas. My daughter had been my sole visitor and I'd
fallen out with her by this time too, for not bringing my 'going home clothes'

to the hospital for me. She had taken my bank card and with no cash in my purse, I walked home in the frost in foam slippers, without a jacket, having lied to the nurses that my son was just downstairs waiting in the car.

Home alone with a palm-full of pills to take everyday, and no invitations for Christmas dinner; I fled to England for another Vipassana, missing Christmas out altogether. Weeping my way through the first few days, this eventually gave way to peace: to bliss. I realised that ecstasy didn't have to be a pill you took with your pals at a house music club night. Here it was naturally, with no nasty come down.

SHE walks off stage
ONE/TWO begin the final breathing, joined by THREE's breathing
curtains are drawn back to reveal THREE completely shrouded in the same cloth
and in the same seated posture she was in when the show first began, but this is in
fact a plaster cast sculpture of SHE (with pre-recorded breath)
the 'real' SHE reappears from the back

SHE

And I felt happy.

I observed how I was transforming.

looks down on self

I made decisions about how I wanted to be treated.

There wasn't the space – and possibly not the time – for anyone who couldn't behave with generosity and kindness towards me, to be in my life.

Even if they're *family*.

And if I wasn't getting loved back

I'd just keep sending it out

especially for myself/

ONE springs forward into light, starts belting out Whitney Houston

ONE

The Greatest Love of All!/

SHE

What are you doing?/

ONE

Is easy to achieve/

SHE

Oi!/

ONE

SHE

Learning to Love Yourse/STOP!

SHE *quietly*

What are you doing?

ONE

I was ... learning to love ...

yourself, isn't that what you're doing?

SHE

Well that's a work in progress.

But let's keep this cool.

You never know, passionate love may still surface

- anybody interested, my contact details are on the programme –

but I *do* have love.

I give my yoga students love, and they love me right back.

My life is filled with love.

It's all Hunky Dory:

ONE/TWO/SHE

reciting the lyrics of Fill Your Heart by David Bowie

Fill your heart with love today

Don't play the game of time

Things that happened in the past

Only happened in your Mind

Only in your Mind

-Forget your Mind

And you'll be free-yea'

The writing's on the wall

Free-yea'

And you can know it all

If you choose

Just remember

Lovers never lose

'Cause they are Free of thoughts,

Un-pure

And of thoughts

Unkind

Gentleness clears the soul

Love cleans the mind

And makes it Free – eeeeeeeee

ONE, TWO & SHE hold this last note as 30-second clip of 'Fill Your Heart' by David Bowie fades in

actors walk around the playing area picking up books and bits of paper and tidying up

back to centre stage, standing in a row

place their hands together in front of their hearts, bowing heads 4 times to the last four notes of the song – and lights snap to black

Bibliography

Adichie, C.N. (2014) *We Should All Be Feminists*. UK: Harper Collins.

Ainsworth, R. and Pippen, J. (Contributors) (2013) In: *Staging Social Justice: Collaborating to Create Activist Theatre*. US: Southern Illinois University Press.

Allen, R.E. (ed.) (1990) *Concise Oxford Dictionary*. Oxford: Oxford University Press.

Beacom, B. (2015) Tommy's Right on Song. *The Evening Times*. 11 May, p.31.

Brennan, M. (2014) Theatre Review: Blood Lines. *The Herald*. 5 July.

Britton, J. (2013) *Encountering Ensemble*. UK: Methuen Drama.

Bharucha, R. (1988) Peter Brook's "Mahabharata": A View from India'. *Economic and Political Weekly*. Vol. 23(32), pp. 1642–1647.

Bharucha, R. (1993) *Theatre and the World: Performance and the Politics of Culture*. UK: Taylor and Francis Ltd.

Bochner, A. and Ellis, C. (2000) *Researcher as Subject: Autoethnography, Personal Narrative, Reflexivity*. In: Denzin, N. and Lincoln, Y. (eds.) Handbook of Qualitative Research. 2nd ed. California: Sage Publications, pp.733–754.

Bogart, A. (2001) *A Director Prepares: seven essays on art and theatre*. Oxon: Routledge.

Bowie, David (2016) *Blackstar*. Record Label: ISO, Columbia, Sony.

Bowles, N. and Nadon, D.R. (2013) *Staging Social Justice: Collaborating to Create Activist Theatre*. US: Southern Illinois University Press.

Blackmore, S. (2005) *Consciousness: A Very Short Introduction*. New York: Oxford University Press.

Bradbury, D. and Delgado, M. (eds.) (2002) *The Paris Jigsaw: Internationalism and the City's Stages*. Manchester: Manchester University Press.

Brask, P. and Meyer-Dinkgräfe, D. (eds.) (2010) *Performing Consciousness*. Newcastle: Cambridge Scholars Publishing.

Brennan, M (2015) Theatre Review: Tommy's Song at Oran Mor, Glasgow. [Online] *Herald Scotland*. 15 May. Available: https://www.heraldscotland.com/life_style/arts_ents/13213377.theatre-review-tommys-song-oran-mor-glasgow/ [15 May 2017].

Brook, P. (1968) *The Empty Space: A Book About the Theatre: Deadly, Holy, Rough, Immediate*. New York: Touchstone Publishing.

Carnicke, S. (2009) *Stanislavski in Focus: An Acting Master for the Twenty-First Century*. London: Routledge.

Carel, H. (2008) *Illness: The Cry of the Flesh*. Durham: Acumen Publishing Ltd.

Choudhury, B. (2007) *Bikram's Beginning Yoga Class, Vol.2*. [CD]. International Friends.

Choudhury, Bikram (2007) *Bikram Yoga*. New York: HarperCollins.

Climenhaga, R. (2010) Anne Bogart and Siti Company: Creating the Moment. In: Hodge, A. (ed.) *Actor Training*. Oxon: Routledge.

Cook, A. (2013) Texts and Embodied Performance. In: Shaughnessy, N. (2013) *Affective Performance and Cognitive Science: Brain, Body, Being*. UK: Bloomsbury Methuen Drama.

Collins, J. (2013) Elevator Repair Service and The Wooster Group: Ensembles Surviving Themselves. In: Britton, J. *Encountering Ensemble.* London: Bloomsbury Methuen Drama.

Cope, S. (2006) *The Wisdom of Yoga: A Seekers Guide to Extraordinary Living.* New York: Bantam.

De Bono, E. (1970) *Lateral Thinking.* England: Penguin Books Ltd.

Denzin, N. K. (2014) *Interpretive Autoethnography.* USA: Sage Publications.

Dolan, J. (2005) *Utopia in Performance: Finding Hope at the Theatre.* USA: University of Michigan press.

Drew, C. (2014) *8-Minute Yoga Workout.* Fitlife TV (subscription).

Edwards, G. (2010) *Conscious Medicine: A Radical New Approach to Creating Health and Wellbeing.* UK: Piatkus.

Ellis, Carolyn (2004) *The Ethnographic I: A Methodological Novel About Autoethnography.* New York: AltaMira Press.

Farhi, D. (2004) *Bringing Yoga to Life: The Everyday Practice of Enlightened Living.* New York: Harper Collins.

Fenemore, A. (2011) (ed.) The Body. In: Pitches, J. and Popat, S. *Performance Perspectives: A Critical Introduction:* UK: Palgrave MacMillan.

Grotowski, J. (1968) *Towards A Poor Theatre.* New York: Routledge.

Gillett, J. (2007) *Acting on Impulse: Reclaiming the Stanislavski Approach.* London: Methuen Drama.

Gallop, J. (2000) *Anecdotal Theory.* Durham: Duke University Press.

Goenka, S.N. (1987) *The Discourse Summaries.* India: Vipassana Research Institute.

Gold, R. (1958) Roles in Sociological Field Observation. *Social Forces.* Vol. 36 (3), pp. 217–213, Oxford: Oxford University Press.

Govan, E. Nicholson, H. and Normington, K. (2007). *Making A Performance: Devising Histories and Contemporary Practices.* Oxon: Routledge.

Hammersley, M. and Atkinson, P. (2007) *Ethnography: Principles in Practice.* New York: Routledge.

Hart, W. (1988) *Vipassana Meditation: The Art of Living as taught by S. N. Goenka.* Maharashtra, India: Vipassana Research Institute.

Haseman, B. & Mafe, D. (2009) *Acquiring Know-how: Research Training for Practice-led Researchers.* In: Smith, H and Dean, R.T. *Practice-led Research, Research-led Practice in the Creative Arts.* Edinburgh: Edinburgh University Press.

Hart, W. (1987) *Vipassana Meditation – The Art of Living.* India: Vipassana Research Institute.

Hearn, J. and Connell, R.W Men (2005) Masculinities in Work, Organisations and Management. ((pp.289–310) In: Kimmel, M., Hearn, J. and Connell, R. W. (2005) Handbook of Studies on Men and Masculinities. London: Sage.

Heddon, D. (2007) *Autobiography in Performance: Performing Selves.* Palgrave McMillan: UK.

Henry, D. (2009) Transnet. In: Allegue, L., Jones, S. and Kershaw, S. (eds.) *Practice-as-Research: In Performance and Screen [With DVD].* UK: AIAA.

Houston, W. (2011) Some Body and No Body: The Body of a Performer. In: Pitches, J. and Popat, S. (eds.) *Performance Perspectives: A Critical Introduction.* UK: Palgrave.

James, E.L. (2012) *Fifty Shades of Grey.* UK: Arrow Books.

Jones, S. (2009) The Courage of Complementarity: Practice-as-Research as a Paradigm Shift in Performance in Performance Studies. In: Allegue, L. (Ed.) *Practice-as-Research in Performance and Screen.* New York: Palgrave Macmillan.

Kawulich, B. (2005) Participant Observation as a Data Collection Method. *Forum: Qualitative Social Research.* Vol. 6(2), pp.1–22.

Kemmis, S. (2008) Critical Theory and Participatory Action Research. In: Reason, P. and Bradbury, H. *The SAGE Handbook of Action Research: Participative Inquiry and Practice.* London: Sage Publishing.

Kershaw, B. (2009) Practice as Research through Performance. In: Smith, H and Dean, R.T. *Practice-led Research, Research-led Practice in the Creative Arts.* Edinburgh: Edinburgh University Press.

Khan, M. (1985) Vipassana Meditation and the Psychobiology of Wilhelm Reich. *Journal of Humanistic Psychology* [online] Vol. 25(3), pp.117–128. Available: https://doi.org/10.1177/0022167885253010 [Accessed: 20 July 2016].

Kimmel, M. S. and Messner. M. A. (2001) *Men's Lives.* Boston: Allyn and Bacon.

Kosmala, K. (2013) *Imagining Masculinities: Spatial and Temporal Representation and Visual Culture.* London: Routledge.

Ladron de Guevera, V. R. (2011) Any body? The Multiple Bodies of the Performer. In: Pitches, J. and Popat, S. (Eds.) *Performance Perspectives: A Critical Introduction.* UK: Red Globe Press.

Lykke, N. (Ed.) *Writing Academic Texts Differently: Intersectional Feminist Methodologies* and the Playful Art of Writing. New York and London: Routledge.

Madison, S. (2011) *Critical Ethnography: Method, Ethics, And Performance.* UK: Sage Publications.

Marley, R. (1981) *Who Feels It Knows It,* Canada: Shanachie Records Corp.

Maté, G (2019) *When the Body Says No: The Cost of Hidden Stress.* London: Vermilion.

McAuley, Gay (2000) *Space in Performance: Making Meaning in the Theatre.* USA: University of Michigan Press.

Meyer-Dinkgräfe, Daniel (2005) *Theatre and Consciousness: Explanatory Scope and Future Potential.* USA: Intellect Books.

McAuley, G. (2000) *Space in Performance: Making Meaning in the Theatre.* US: University of Michigan Press.

Mohanty, C. T. (2003) *Feminism Without Borders: Decolonising Theory, Practicing Solidarity*. Durham, USA: Duke University Press.

Morris, M. (2015) *Scotland and the Caribbean, c.1740–1833 Atlantic Archipelagos.* Oxon: Routledge.

Morris, M. (2015) Yonder Awa: Slavery and Distancing Strategies in Scottish Literature. In: Devine, T. (ed.) *Recovering Scotland's Slavery Past*. Edinburgh: Edinburgh University Press.

Mower, S. (2010) Etienne Decroux: A Corporeal Consciousness. In: Brask, P. and Meyer-Dinkgräfe, D. (eds.) *Performing Consciousness*. Newcastle: Cambridge Scholars Publishing.

Mullen, S. (2009) *It Wisnae Us: The Truth About Glasgow and Slavery*. UK: The Royal Incorporation of Architects in Scotland.

Murray, R. (2002) *How to Write a Thesis*. London: Open University Press.

Nakazawa, D. J. (2015) *Childhood Disrupted: How Your Biography Becomes Your Biology, and How You Can Heal*. New York: Atria.

Nelson, R. (2006) Practice-as-research and the Problem of Knowledge. *Performance Research* [online] Vol. 11(4), pp. 105–116 Available: DOI: 10.1080/13528160701363556 [Accessed: 7 April 2014].

Nelson, R. (2009) Modes of Practice-as-Research Knowledge and their Place in the Academy. In: Allegue, L., Jones, S. and Kershaw, B. (eds.) *Practice-as-Research: In Performance and Screen [With DVD]*. UK: AIAA.

Nelson, Robin (2013) *Practice as Research in the Arts: Principles, Protocols, Pedagogies, Resistances.* London: Palgrave Macmillan.

Núñez, N. (1997) *Anthropocosmic Theatre: Rite in the Dynamics of Theatre*. UK: Harwood Academic Publishers.

O'Reilly, K. (2016) *Atypical Plays for Atypical Actors: Selected Plays by Katie O'Reilly*. London: Oberon Books.

O'Reilly, K. (2005) *Ethnographic Methods*. Oxon: Routledge.

Pearson, M. & Shanks, M. (2001) *Theatre/Archaeology*. London: Routledge.

Performance and Mindfulness Symposium (June 2016), Centre for Psychophysical Performance Research, Huddersfield University, UK.

Phelen, P. Foreword: Performing Questions; Producing Witnesses. In: Etchells, T. (1999) *Certain Fragments: Texts and Writings on Performance*. London and New York: Routledge.

Prendergast, L. (2014) *Blood Lines* theatre production. Glasgow: Arches Theatre.

Prendergast, L. (2015) *Tommy's Song* theatre production. Glasgow: Oran Mor.

Ramacharaka (2007) *Hatha Yoga or The Yogi Philosophy of Physical Well-Being*, New York: Cosmo Classics.

Ramacharaka (2008) *Raja Yoga or Mental Development.* London: Forgotten Books.

Reynolds, D. and Reason, M. (2012) *Kinesthetic Empathy in Creative and Cultural Practices.* Bristol: Intellect Books.

Richardson, L. (2000) Evaluating Ethnography. *Qualitative Enquiry* [online] Vol. 6(2), pp. 253–255 Available: https://doi.org/10.1177/10778004000600207 [Accessed: January 10, 2016].

Richmond, F. P., Swann, D. L., Zarrilli, P. B. (Eds.) (1990) *Indian Theatre: Traditions of Performance*. Honolulu: Hawaii.

Shapiro, D. (1990) *The Bodymind Workbook: Exploring how the Mind and the Body Work Together*. Dorset, UK: Element Books Ltd.

Sheets-Johnstone, M. (2009) *The Corporeal Turn: An Interdisciplinary Reader*. UK: Imprint Academic Books.

Shusterman, Richard (2008) *Body Consciousness: A Philosophy of Mindfulness and Somaesthetics*. Cambridge University Press: New York

Shusterman, Richard (2012) *Thinking Through the Body: essays in Somaesthetics*. Cambridge University Press: New York

Spry, Tammy (2011) *Body, Paper, Stage: Writing and Performing Autoethnography*. USA: Left Coast Press

Swami Sivananda (1971) *Science of Yoga Vol. 11: Jnana Yoga*. India: Sivananda Int.

Taylor, C. (1992) *The Ethics of Authenticity*. Cambridge, MA: Harvard University Press.

Varley, J. (2013) Ensembles, Groups, Networks. In: Britton, J. *Encountering Ensemble* London: Methuen Drama.

Weiss, W. (2010) The Ego and the Self in Actor Training. In: Brask, P. and Meyer-Dinkgräfe, D. (eds.) (2010) *Performing Consciousness*. Newcastle: Cambridge Scholars Publishing.

White, A. (ed.) (2014) *The Routledge Companion to Stanislavsky*. Oxon: Routledge.

Wirth, L. (1945) The Problem of Minority Groups. In: Linton, R. (ed.) *The Science of Man in the World Crisis*. New York: Columbia University Press.

Wolford, L. (1996) *Grotowski's Objective Drama Research*. US: University Press of Mississippi.

Worley, L. (2001) *Coming from Nothing: the Sacred Art of Acting*. US: Turquoise Dragon Press.

Zarilli, P. B. (2009) *Psychophysical Acting: An Intercultural Approach*. London and New York: Routledge.

Additional Web Resources

Brennan, M. (2012) Arches Live '12, Glasgow. [Online] *Herald Scotland*. 2 October. Available: http://www.heraldscotland.com/arts-ents/stage/arches-live-12-glasgow.19029901 [20 December 2017].

Glas(s) Performance. (n.d.) [Online] Available: http://www.glassperformance.co.uk/what-we-do/[Accessed: 7 September 2016].

Irvine, L. (2015) Theatre Review: Tommy's Song Across the Arts. [Online] May 16. Available: http://www.acrossthearts.co.uk/news/artsblog/theatre-review-tommys-song-/[Accessed: May 17 2015].

Karoulla, E. (2012) Whatever Happened to Harry @ Arched Live. The Skinny. [Online] November 5. Available: http://www.theskinny.co.uk/theatre/shows/reviews/whatever-happened-to-harry-arches-live [Accessed: December 2013].

McMillan, J. (2014) Blood Lines. Joyce McMillan – Online. [Online] 5 July. Available: https://joycemcmillan.wordpress.com/2014/07/05/44-stories-blood-lines-one-man-two-guvnors/[Accessed: 6 July 2014].

Nephrotic Syndrome in Adults. (n.d.) [online] Available: https://www.niddk.nih.gov/health-information/kidney-disease/nephrotic-syndrome-adults [Accessed: 29 September 2013].

Pulmonary Embolism. (n.d.) [Online] Available: https://www.nhs.uk/conditions/pulmonary-embolism/[Accessed: January 7, 2015].

UWS (n.d.) Study Skills. [Online] Available: https://www.uws.ac.uk/current-students/supporting-your-studies/study-skills/[Accessed: December 2013].

20 for 14 Fund. (n.d.) [Online] Available: http://www.creativescotland.com/funding/archive/20-for-14-fund [Accessed: October 2014].

Willett, Cynthia, Anderson, Ellen and Meyers, Diana, "Feminist Perspectives on the Self", *The Stanford Encyclopaedia of Philosophy* (Winter 2016 Edition), Edward N. Zalta (ed.), https://plato.stanford.edu/archives/win2016/entries/feminism-self/ [Accessed: April 2019]

Index of Names

Ainsworth, R.   158–159
Atkinson, William Walker   39, 40, 53, 157, 159, 160

Blackmore, Susan   11
Bochner, Arthur   47, 50, 53
Bogart, Anne   35, 115, 116, 140
Britton, John   103, 104, 138, 163, 164
Brook, Peter   10, 11, 21, 26, 43, 44, 97, 119, 141, 155, 161

Callery, Dymphna   142
Carel, Havi   19, 20, 166
Carnicke, Sharon   39, 41
Choudhury, Bikram   8, 12, 30–34, 54, 104, 143, 156, 166
Climenhaga, Royd   140
Collins, John   164
Collinson, David   118
Cope, Stephen   30–31

de Bono, Edward   88–89
Decroux, Etienne   9, 89
Delgado, M.   98
Denzin, Norman   13–14
Dolan, Jill   10, 41, 87, 120, 161

Edwards, Gill   20, 27–29, 90
Ellis, Carolyn   13, 47, 48, 50

Farhi, Donna   34
Fenemore, Anna   140, 141

Gallop, Jane   14
Gillett, John   45
Goenka, Satya Narayan   8, 30–32, 37, 58, 60, 61, 64–70
Govan, Emma   49, 100–102, 141–143
Grotowski, Jerzy   21, 26, 42, 44–46, 51, 103, 119, 141, 156, 161, 167

Hammersley, M.   39, 40, 53, 157, 159, 160
Hart, William   31, 35, 37, 38, 45, 95
Haseman, B.   8, 48–50
Hearn, Jeff   118

Heddon, Dierdre (Dee)   14, 100–101
Henry, Daniel   89
Hollinshead, Lee   167
Houston, Wendy   142, 144

Katie Normington   49, 100–102, 141–143
Kawulich, Barbara   52–53
Kemmis, S.   22, 153
Kershaw, Baz   48
Kimmel, Michael   117, 118
Kosmala, Katarzyna   111, 116–119

Lykke, Nina   16–18

Madison, Soyini   52, 89
Mafe, D.   8, 48–50
Mate, Gabor   161–162
McAuley, Gay   15–16, 19, 28, 36, 39, 102
McKendrick, Alan   159
McTaggart   22, 153
Meyer-Dinkgrafe, Daniel   7, 9–13, 22, 39–40, 44, 51, 53, 90, 96–98, 154, 161, 166
Middleton, Deborah   42–43, 50
Milling, Jane   100
Mohanty, Chandra T   17–18
Morris, Michael   99, 102
Mullen, Stephen   102

Nakazawa, Donna Jackson   17–18, 162
Nelson, Robin   7, 19, 27, 28, 49
Nicholson, Helen   49, 100–102, 141–143
Nunez, Nicolas   21, 26, 42–43, 45, 50, 103, 142, 161

O'Reilly, Karen   53–55, 153, 157–158

Phelan, Peggy   102
Pippen, J.   158–159

Ramacharaka, Yogi   26, 39, 40

Shapiro, Debbie   28, 29
Sheets-Johnstone, Maxine   19, 35
Shusterman, Richard   21, 27, 29, 34, 35, 37
Sivananda, Swami   168

Spry, Tami   10, 13, 14, 50, 52, 55, 89, 139,
    159, 160
Stanislavsky, Konstantin   25–26, 41–43, 45

Taylor, Charles   96
TCTSY   22, 166
Templeton, Deborah   21
Travers, Martin   167

Varley, Julia   50

Weiss, William   43
Wolford, Lisa   44
Worley, Lee   21, 50, 103, 140, 144, 148, 163

Zarrilli, Phillip   21, 26, 28–30, 32–33, 38–42,
    50, 104, 161, 166